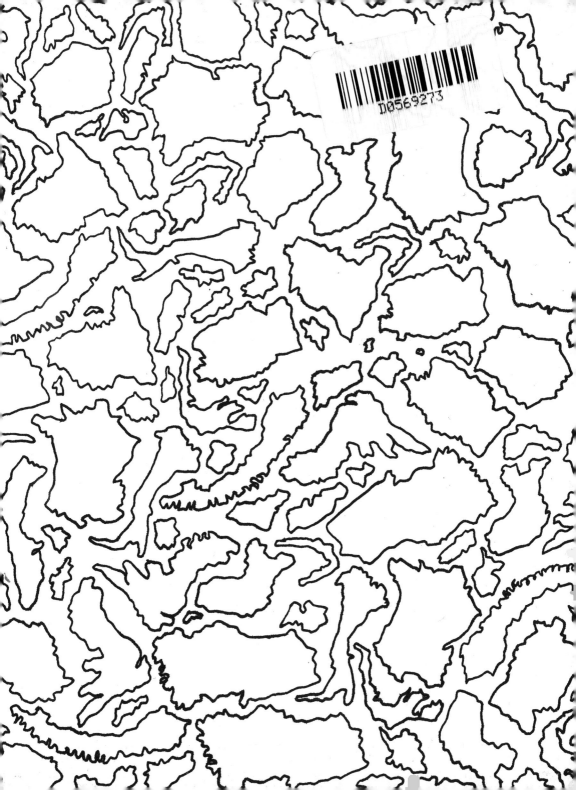

GRAPHIC EUROPE

AN ALTERNATIVE GUIDE TO 31 EUROPEAN CITIES

1—
FH52

Published by Cicada Books Limited

Edited by Ziggy Hanaor
Designed by April, www.studio-april.com
Text and images by the contributors as specified
Set in LL Gravur Condensed, www.lineto.com

British Library Cataloguing-in-Publication Data.

A CIP record for this book is available from
the British Library.
ISBN: 978-0-9562053-0-8

Cicada Books Limited
76 Lissenden Mansions
Lissenden Gardens
London, NW5 1PR

T: +44 207 267 5208
E: ziggy@cicadabooks.co.uk
W: www.cicadabooks.co.uk

CONTENTS

EDITOR'S NOTE

This project was started over a Skype conversation between myself and the designer, Joana Niemeyer. Joana had thought of creating a guide to Europe written and illustrated by designers, and asked me to come on board as an editor. After some thought, it came to me that rather than pitching it around the publishing houses, we could put it together ourselves, and so the process began.

We started out by sourcing designers to represent the countries we had decided to include. We chose to focus on individual freelance designers rather than studios, in order get a more intimate, personal view of the city. Starting with the contacts made by Joana on a previous project, we built up a list of contributors whose work we thought was distinctive and inspiring, and asked whether they'd like to participate. It was an overwhelmingly positive response, and without exception, they threw themselves into the work with complete dedication and enthusiasm.

The European design community is a big and tangled web, with its cities at its joins. The urban centres of Europe incubate talent – drawing it in, nurturing it and allowing it to move freely away and back, bringing with it all the influences of its previous destinations. Added to this, graphic designers tend to be web-savvy people (the internet being a great source of inspiration as well as the world's most accessible distraction activity). And what this means is that there is a constant cross-boundary dialogue between individuals. Although each city that features in this book is completely unique in what it has to offer, their artistic nerve-centres are very much influenced by the multi-national affiliations of their clientele.

It was tremendous fun tapping into this diverse community of like-minded people. And although I still haven't met many of them in person (and many of them still think I'm a man), I felt like I got to know a lot of them over the course of the project, through their e-mails and work. They all wrote texts in English despite this often being their second language, and supplied fantastic imagery that had really been thought through. Joana Niemeyer then put the book together with inimitable flair, somehow managing to fit long texts and detailed imagery together without compromising either. A lot of love went into this book – from every single person involved.

Graphic Europe is intended to be a beautiful object, but also one that is a usable, functioning travel guide. The illustrations do not depict the venues listed, but rather a personal interpretation of the cities in which the individual designers live. Although there were no highly skilled teams of researchers drawing up detailed surveys of venues to recommend, I hope that the individual opinions and illustrations of the designers can provide a more informal, intimate insight into the cities. Kind of like a friend showing you their favourite places to go – and then telling you how their city makes them feel. I hope that this book inspires people to travel and to create. After all, it seems like the two are often interconnected.

Ziggy Hanaor

Illustration by Radovan Jenko

CHRISTOF NARDIN'S VIENNA

It's been almost a century since the collapse of the Austro-Hungarian Empire, but the echoes of that moment of glory in Austria's history still resound loudly in Vienna. The legendary cafes around the city cling onto the antiquated mannerisms of days gone by, and the older generation can harp on endlessly about the good old days. The aesthetics of the city also reflect a degree of nostalgia – a lot of shops still use traditional typographies, their ornate windows evoking images of horse-drawn carriages, fur coats and big hair. Behind them, narrow alleyways hold dark and dusty shops that sell the most bizarre things. This combination of glamour and fustiness is very characteristic of Vienna, and can be very inspiring.

There is also a new Vienna that has grown out of all this historical baggage. As the only real city in Austria, it is the place where the country's young people gravitate towards, and where the international community congregates. It has been a centre for cultural production since the days of Mozart, and there is a fantastic variety of cultural venues, festivals and projects going on at any given time, fostering a vibrant scene in music, performance, theatre, design and the arts. This tension between morbid nostalgia and euphoric movement forward is what makes Vienna interesting. Sigmund Freud described Vienna as a place of 'hate/love'. It's a city where new things happen but nothing much becomes trendy, where big city meets small town mentality, new meets old. It is socialistic and capitalistic and generally militant in its views.

Geographically, Vienna is divided into 23 districts. The first district is encircled by a boulevard called the Ringstraße, which takes the place of the walls that used to surround the city, and the eight central districts are arranged around it. These are then in turn encircled by a ring road called the Gürtel, and the remaining 14 districts are spread around that. Outside the city is the idyllic Wienerwald. My life mostly happens in districts 4-7, where the interesting galleries, nice bars and good restaurants can be found, as well as the Naschmarkt, Vienna's central marketplace.

DAS TRIEST An old house luxuriously done up in contemporary style. The Silverbar is one of the best hotel bars in town. Wiedner Hauptstraße 12, 1040 Vienna, www.dastriest.at

ALTSTADT VIENNA The residence of a wealthy industrialist built in 1902 has been turned into a posh hotel with 42 individually designed rooms by designers and architects including Polka and Mattheo Thun. It's centrally located behind MuseumsQuartier. Kirchengasse 41, 1070 Vienna, www.altstadt.at

BEDINVIENNA AT JOSEPHINE Josephine rents out her wonderfully light, 70m² two-bedroom flat at Spittelmarkt in district 7. It's very reasonably priced. Sigmundgasse, 1070 Vienna, www.bedinvienna.com

HOTEL ORIENT This place has been a discreet refuge for lovers for the past hundred and something years. It's not exactly a place to stay... the rooms are rented by the hour. But they're big and clean and romantic in a slightly kinky kind of way – each one is individually themed. The staff are the picture of discretion. Tiefer Graben 30, 1010 Vienna, www.hotelorient.at

PLACES TO STAY

CAFE AM HEUMARKT The cafe at the Heumarkt Road had its best days around 50 years ago. The interior is pretty much stripped back to the basics, but worn flooring and nicotine-stained furniture has its own earthy charm. It serves the best Wiener Schnitzel at the best price in town. Closed at weekends. Am Heumarkt 15, 1030 Vienna

FINKH Modern, innovative Austrian cuisine in simple but stylish surrounds. The guys who run this place have worked in the best kitchens in the country. Make sure you book in advance. Esterhazygasse 12, 1060 Vienna, www.finkh.at

AM NORDPOL 3 The Nordpol is tucked behind the Augarten Park, in the middle of nowhere, but every step of the trip is part of the experience. The interior is charmingly eclectic, the service is friendly and hectic and the food and the beer is fantastic. Try the Blunzengröstl. Nordwestbahnstraße 17, 1020 Vienna, www.amnordpol3.at

CAFE ANZENGRUBER This is a down to earth, totally run-of-the-mill place that happens to serve fantastic food with great service, attracting a friendly crowd and broadcasting live transfers of the Croatian national football team. Legendary! Schleifmühlgasse 19, 1040 Vienna

KIOSK The sausages at Kiosk taste better than anywhere else, and it also serves a range of beers, and excellent Austrian wine. Schleifmühlgasse 7, 1040 Vienna

AROMAT Small and nice. Very nice. Sometimes you bump into the owner, Oliver, during the day at the Naschmarkt, shopping for fresh ingredients for the evening. The menu changes daily, and sometimes guest chefs are invited to cook. Magaretenstraße 52, 1040 Vienna, www.arom.at

AIDA – VIENNA PASTRY SHOPS Aida is a pastry shop chain with 20-odd branches around the city serving the best coffee and the finest cakes in town. Forget the sachertortes, there's so much more on offer! www.aida.at

LOOSBAR Architect Adolf Loos designed this bar in wood, glass, brass, marble and onyx, inspired by a visit to the United States. It's now a historical monument serving excellent cocktails. Kärntner Passage 10, 1010 Vienna

FUTUREGARDEN This is a piece of Berlin in Vienna – a bar where the art-crowd converges to get drunk, chat and sometimes dance. There are exhibitions every month, live DJs and an urban atmosphere. Schadekgasse 6, 1060 Vienna

JOANELLI This place used to be the oldest ice-cream parlour in Vienna. Now it's where all the architects, artists and posh hairdressers go. Perfect for an after work beer or three. Gumpendorferstraße 47, 1060 Vienna

BARS

FLUC The Fluc is one of the most important addresses in terms of experimental electronic music. This weird party joint holds a free concert every night. You can find bigger events with international acts at the Fluc Wanne in the old pedestrian underpass under the Fluc. Praterstern 5, 1020 Vienna, www.fluc.at

A BAR SHABU A former brothel that is now a charming hide-away in the second quarter. You can eat hearty regional classics, and drink the best Austrian wine, liquors and schnapps. All at trade prices. Rotensterngasse 8, 1020 Vienna

CLUB NIGHTS There are a few legendary parties with great DJs that happen in various venues around the city. Check on the websites for details:
WURSTSALON www.myspace.com/wurstsalon
TINGEL TANGEL www.tingeltangel.at
RHINOPLASTY www.myspace.com/rhinoplastyclub
MEAT MARKET www.myspace.com/clubmeatmarket
PLING PLONG www.myspace.com/plingplongklub
SUSI KLUB www.myspace.com/susiklub

PARK A concept store for contemporary design – stocking fashion, streetwear, accessories, magazines, books and furniture. Mondscheingasse 20, 1070 Vienna, www.park.co.at

PHIL A bookshop/cafe where you can sit on vintage furniture with a beer or a coffee, listen to the music and leaf through a book. If you like the chair more than the book, you can buy that instead. Great for breakfast. Gumpendorferstraße 10-12, 1060 Vienna, www.phil.info

BOOKSHOP LIA WOLF Lia's small bookshop is the best place to go for art and design books. She knows every title she has in stock, and will help you find whatever you're after. Bäckerstraße 2, 1010 Vienna, www.wolf.at

DAS MÖBEL This place serves coffee, cakes and a breakfast buffet, which you can eat sitting at a regularly changing exhibition by an Austrian furniture designer. If there's anything that takes your fancy you can buy it at the shop in Gumpendorferstraße. Cafe – Burggasse 10, 1070 Vienna, Shop – Gumpendorferstraße 11, 1060 Vienna, www.dasmoebel.at

LITTLE JOE'S GANG-FANSHOP A great little treasure trove selling shoes, sunglasses, music, shirts and bags. If you can't find a memento of your favourite subject, it can be printed for you. You must go! Operngasse 34, 1040 Vienna

NASCHMARKT This market sells fresh fish, exotic fruit, herbs, and anything else your heart desires. The media scene convenes in the cafes around the market on warm summer evenings, and on Saturdays, the parking lot is used for a flea market. Between Linke Wienzeile and Rechte Wienzeile, 1040 Vienna

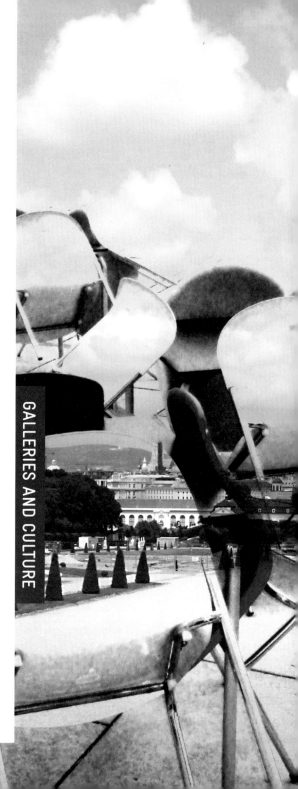

GALLERIES AND CULTURE

COCO (CONTEMPORARY CONCERNS)
In a passage in the city centre, this brand new contemporary art space runs two exhibition spaces and a bar. COCO presents thematic group shows and a lecture/events programme. Bauernmarkt 9, 1010 Vienna, www.co-co.at

SALON FÜR KUNSTBUCH This is a concept space established by local artist Bernhard Cella, who produces beautiful books. It focuses on creating a dialogue between art-book publishers around the world, and the exhibitions include dramatic book arrangements. Mondscheingasse 11, 1070 Vienna, www.salon-fuer-kunstbuch.at

MUSEUMSQUARTIER WIEN The MQW is basically a really large cultural complex, which holds within it institutions including big museums, small galleries, architectural exhibition spaces, and performance venues. Just a few worth mentioning are the TanzQuartier, an international, state-of-the-art centre for dance, Quartier21, a support structure that offers space to more than 40 autonomous cultural initiatives, and the Zoom Children's Museum. It also has some great cafes, restaurants and shops. In the summer, I love hanging round the courtyards designed by PPAG architects. Museumsplatz 1, 1070 Vienna, www.mqw.at

BRUT A theatre with two spaces presenting a refreshing programme of contemporary dance and performance. The Karlsplatz venue has the added bonus of the Bar Brut Deluxe that opens after performances for artistic mingling. Karlsplatz 5 (Künstlerhaus), 1010 Vienna, Lothringerstraße 20 (Konzerthaus), 1030 Vienna, www.brut-wien.at

GOTO An initiative of young artists from different disciplines, GOTO holds events such as readings, exhibitions, parties, etc. Ottakringerstraße 77, 1160 Vienna, www.gotoclub.org

GALLERIES IN ESCHENBACHGASSE

The neighbourhood of Eschenbachgasse in the Gumpendorferstraße district has lots of cool galleries and shops (some of which I've recommended). MuseumsQuartier and Mariahilferstraße are not far away. Have a stroll around the area, and check out the following galleries:

MEYERKAINER Eschenbachgasse 9, 1010 Vienna, www.meyerkainer.com

MEZZANIN Eschenbachgasse 1/ Getreidemarkt 14, www.galeriemezzanin.com

MARTIN JANDA Eschenbachgasse 11, www.martinjanda.at

GALERIE STEINEK Eschenbachgasse 4, www.galerie.steinek.at

GALLERIES IN SCHLEIFMÜHLGASSE

Another good place for contemporary art galleries. Keep an eye out for Ve.Sch/Friends and Art in particular— it's a really nice space with opening parties on Wednesdays. Grab a bite to eat at the Naschmarkt at the end of the street.

ENGHOLM ENGELHORN Schleifmühlgasse 3A, 1040 Vienna, www.engholmengelhorn.com

GEORG KARGL Schleifmühlgasse 5, www.georgkargl.com

GALERIE SENN Schleifmühlgasse 1A, www.galeriesenn.at

CHRISTINE KÖNIG GALERIE Schleifmühlgasse 1A, www.christinekoeniggalerie.com

VE.SCH/FRIENDS AND ART Schikanedergasse 11/3, www.friendsandart.at

PRATER The Wiener Prater is a large park mostly consisting of wetlands. There's a main avenue running through it for walking, jogging and cycling. You'll also find an amusement park, lawns, forested areas and a swimming pool.

DONAUKANAL When the weather is nice, the walk along the urban, concrete Danube canal can be very nice. On the way, you'll pass some good graffiti, the lock and the 'Friedensbrücke' by Otto Wagner, a house by Zaha Hadid, the incinerator of Hundertwasser, the skyscraper designed by Jean Nouvel and the Urania and Uniqua Tower, with its innovative media facade.

ALTE DONAU The old Danube is one of the green lungs of the city. You can picnic, swim (naked), and rent electric boats, all with the city skyline in the background. On the nights of the full moon, the boat rental companies extend their opening hours, and provide a lantern and a picnic basket with a bottle of prosecco for romantic boat trips.

KARL-MARX-HOF One of the best-known municipal buildings in Vienna is the Karl-Marx-Hof in Heiligenstadt. Built between 1927 and 1930 it follows the concept of a 'city within a city', harbouring 1382 homes, laundries, kindergartens, a library, medical facilities and shops. It's four tram stops long, making it the longest continuous building in the world.

WERKBUNDSIEDLUNG WIEN The Werkbundsiedlung at the western edge of Vienna is an urban planning experiment initiated in the 1930s by Josef Frank to provide the city with affordable family housing. It includes 70 buildings by 32 international architects including Richard Bauer, Karl A Bieber, Max Fellerer, Helmut Wagner Freynsheim, Hugo Häring and Adolf Loos. Unfortunately, the house by Oskar Strnad was destroyed in the war alongside five others. Some have been renovated by the current residents with a few slightly amusing results.

VIENNA DESIGN WEEK OCTOBER Annual design festival. www.viennadesignweek.at

FESTIVAL FOR FASHION AND PHOTOGRAPHY MAY-JUNE Amazing shows, exhibitions and parties. www.10festival.at, www.unit-f.at

IMPULSTANZ JULY-AUGUST Festival for contemporary dance and performance. www.impulstanz.com

ACCORDION FESTIVAL FEBRUARY-APRIL Sounds boring, but it isn't! www.akkordeonfestival.at

SOHO IN OTTAKRING SUMMER Urban art project in the 16th district. www.sohoinottakring.at

OPEN AIR CINEMA SUMMER In Augarten near the Austrian Film Archive. www.filmarchiv.at

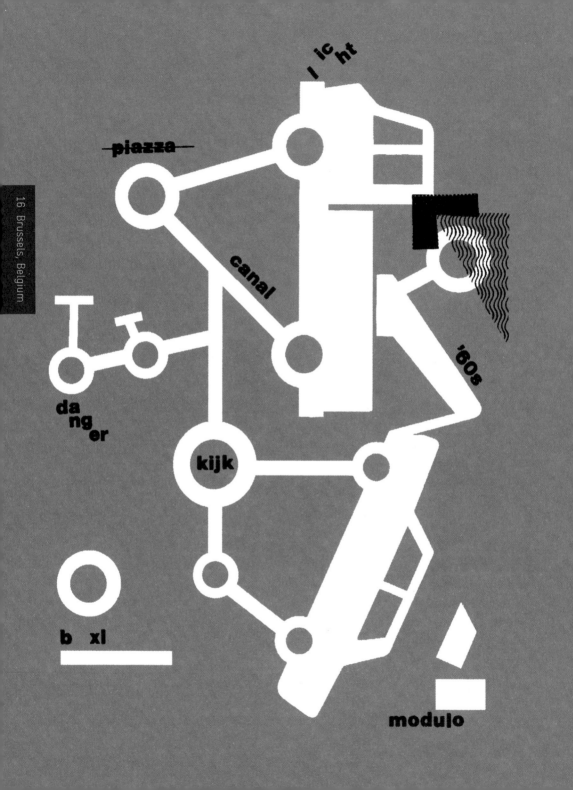

TERESA SDRALEVICH'S BRUSSELS

Known variously as BXXL, Bruxel, Brüsel, BXL and various other acronyms, Brussels is a city in search of an identity. It is officially a bilingual capital – speaking both Dutch and French – but with 46 per cent of the population being of non-Belgian origin, many other idioms can be heard. Its population stands at just over one million, but each week from Monday to Friday it hosts a further 200,000 commuters. It is, of course, the European capital, and as such has a lot of wealth – but simultaneously 20 per cent of the population live in poverty.

Architecturally as well, Brussels has no clear visual character – or rather its character is the result of destruction and mistakes, layered in strata of disorder around a handful of coherent spots (such as the 17th Century 'Grand Place'). It's such palpably bad urban planning that it has provided the root for two shameful words in urbanist jargon: 'Brusselisation' and 'facadism' (check them out on Wikipedia).

Brussels is a conglomerate of 19 communes, each of which preserve a certain village-like character. To generalise, the northern part of the city is poor and run down, whilst the southern part is wealthy and luxuriant. A steep hill divides the upper town and downtown. The centre is a hybrid that was deserted in the 1970s and 80s, and was resuscitated in the 90s, with the opening of bars, restaurants and trendy shops. The canal and port area have also seen recent redevelopment, with some interesting shops and cultural spaces popping up. Students and artists are concentrated in Ixelles, where the art schools and universities can be found, as well as Saint-Gilles.

I have lived in Brussels for the past 15 years. Before then I lived in beautiful Italian cities like Pavia and Bologna, and I never could have imagined that I would fall in love with the Nordic-Latin spirit of Brussels, its architectural disasters and incongruous skyline. And yet, despite all its imperfections, there is still something in it that appeals to me. It is the perfect sized city – big enough to preserve your anonymity, but small enough to cycle round and bump into friends occasionally. There is a great mix of residential, industrial and green spaces, and of course its multicultural nature has many benefits. But the thing I appreciate most is the way that Brussels constantly gives reason to be upset, or pleased, or revolted, because, thanks to its lack of firm identity, it is constantly changing and reinventing itself.

BIBLIOTHÈQUE ROYALE DE BELGIQUE

The Monts des Arts is a complex of cultural buildings in the middle of a no-man's land of run-down buildings covered with graffiti. The square and gardens are currently being renovated, and the library building has been spruced up in pure Belgian-International style with mini lamps and odd Starck chairs. The cafe is on the fifth floor, and has maintained its original 1970s décor of orange chairs and glass and wood furniture. You get a great view of the messed up city centre from up here. Not open at weekends. Boulevard de l'Empereur 4, 1000 Brussels, www.kbr.be

ENSAV LA CAMBRE CAFETERIA Another place not open at weekends (I can foresee your objections, but you'll only get the real city during the week!). This is the restaurant and bar of the School of Visual Arts in the beautiful grounds of the La Cambre Abbey in Ixelles. It is reasonably priced, and you can pretend to be a student and try to sneak into the printing and engraving workshop on the ground floor, or the charming bookbinding department (1st floor). Abbaye de La Cambre 21, Brussels 1000, www.lacambre.be

PLACES TO EAT

PLACES TO STAY

BRUXELLES EUROPE À CIEL OUVERT
This is a surreal campsite in the heart of the European Quarter that very few people know about. It's only open from the beginning of July to the end of August and only tents are allowed. At €6 per person per night, it's the cheapest way to experience the city. Chaussée de Wavre 205, 1050 Brussels, www.cielouvertcamping.wordpress.com

HÔTEL METROPOLE If you stay in Brussels, make it grand, at least for one night! Hôtel Metropole is a magnificent hotel in the city centre, dripping with old-school European splendour. Make a reservation online (not through their website) and you'll get half the official prices. Place De Brouckèreplein 31, 1000 Brussels, www.metropolehotel.com

HÔTEL GALIA Overlooking the famous flea market that takes place every single day of the year, this is an affordable hotel – especially mid-week. It's decorated with 'bd' or bandes dessinées (cartoons by Belgian creators), and is located in the heart of Marolles – once the poorest neigbourhood, and still an intriguing mixture of expensive antiques shops and crumbling houses. Place du Jeu de Balle 15-16, 1000 Brussels, www.hotelgalia.com

THE WHITE HOTEL Situated in the wealthy Quartier Louise in Ixelles, this is an upmarket design hotel with extremely high profile design furniture. It regularly hosts exhibitions by young designers and artists, often coupled with parties or DJ sessions. Oddly, it's cheaper at weekends – although still not cheap! Avenue Louise 212, 1050 Brussels, www.thewhitehotel.be

HOTEL REMBRANDT A warm, old-fashioned and friendly B&B. Rue de la Concorde 42, 1050 Brussels, www.hotel-rembrandt.be

LE FIN DU SIÈCLE This is a more traditional restaurant next to the Bourse (Stock Exchange). It serves good food at fair prices, and is in a charming street, which also houses a tiny vintage shop and the Greenwich Bar that, despite the arrival of a huge plasma screen, remains the rendez-vous of choice for all chess players in Brussels. Kartuizerstraat 10, Rue des Chartreux, 1000 Brussels

LA CLEF D'OR If you happen to be around the flea market, stop by this atmospheric traditional Brussels tavern run by a fantastic character called Jo Jo. It serves soup and tartines at very cheap prices, and if you're lucky, Jo Jo will play his accordion. Place du Jeu de Balle 1, 1000 Brussels

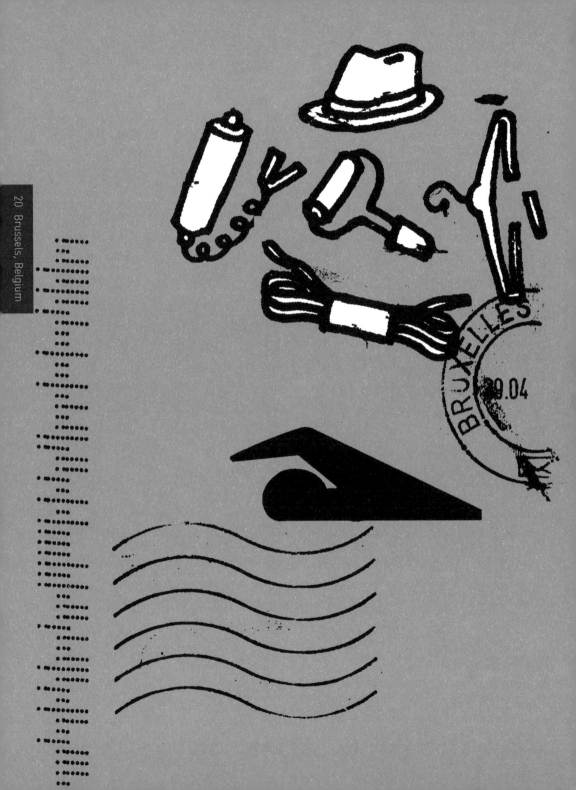

L'ARCHIDUC This is a well-known venue, but its immaculately preserved Art Deco design and architecture still make it worth a visit. Check out the Depero-style fabric on the couches, and the original neon sign. It is a jazz bar with free concerts every Saturday at 5pm. Rue Dansaertstraat 6, 1000 Brussels, www.archiduc.net

BELGA In the newly revamped Place Flagey in Ixelles, this is the place to be. It's spacious and nicely decorated with good attention to detail (even in the toilets!) Don't wait for table service – help yourself at the bar. Place Eugène Flagey 18, 1050 Brussels

BARS

MONK BAR A regular hangout for me and my friends, this is a traditional Belgian Art Nouveau pub with fantastic tiled floors and 40 different beers. Rue St Catherine 42, 1000 Brussels

DE DARINGMAN A tiny bar a stone's throw away from Place St Catherine. It's run by a guy called Martine, who is a supporter of the glorious RWDM Molenbeek football club, which sadly no longer exists. On the same street you'll find a charming bike workshop in an old movie theatre. Rue de Flandres 37, 1000 Brussels

WALVIS CAFE Another one of my favourites, this is a trendy bar in the Dansaert area, near the canal. It's done in Art Deco style and has regular live events. Rue Antoine Dansaertstraat 209, 1000 Brussels, www.cafewalvis.be

SHOPPING

LE TYPOGRAPHE This shop stocks a wide range of writing instruments, papers, notebooks and typographic postcards, and also serves as a mini print-shop – the owner operates a one-colour Heidelberg Press and metal type as you watch. Print a business card or a wedding invitation, and it will be much more interesting than a computer generated composition. It's a little bit out of the way but still in Ixelles. Rue Franz Merjay 167, 1050 Brussels

MICROMARCHÉMIDI This is an association of independent sellers specialising in biological or eco-friendly designer products. It's usually an open-air market, but it's currently looking for a new location. Check their website to see where it's based. www.micromarchemidi.be

77 A shop in Ixelles selling clothes for adults and children by local designers at affordable prices. Rue du Page 77, 1050 Brussels, www.septante-sept.be

OXFAM VINTAGE AND SALVATION ARMY Second hand clothing is very popular in Brussels. The Oxfam Vintage shop has carefully selected stock, and just down the road is the big Salvation Army warehouse, where with a bit of luck you might find THE piece you were looking for at a dirt-cheap price. Rue de Flandre 104 and Boulevard d'Ypres 24 respectively, 1000 Brussels

PEINTURE FRAÎCHE The best art bookshop in town stocking architecture, art and design publications in a very relaxing atmosphere. Rue du Tabellion 10, 1050 Brussels

PLAIZIER 'Plaizier' means 'plaisir' in some Brussels jargon, but in this instance it's the family name of the owner of this beautiful shop. Situated just behind the Grand Place, it specialises in postcards and prints with a focus on local 'ligne claire' illustrators. Rue des Eperonniers 50, 1000 Brussels

THE PLASTICARIUM An impressive private collection of several thousand plastic objects made by top designers between 1960 and 1973. The owner, Philippe Decelle, lends pieces out to the most famous design museums in the world. It only takes groups of 10-20 people, and you have to book in advance. Rue Locquenghien 35, 1000 Brussels

ESPACE ARCHITECTURE LA CAMBRE An extraordinary building situated in Place Flagey, next to the cultural centre, hosting temporary architecture, design and popular culture exhibitions. It's called 'le petit Guggenheim', but it's a sort of Modernist garage in white, red and black, with two ramps running along the building in an unexpected asymmetric scheme. Place Eugène Flagey 19, 1050 Brussels, www.lacambre-archi.be

NOVA CINEMA This cinema is so underground you feel like you're in a bunker. During the day it hosts exhibitions, and you can have a beer at the bar. At night there's a good selection of art-house films and special events. Mind the chairs – they're very uncomfortable! Rue d'Arenbergstraat 3, 1000 Brussels, www.nova-cinema.org

GALLERIES AND CULTURE

THE CANAL AND THE HARBOUR Either walk or take the train to Yser/Ysère metro station and head for the unmissable white silhouette of the beautiful Citroën warehouse. Cross the canal on the 1930s bridge and look back to get one of the nicest views of Brussels – the recently renovated 'Bassin Béco'. If you're lucky, a barge will be passing by; the equivalent of 250,000 trucks of industrial materials pass through the harbour every year. Follow the canal towards the Tour et Taxis site (www.tourtaxis.be). This is a slightly over-refurbished maritime warehouse that now houses shops, restaurants and offices. Cross the canal again and you'll find yourself in front of a huge dock, with mountains of rusting cars, wood and sand alongside it. Just before the bridge you'll see a nice 1930s building. This is the headquarters of the Port de Bruxelles, which starts here and stretches for several kilometres along the canal. Boat tours of the harbour are organised every day in summertime: www.brusselsbywater.be

THE SWIMMING POOL (UNGUIDED) TOUR Brussels is home to a number of beautiful swimming pools that were built from the 1940s onwards, to provide the population with cheap bathing facilities. They're all worth visiting – but I especially love the Bains du Centre. Prices are between two and three euros. **BAINS DU CENTRE** Just next to the flea market, this pool was built in 1949. It's on the third floor and the architecture and furnishings are remarkable. Rue du Chevreuil 28, 1000 Brussels **BASSIN DE NATATION** In St Josse, near the Jardin Botanique. Rue St François 23-27, 1210 Brussels **PISCINE VICTOR BOIN** An old fashioned pool in St Gilles. Rue de la Perche 38, 1060 Brussels

WALKS AND ARCHITECTURE

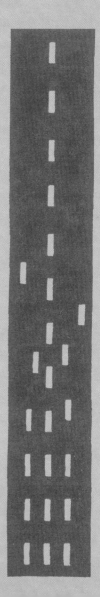

goiedag
bonjour

B BRUXEL ✈

EVENTS

PLEINOPENAIR AUGUST Every summer the Cinema Nova hosts a festival, in which they arrange thematic evenings with a concert and two movies in a derelict building, or other neglected space in Brussels. It's free and there's beer and food on offer. www.nova-cinema.org

ANIMA FESTIVAL FEBRUARY The animated film festival in Flagey has a great reputation. It screens both local and international films. www.animatv.be

AGE D'OR/THE BRUSSELS FILM FESTIVAL JUNE Featuring the best films of the European festivals, free concerts and open-air screenings. It mostly takes place in the newly renovated Film Museum and Cinematek. www.cinematek.be

KUNSTENFESTIVALDESARTS MAY This festival (whose name is a strange hybrid of Dutch and French) showcases innovative theatre and dance performances, as well as installations and lectures. www.kunstenfestivaldesarts.be

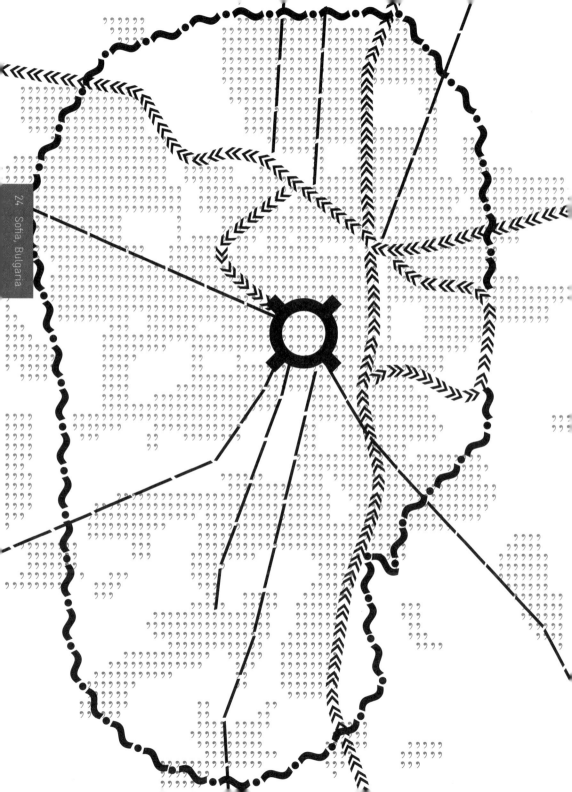

BORIS BONEV'S SOFIA

Even if you've never been to Sofia before, you'll find that there is something familiar about it — as though you visited it once in your childhood. It's a friendly place, and the people — especially the young ones — are hospitable and warm to newcomers, no matter who you are or where you come from. Visually, the thing that will stand out most as you walk around will be the contradiction between the old Baroque architecture and the Constructivist buildings left over from the days of communism. As in many Eastern European cities, it can be a bit disconcerting, as you never get a sense of a specific era — but I like the way the entire history of the city is with you at any given time — it's kind of exotic in a way.

In terms of stuff to see, there's no shortage. Sofia (and actually Bulgaria as a whole) is not a big tourist destination, but actually it should be. You could start your visit at the National Palace of Culture (NDK) — an interesting building that is now 30 years old, but still feels fresh. There is a big open space at the front, where kids like to skate, do tricks and just hang around. Alternatively you could start in one of the older parts of the city — which is where I tend to spend my time. The space in front of the Ivan Vaznov theatre is a popular meeting place, and is also one of the most beautiful Baroque buildings in Sofia. I meet my friends by the fountain, and we sit around having a drink and playing music. Take a walk around. Most of the city centre is accessible on foot, although the tram and bus system is pretty good too. In the evening you can enjoy Sofia's buzzing nightlife — there are a few mafia-run clubs and Eurotrash discos you'd do well to avoid, but also plenty of places where you can find underground culture, and friendly, like-minded artists and intellectuals.

One of the best things about the city of Sofia is the Vitosha Mountain, which is just a stone's throw away. In the summer you can go hiking — try and find the 'Boyanskata Tsarkva' — Church of Boyana, which features the remains of some beautiful murals. In winter you can ski there. In fact you can pick up some cheap skis in the market in the morning and be on the slopes by midday. If you need a proper break from the city, you can even stay in one of the many cabins that pepper the mountain.

PLACES TO STAY

ART HOSTEL This place is a cultural hub as well as a place to bed down for the night. It has a very funky downstairs bar (see Bars), a nice garden, and regular exhibitions. It also has holiday apartments to rent – all at bargain basement prices. 21A Angel Kanchev Street, www.art-hostel.com

RADISSON BLU GRAND HOTEL An international standard five-star business hotel. It has great views over the city from the business class doubles and the junior suites, and a good central location. 4 Narodno Sabranie Square, www.radissonblu.com/hotel-sofia

CRYSTAL PALACE BOUTIQUE HOTEL A 19th Century apartment block, that was renovated and extended with a huge glass and steel cube on the top. It's one of the best hotels in the city, and has funky retro décor, cool lighting and a relaxed vibe. 14 Shipka Street, www.crystalpalace-sofia.com

LES FLEURS Another boutique hotel in the centre, with friendly staff, comfortable rooms and nice design (although they might have been a little bit enthusiastic on the floral motifs!) 21 Vitosha Blvd, www.lesfleurs.com

BRASSERIE Sleek and chic dining. It serves Asian fusion food, and has a nice bar as well as a pleasant garden seating area. I like coming here for lunch. 3 Rayko Daskalov Square, www.brasserie-bg.com

MANASTIRSKA MAGERNITSA This is the place for Bulgarian cuisine. It's in a 19th Century house with a nice shady courtyard. The menu was apparently researched from the traditions of over 160 monasteries from all over the country. 67 Han Asparuh Street, www.magernitsa.com

BISTRO N8 A friendly restaurant, split over two storeys, serving European food. It has funky design (exposed bricks and contemporary furniture), and a decent bar tucked away. 8 Tzar Ivan Shishman Street

PLACES TO EAT

CLOCK HOUSE An elegant but intimate restaurant with a beautiful outdoor seating area, serving international cuisine. It takes up an entire old two-storey house, so there are different areas – all are nice. 15 Moskovska Street, www.clockhousebg.com

MOTTO Chilled out, lounge-style restaurant with funky contemporary design and a nice garden. It serves 'modern' cuisine and has a good cocktail list. 18 Asakov, www.motto-bg.com

BILKOVA One of the coolest bars in Sofia. Everyone knows it, so it's easy to find. It's not fancy, but has a nice, urban atmosphere, attracting artists, musicians and other interesting people. I especially like coming here in summer when people spill outside onto the street. 22 Tzar Ivan Shishman Street

BLAZE A bit fancier than Bilkova, but still not expensive. There's always nice house music playing (not too intrusive), and a cool crowd. The interior is well designed, and it also has an outdoor space — but not a particularly nice one — I prefer coming here in the colder months. On Fridays it can get packed. 36 Slavyanska Street

LODKI A really interesting place, located in Sofia's biggest park, Borisova Gradina, alongside an artificial canal for toy boats ('lodki' actually means 'boats'). Today the canal is empty, and is just a place to sit. It's open 24 hours a day throughout the summer months, and as it's in the middle of the park, you don't have to worry about disturbing anyone. The music is mostly reggae/ragga — that kind of thing. Lots of fun! Borisova Gradina

BUTCHERS BAR A very nice, atmospheric artist-hangout in urban minimalist design with a vaguely Constructivist-socialist vibe. There's a pretty good restaurant next door owned by the same people. Unfortunately there's no outside space. 4A Sheinovo Street

BARS

TOBA&CO BAR In the cast iron pavilion in the garden behind the National Art Gallery, you'll find this nice, old-school Parisian style bar, with plenty of outdoor seating. After 10pm, they have DJs playing decent music, and the atmosphere goes up a notch. 6A Moskovska Street

ART HOSTEL BAR Even if you're not staying at the hostel, this is a pretty interesting place to party. It's got funky design, with paintings on the walls, and lots of foreigners and locals mixing it up. Worth going to. 21A Angel Kanchev Street

SHOPPING

VITOSHA BOULEVARD Most of the high end shopping in Sofia takes place along the pedestrianised Vitosha Boulevard. You'll find all the D&G/Gucci/Lacoste labels your heart desires in and amongst the old buildings. Everything else can mostly be found in the shopping malls or the markets.

CITY CENTRE SOFIA A new mall with all the things you would expect — restaurants, fashion, a cinema, banks, etc. 2 Arenalski Blvd, www.ccs-mall.com

PUNTO & KANELA Trendy, locally designed woollen garments and accessories. 52 Neofit Rilski Street

PLOSHTAD ALEKSANDAR NEVSKI (ANTIQUES MARKET) You can always find something interesting at the antiques market — Soviet memorabilia, musical instruments and old weapons, as well as an awful lot of tat — it's all here. In the middle of the market, there's a small side street, where Bulgarian artists sell their work. The whole thing is fairly contained, but definitely worth a visit. Corner of Aleksandar Nevski Square and 11 August Street

SLAVEIKOV SQUARE Even if you can't read Bulgarian, this book market is lots of fun. It's open every day, and it sells every type of book imaginable — including old-school art and design publications. Ploshtad Slaveykov

CENTRAL SOFIA MARKET This is the big covered market in the centre of Sofia, with stalls and shops spread over three floors selling foods, jewellery, fashion and fast food. 41 Sitniakovo Blvd

TESTA GALLERY A really interesting exhibition space where you can find fresh and exciting pieces in fields as varied as ceramics, graphics, sculpture, jewellery and everything else in between. It's a cosy and friendly space. Highly recommended. 8 Tsar Ivan Shishman Street

NATIONAL ART GALLERY Situated in the former Bulgarian Royal Palace, this is a spacious 19th Century building that now houses a massive collection of Bulgarian works of art, including a particularly large medieval collection. 1 Knyaz Battenberg Square

SHIPKA 6 AND RAYKO ALEXIEV GALLERY The Union of Bulgarian Artists is a non-profit organisation protecting the interests of the nation's artists. These are its two big exhibition spaces, between them hosting around eight exhibitions a month of both local and international artists in all the visual art forms. Shipka 6, 2nd Floor and 125 Rakovski Street respectively, www.sbhart.com

FOREIGN ART GALLERY This gallery, which has an eclectic collection of classic, modern and ancient exotic art, is housed in the State Printing House designed by the Viennese architect Friedrich Schwanberg. It has an impressive collection of graphic prints and illustrations through the ages. 1 Alexandar Nevski Square, www.foreignartmuseum.bg

1908 GALLERY This is the newest gallery in Sofia. Run by a violinist, a conductor and a ballet director, it's a small but interesting space. It's got an open policy for artists working in a variety of mediums. 1 Angel Kanchev Street

WALKS AND ACRHITECURE

GALLERIES AND CULTURE

IVAN VAZOV THEATRE AND SURROUNDS The national theatre is located in an ornate Neo-classical building. It hosts some interesting productions (and at €5 a ticket, it's worth going even if you don't understand anything), but its location is what really makes it nice. There's a pedestrianised area and a small park in front of it, with a fountain and statues. It offers a refreshing break from the city, hosting open-air concerts and events in the summer. If you come here during the day take a walk around. The area is paved with yellow flagstones that were a gift from the Russian government in the Soviet era. If you come here at night, you'll find that the area has a pleasant buzz about it, with a handful of cafes and old guys playing chess on the outdoor tables. 5 Dyakon Ignatiy Street

SOFIA'S CHURCHES You can't miss the churches as you walk around the city. Built in Eastern-Orthodox style, they're very bling. The 'Russian Church' (aka St Nikolay Mirikliiski Church) was built in 1923 in the architectural style of 17th Century Moscow, with gold domes and fairy-cake detailing. It has some crazy murals inside, painted in the 1940s. Aleksandar Nevski Cathedral is a more squat building, but equally elaborate. It has one of the largest collections of orthodox icons in Europe (if you're into that kind of thing), and has a small flea market in front of it on most days.

NDK This impressive modern fortress of a building is the largest multifunctional conference and exhibition centre in the region. It was opened in 1981 and has an area of 123,000m^2 over 11 floors. There is more steel used in it than in the Eiffel Tower – apparently. It sometimes hosts interesting exhibitions. www.ndk.bg

VITOSHA MOUNTAIN The Vitosha Mountain borders the suburbs of Sofia, and is preserved as part of a national park encompassing over 250km^2. It has forests, rivers, springs and a ski resort. Get a map from the tourist office and hike around. Try to get to the Boyana Waterfall, which has an impressive 15m drop into the Boyanska river. Alternatively you can bathe in the thermal springs at Knyazheno, Rondantsy, Boyana or Simeonovo. They're said to have curative powers. If you're into skiing, the Aleko ski resort is very popular, and is only 22km away from the city centre.

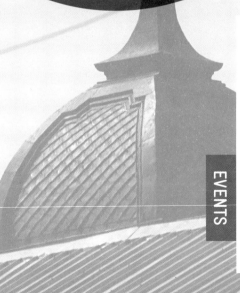

EVENTS

SOFIA DESIGN WEEK JUNE
Workshops, exhibitions and
talks by an impressive selection
of international designers.
sofiadesignweek.com

SOFIA FILMFEST MARCH A big,
fun event held in the National
Art Gallery. www.cinema.bg

PARK LIVE MUSIC FESTIVAL JUNE
A three day music festival held
in the cycling park and featuring
international DJs and acts in
hip-hop, pop and electronica.
www.parklivefest.com

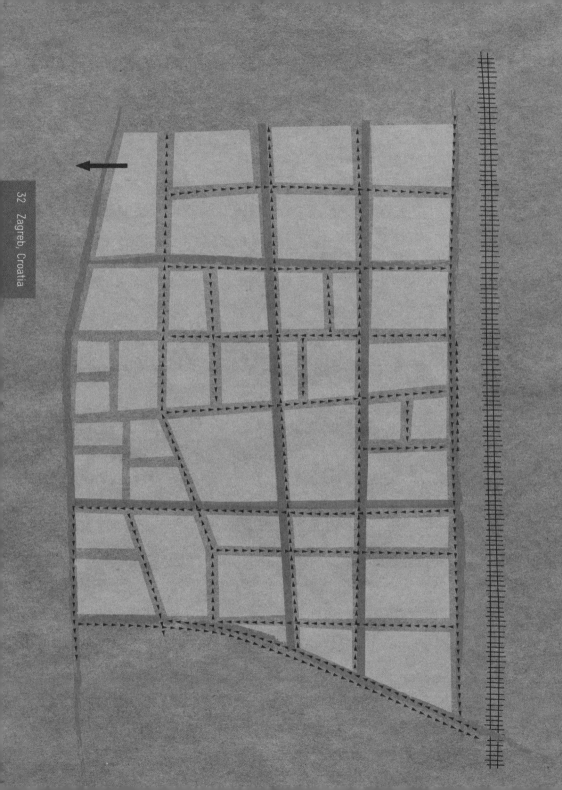

martina skender's ZAGREB

Zagreb is a surprising city on many fronts. Geographically it's wedged between the Medvednica Mountain and the River Sava. Throughout the ages it has had a strategic significance, being ideally located on the routes connecting Western Europe to the East, via the Adriatic Sea. It's home to more than a quarter of Croatia's population, around 1.2 million people, but it doesn't feel like a metropolis. It's got virtually no skyscrapers or tall buildings, and thanks to its hemmed-in geography, its layout is contained and comforting – you often bump into people you know. There's a friendly atmosphere that you don't often find in cities – people are always happy to help you with directions, advice, or maybe just have a conversation over a beer. It's not long before you start feeling like you know everyone in the city.

Croatia is often criticised for being overly centralised, and Zagreb is very much that centre. All the culture, arts, sports and academic institutions are concentrated here. The university faculties are spread all over the city, and the large student population keeps Zagreb vibrant, colourful, fresh and young. You'll notice that the city is wallpapered with posters for concerts, theatre and festivals, and most of the year it's buzzing with events and happenings. I'm sure you'll find something to take your fancy – and let's not even start on the street art – just go and explore – you'll find the streets speaking to you with a specifically Balkan sense of humour and social engagement.

Architecturally, the city is reminiscent of Vienna, Budapest and Prague – with a bit of Italy mixed in there as well. It has broad, manicured boulevards, little courtyards and a medieval Old Town with steep cobbled streets. The centre is divided into two parts – Gornji Grad (Upper Town) and Donji Grad (Lower Town) that are connected by a funicular railway. The river is not really a focal point for the city, except that it separates the centre from the ugly modern suburb of Novi Zagreb (there is a serious lack of urban planning in the newer neighbourhoods). In general, as you move away from the centre, the more the Yugoslavian and Balkan part of the city's history becomes apparent in the socialist architecture.

A couple more things to add: Zagreb is a fairly safe city and it is an easy city to navigate. It has shiny, new air-conditioned trams, many bicycle lanes and most of it is walkable. Enjoy!

PLACES TO STAY

ARCOTEL ALLEGRA ZAGREB
Zagreb's first designer hotel. It's done in tasteful Mediterranean style, and it shares a building with a multiplex cinema. Try the wellness area at the top of the building – apart from anything else you'll get a great view. Branimirova 29, www.arcotel.at

ASTORIA BEST WESTERN PREMIER HOTEL A newly refurbished hotel built in 1932. It's friendly and serves a nice breakfast. Petrinjska 71

HOBO BEAR HOSTEL A laid-back hostel in an old building with a comfortable, contemporary soul. Whether you're a modern day hobo, or just a budget traveller, you'll find yourself welcome here. Andrije Medulićeva 4, www.hobobearhostel.com

PLACES TO EAT

PEKARNICA DINARA Fast food in Zagreb is traditionally baked goods – pitas, pastry and burek (puff pastry filled with cheese, meat or vegetables). You'll recognise this small chain of bakeries by the queues outside and the tantalising smell. They sell 150 types of bread here! Multiple stores; Britanski trg, Gajeva ulica, Dolac Market

BOBAN Owned by the famous Croatian football player, Zvoninier Boban, this is an Italian restaurant in a rustic cellar setting. It's laid-back but sophisticated, and has a big menu with a good wine list. Upstairs there's a cafe where the rich and the beautiful hang out. If you want to come for lunch, make sure to book in advance. Gajeva 9, www.boban.hr

TRILOGIJA If you're in the Old City and you need a bite, this intimate little place is a good bet. It has an intriguing and imaginative menu that changes according to which fresh ingredients can be bought at Dolac Market, and a great international wine list. Kamenita 5, www.trilogija.com

RESTORAN NOVA Irresistible vegan specialties based on macrobiotic principles that attract both foreigners and locals. It's a peaceful retreat – so if you've been tired out by the day it might just restore your calmness, concentration and focus. Ilica 72/I, www.novarestoran.com.hr

IVICA I MARICA This restaurant, which is named after the Croatian version of Hansel and Gretel, started as an oasis of healthy desserts, made using wholemeal flour, brown sugar and organic ingredients. Later on they added a restaurant serving traditional Croatian food with a fairytale theme. There's a strong organic/ethical approach to the food here too. You can't mistake the gingerbread house – but don't worry – Zagreb's witch is long gone. Tkalčićeva 70, www.ivicaimarica.com

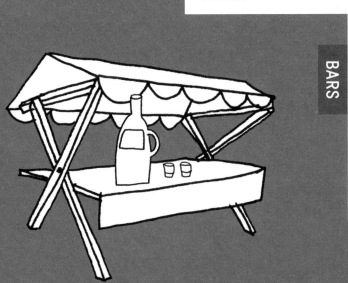

THE JAZZ CLUB ZAGREB A relatively new addition to Zagreb's nightlife, this is an intimate basement venue playing great jazz, and promoting emerging artists. Young musicians perform, filmmakers hold screenings, and new artists use the walls to exhibit their work. Gundulićeva 11

SEDMICA Located between the Faculty of Architecture and the Art Academy, this relaxed, clandestine cafe/bar is a popular hangout for students and art professionals. It's a great place to find out what's new on the art scene. Kačićeva 7A

KIC Kic – or Cultural Informational Centre – has a lot of good spaces to hang out in. On the ground floor is a famous terrace cafe/bar. On the first floor you'll find an internet corner. The second floor has another cafe/bar with comfy sofas, and a screening/ lecture room. Pick whichever you like the best. Around the corner you'll find Gallery Forum – one of Zagreb's most famous galleries. Preradovićeva 5, www.kic.hr

BARS

CICA Tkalčićeva Street is packed with cafes that turn into bars in the evening. Cica ('Boob') Bar is a small, well-designed place at the beginning of the street. It's known for its variety of 'rakija' and for its cool crowd. It occasionally hosts poetry readings, exhibitions and screenings. Tkalčićeva 18

KRIVI PUT Translating as 'Wrong Way', this bar is a very local venue that stays open till 2am. It's in a small warehouse covered with graffiti and shares a yard with a gallery and a fast food stand that sells sausages. Sometimes it holds concerts, but mostly there is just good music, a jolly atmosphere and cheap drinks. Runjaninova 3

PROFIL MEGASTORE Zagreb's book heaven. Really. I go there at least once a week. It has a great selection of literature, philosophy, sociology and of course, art and design books. Don't miss the upstairs cafe, which is a great place to go in winter months. Oops! I almost forgot to mention the multimedia store in the basement! Bogovićeva 7, www.profil.hr

CROATA KRAVATA Croats make some of the finest ties and cravats in the world, and this is the place to buy them. They use high quality silk and different weaving techniques. The intricate details and patterns are impressive. Oktogon Passage near Ilica

NEBO In Importanne Mall, this very cool shop stocks the minimalist style of designer Dinka Grubišić. Radićeva 17

SHOPPING

DOLAC MARKET Dolac market represents the heart of the city. Farmers still come here from miles away to sell their goods. Walk up the stairs north of Jelačić Square, and you'll find yourself in an open-air market surrounded by fruits and vegetables. A bit further along you'll find handmade baskets, textiles and other Croatian products. In the enclosed bit they sell fresh meat, fish, cheese and pasta. It's one of the best European markets. Tkalčićeva

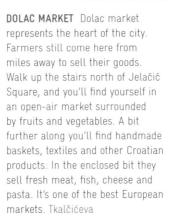

ANTIQUES MARKET BRITANAC The Britanac farmers' market, which takes place every day, is transformed on Sundays into an antiques/flea market. This is a good way to get a taste of the old Zagreb – you'll find old photos, tableware, jewellery and furniture, as well as tales of the 'good old days' from the sellers. Britanski trg

I-GLE Croatian fashion design has taken a while to break through, but there are a few designers that have finally begun to make an impact, and even to gain an international following. I-gle is one of them – they make strikingly dramatic dresses that have gained cult status. Dežmanov prolaz 4, www.i-gle.com

BOUDOIR Another dramatic fashion label selling feminine, nostalgic and romantic clothes. Radićeva 25

PRODAVAONICA KARAS The oldest art supply store in Zagreb with a wide variety of materials. It has an adjacent gallery – Galerija Likum. Dežmanov prolaz 2

FILMSKI PROGRAMI This is a programme of alternative, art-house, classic and amateur films that takes place at the wonderful 19th Century Tuškanac Cinema. There is also a series of workshops, director talks and other events (check the website). Tuškanac 1, www.filmski-programi.hr

HDD GALERIJA The Croatian Design Society (HDD) is a voluntary, non-profit professional association that serves to improve the working conditions of its members. This newly opened gallery offers exhibitions, lectures and information about design in Croatia. Boškovićeva 18, www.hdd.hr

ULUPUH GALLERY This is the gallery of the Association of Artists of Applied Arts, and has exhibitions on everything from architecture, to industrial design, photography, ceramics, textile design and jewellery. Tkalčićeva 14

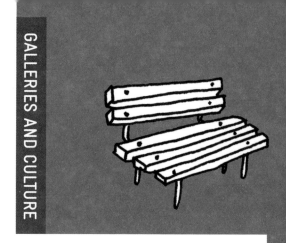

HDLU HDLU (Croatian Association of Artists) is situated in the first circular museum ever built, which was designed by Croatian sculptor Ivan Mestrovic in 1938. Over the course of its history it has been used as a mosque, a pavilion and finally this open gallery space and multi-platform cultural centre. It holds international level exhibitions and is well worth a visit. Trg žrtava fašizma, www.hdlu.hr

STUDENTSKI CENTAR One way or another you will probably end up at the student centre at some point – whether to check out an exhibition, to watch a play or concert, to see a movie in Zagreb's biggest cinema or to go to a bar/club night. It's situated in the buildings that held Zagreb's first international fair. Some have been renovated and others are still in disrepair. In some ways, this is the heart of alternative Croatian culture. Savska 5, www.sczg.hr

ZAGREB'S ARCHITECTURE Your architectural tour of Zagreb can start with the Baroque architecture of the Upper Town. From there, make your way downtown to see the turn-of-the-century buildings, including some excellent examples of Secession architecture. After that, have a stroll down Vukovarska Street where you can see socialist architecture at its best. You'll also pass by the new National University Library (NSB), a good example of contemporary architecture (built in 1995), and finally end up in front of the newest building in Zagreb, the Museum of Contemporary Art (at the time of writing it's still under construction). If you then need a bit of peace and quiet you can go to the beautiful Mirogoj Cemetery – one of the nicest in Europe. It's located on Mirogojska Road and Hermann Bollé Street, and architect Hermann Bollé himself designed the main building.

GREEN ZAGREB There are many beautiful places for nature walks in and around Zagreb. Sljeme on top of Medvjednica Mountain is just a train ride away. Or you can follow the long green space that runs along the River Sava – where I often come to clear my mind – even on a rainy day. Alternatively you can check out Maksimir Park in the east of the city, which has some lovely meadows and a zoo. If you come in summer, make sure to take a dip in Jarun – Zagreb's famous lake.

EVENTS

Almost every week starting from September to
June there is some kind of event or happening
going on. These are some of my favourites:

ANIMAFEST JUNE This is the second oldest
animation festival in Europe. It is built on
the tradition of the famous Zagreb School
of Animation. www.animafest.hr

MUSIC BIENNALE ZAGREB MAY An international
festival of contemporary music that has been
running since 1961. www.biennale-zagreb.hr

ZAGREBDOX FEBRUARY-MARCH The
biggest international documentary film
festival in the region. www.zagrebdox.net

ZAGREB FILM FESTIVAL OCTOBER Our
version of Berlin or Cannes gets better
by the year. It also has some great
parties. www.zagrebfilmfestival.com

TJEDAN SUVREMENOG PLESA MAY-JUNE
This week-long dance festival is a great
way to see cutting edge contemporary
dance, physical theatre and mime.
www.danceweekfestival.com

evripides zantides's Lefkosia

Nicosia, or Lefkosia, as it is known to locals, has a rich history, which is apparent wherever you go. Its ideal geographical location means that it has been conquered by countless nations over the years, most importantly the Venetians in the 15th Century, who built the fortifying walls that still envelop the Old City, and the Ottomans in the 16th Century, who occupied the city for three centuries, leaving a clear cultural imprint.

Just before Cypriot independence in 1960, the city was racked with violence between the Greek and Turkish populations, and this eventually led to a Greek-supported coup followed by a Turkish invasion in 1974. For the past 35 years, the northern sector of the city has been divided by a wall known as 'the Green Line' separating the Turkish Cypriot community in the north and the Greek Cypriot south. In 2008 the wall on the main shopping street, Ledra Street, was torn down in an effort to reunify the two communities.

Architecturally this is also a divided city. There is an old part and a new part, built after the war. I find the Old City much more interesting, with its never-ending windy roads bustling with activity and rich with authentic character. You'll notice that there are very few examples of residential architecture in the main parts of the Old City. Most of the buildings that were once domestic are now used for commercial purposes – many of them specialising in carpentry or glass works. However, if you look more closely, there are residential areas tucked away where you might find an older generation that have been there for many years, or younger people who have been helped by the government to revitalise the area. It's also in these areas that you will find some more off-beat establishments run by a younger generation, and small businesses set up by foreign nationals.

I have lived in Lefkosia all my life, leaving to go to university and then coming back. What I like most are the summer nights in the open-air cinemas under a full moon. The city has grown since Cyprus joined the European Union, and now has a population of around 300,000. Even so, the distances are easily traversed – with a good bus network and taxis that are cheap, friendly and easy to flag down. There is a warm, welcoming atmosphere that I miss when I leave. Friends have verandahs and big gardens that are always open for visitors to sit up late chatting and eating halloumi and watermelon.

ALMOND HOTEL This is a business hotel, but I really like its style – very small and comfortable and quite boutique-y. It's situated a little outside of the centre so it's quiet but still easily accessible. 25th March Street 11, Ayioi Omologites, www.almond-businesshotel.com

CROWN INN HOTEL This is a quiet, local hotel in the area of Ayios Andreas, a really lovely residential neighbourhood just outside the city. It's been revamped, and if you walk around you'll get an idea of what the city is trying to make of its antiquities. 13 Philellinon Street, Ayios Andreas, www.crowninnhotel.com

HOTEL AVEROF A locally owned hotel in the centre of the city with rustic décor, predominantly dressed with wood and wrought iron and locally produced furniture. 19 Averof Street, Ayios Andreas, www.averof.com.cy

CLASSIC HOTEL This hotel is well known for short stays and I've had a few friends and colleagues stay here. It's got a modern, minimalist interior but it's quite cosy, and is very well situated in the centre of the city. 94 Rigenis Street, www.classic.com.cy

ZANETTOS This is one of my favourites – a family-run restaurant open only at night that serves mezze plates. I like to make myself comfortable here, and whatever they have on offer eventually makes its way to the table. It's got a lively local atmosphere – especially at weekends. 65 Trikoupi Street, www.zanettos.com

IL FORNO I often end up at this restaurant having work meetings or brainstorming sessions. Many design ideas were cooked up over a plate of pasta made by the owner, who I know well. It's quite a small place but the portions of food are huge – great value for money! 216-218 Ledras Street

MAT-THAIOS Another local diner set in a narrow street where you can get the feel of city life. It serves authentic Cypriot dishes, always tasty and fresh. 4 Platia 28 Oktovriou

AYIOS YIORGOS (ST. GEORGE) This is a traditional Cypriot diner that only serves local foods. I like coming here on market days (Wednesday and Saturday) because it is located on the market square and you end up eating alongside the stall holders. Sometimes at night, you'll find yourself listening to an impromptu Bouzouki performance by some of the old regulars. 27 Platia Paliou Dimarchiou

BARS

KALA KATHOUMENA A low key, traditional coffee shop in the Old City that stays open until late. It's in an old, peculiarly shaped house, shaded by trees and local plants. The owner is always really friendly and it's predominantly frequented by musicians. 21 Nicocleous, Stoa Faneromenis

NEW DIVISION This has got to be my favourite bar in Lefkosia, and is often where my friends and I end up. It is set in a traditional colonial house with a courtyard, and always plays a great selection of alternative music, attracting a really good mix of customers. 2 V Frederikis Street

TRITOS Open on an event-only basis, Tritos is set on the third floor of a building in an old apartment that was creatively transformed into a bar. It hosts live music events and is a key part of the cultural scene. 40 Leoforos Evagorou, Pantheon Building, 3rd Floor, www.pantheongallery.org

BREW Although it is right in the heart of the touristy area of Lefkosia (Laiki Gitonia), Brew is still worth a visit. During the day it serves tea and food, and at night it is a lively bar that is a local hangout for young artists and students. 30B Hippocratous

PLATOS Platos has existed forever and is a true Cypriot pub in the heart of the Old City. It has a nice courtyard in the summer and a cozy fireplace in the winter. 8-10 Platonos Street

MOUFFLON BOOKSHOP This is a quaint bookshop in the centre of town that is also a publishers. It's into promoting art and design books as well as local publications. 1 Sofouli Street, www.moufflon.com.cy

TWENTYTHREE A design shop owned by a local couple, who make most of the products themselves. They also organise fairs every few months where they invite local designers to sell their products. 86 Aisxilou Street

MIDGET FACTORY A shop window that is designed by up and coming artists. Nothing to buy but lots to see! Eptanisiou Street.

KITIOPIO A shop dedicated exclusively to handmade boxes of any size. Nice to see in action. 4 Achilleos Street

BOMBA BOOKS Bomba Books is a publishing house specialising in illustrated books and other printed matter. It also has a screen-printing studio and its shop sells limited edition t-shirts and prints made there, as well as other design products. 4 Mouson, www.bombabooks.com

MUNICIPAL MARKET Every Wednesday and Saturday morning you will find a vibrant food market in the Old City. I like to go to the fruit section on Saturdays where you can try everything before you buy. Platia Paliou Dimarchiou

INTERNATIONAL MARKET Every Sunday morning, the Lefkosia municipality gives a space to locals and immigrants to sell anything from food, second-hand items and clothes, to cheap bric-a-brac. Arasta Street

SHOPPING

WALKS AND ARCHITECTURE

HISTORICAL LEFKOSIA The architecture of Lefkosia is typically low buildings with large gardens and internal courtyards that you can catch glimpses of through doorways. The Old City is surrounded by Venetian walls and you can follow a nice little trail along the moat at the base of the walls.

There are plenty of historical buildings worth a look, such as the house of Dragoman Hadjigeorgakis Kornissios – a good example of urban architecture from the Ottoman Rule. The Turkish Baths (Hammam Omerye) and the mosque standing in front of it are both well worth a visit.

Keep an eye out for the handful of mud buildings that are still standing. There are some very elegant, well-preserved houses that will jump out at you. These are mostly from colonial times and are held in high regard.

PANTHEON CULTURAL ASSOCIATION This is a non-profit organisation that is involved in festivals, workshops and music/stage productions. It provides great opportunities for young artists. 40 Leoforos Evagorou, 2nd Floor, www.pantheongallery.org

STOA AESCHYLOU An interesting space dedicated to experimental art projects. 5 Aisxilou Street, www.stoaaeschylou.blogspot.com

ARTOS CULTURAL AND RESEARCH FOUNDATION A contemporary arts and sciences centre that often hosts interesting events. 64 Ayios Omoloyiton Avenue, www.artosfoundation.org

LEFKOSIA MUNICIPAL CENTRE OF THE ARTS (POWER HOUSE) This is a really interesting architectural space built in Bauhaus style out of an old power station. It was left derelict for 20 years, and was restored in 1994 to host important cultural events. 19 Apostolou Varnava Street, www.nimac.com.cy

IS NOT GALLERY This gallery presents mostly photography exhibitions. It's located in the Old City, and promotes underground art. 11 Odysseos Street

DIATOPOS GALLERY An experimental space that hosts alternative art projects and video installations. Very dynamic. 11 Kritis, www.diatopos.com

EVENTS

KYPRIA FESTIVAL SEPTEMBER-OCTOBER An annual Cyprus-wide arts festival organised by the Ministry of Education and Culture.

INTERNATIONAL DOCUMENTARY FILM FESTIVAL OF LEFKOSIA JULY-AUGUST A week-long festival featuring a fantastic selection of international documentaries. www.cyprusdocfest.org

RAINBOW FESTIVAL NOVEMBER KISA (Action for Equality, Support, Antiracism) organises an annual festival in the heart of the city that encourages all nationalities to present their culture through traditional dancing, singing, theatre and food. www.kisa.org.cy

This is a map of my city. It is a structure of the different ways in which I orientate myself in the city.

Filip Blažek's PRAGUE

Prague is a picturesque city. It managed to escape most of the bombing in the Second World War, and the Gothic spires, Renaissance mansions, Cubist architecture and Art Deco blocks sit side by side in harmony, with the Vltava River running through it all. The downside is that Prague has become a tourist hotspot. It's the sixth most visited European city, and thanks to its cheap beer and nightclubs, has become a big stag weekend destination. Try to avoid tourist traps and overpriced restaurants (which are easily recognised by the absence of the Czech language), and I assure you, you won't forget the trip.

Almost all places of interest are within walking distance from the city centre. If you want to explore more remote areas, there's an efficient public transport system consisting of a metro, trams, buses, one spectacular funicular line to Petřín hill, and even several ferries connecting the islands on the Vltava River. One important warning: if you plan to use a taxi, call one of the recommended taxi companies or ask the bartender or receptionist to call you one. Never ever pick up a cab from Wenceslas Square or Old Town Square if you don't want to spend your daily budget on a 500m ride.

The area I'll focus most on is Holešovice, which is where I live and work. Once an industrial suburb, this is a rapidly developing area with a river port from the turn of the century, and beautiful factory spaces that are being converted into art institutions and commercial premises. The modern art arm of the National Gallery is also based here in the impressive Veletržní Palace, and the former game reserve of Stromovka has been transformed into a huge park surrounded by exhibition grounds, the river and Letná Hill. A great place for resting, biking, walking, running or picnicking. Holešovice is less touristy than most areas, and has a fantastic atmosphere, with loads of hidden gems, which is why most of my recommendations are in this area.

Please take an invitation to Holešovice as a general invitation to explore the parts of the city that lie outside of the central area. Not spoiled by tourism, you can check out dozens of traditional beer pubs in the Žižkov area, modern architecture by Jean Nouvelle in the former industrial area of Anděl, or one of the many Functionalist villas built by famous architects in the Prague suburbs.

Don't get taken for a ride!
A few reliable cab companies:
AAA RADIOTAXI Call +420
222 333 222 or order online:
www.radiotaxiaaa.cz
CITYTAXI Call +420 257 257
257 or send an SMS to +420
777 257 257, www.citytaxi.cz
MODRÝ ANDĚL +420 272 700
202, or book online:
www.modryandel.cz.

PLACES TO STAY

SIR TOBY'S This hostel is probably the most popular one in Prague. Located in Holešovice, it's ten minutes away from downtown by tram (which operates throughout the night) and has plenty of private rooms. There is a pub in the cellar, which occasionally hosts movie screenings and live gigs, and a couple of decent clubs (Mecca and the more alternative Cross) are nearby. The Italian next door, Lucky Luciano, is a popular 'mafia' restaurant. Dělnická 24, Prague 7, www.sirtobys.com

HOTEL JOSEF The mania of design hotels came to Prague quite recently. This was one of the first. It was designed by famous Czech architect Eva Jiřičná, and is located in the heart of downtown, ten minutes from Old Town Square. The logotype and signage were designed by Zuzana Lednická from the prominent design studio Najbrt. Rybná 20, Prague 1, www.hoteljosef.com

PLACES TO EAT

U HOUBAŘE Traditional beer houses in downtown Prague have almost disappeared over the past 20 years, replaced by restaurants, bars and pubs. U Houbaře, opposite the Veletržní palace in Holešovice, is one of the few left standing, where you can enjoy cheap goulash, roasted game and excellent Pilsner Urquell in an authentic atmosphere devoid of tourists. Dukelských hrdinů 30, Prague 7

ESSE A recent addition to Holešovice's dining scene, Esse is a bar, restaurant and club, with a large room for non-smokers (very unusual in Prague). The food is delicate and service perfect – which means that it gets quite busy, so make sure to book in advance. I had a lunch here for all my best clients and it was a great success. Dukelských hrdinů 696/43, Prague 7, www.esse.cz

PRVNÍ HOLEŠOVICKÁ KAVÁRNA This cafe, which opened in the early 1990s, was one of the reasons I first started to visit Holešovice. It's a friendly place with great food and cheap beer that is packed in the evenings with locals, artists and writers. There are regular exhibitions of work for sale by young artists. If the cigarette smoke gets to you, go to the 'open space' of the old factory next door, La Fabrika. Komunardů 30, Prague 7, www.kavoska.cz

HOTEL YASMIN Studio Najbrt were also involved in this hotel, which was designed in collaboration with architecture studio Mimolimit. It's well located and gets good web reviews for its interior and food. Politických vězňů 913/12, Prague 1, www.hotel-yasmin.cz

DŮM U VELKÉ BOTY My friends run a small family hotel (in English 'House at the Big Boot') in an old Renaissance house in Malá Strana (Lesser Town). It's located ten minutes walk from the Prague Castle, in a small square just opposite the Lobkowitz Palace. Everyone I know who's stayed in this hotel was very satisfied with the quality of the service and the friendly family atmosphere. In fact, it's one of the top B&Bs in Prague according to the travellers' websites! Vlašská 30/333, Prague 1, www.dumuvelkeboty.cz

The public transport system: there are three metro lines. The tramlines (marked in pink) bring business to the streets they run through. The areas around most of the tramlines are filled with shops. The train (black) is not really used in the city centre.

OKO Oko Cinema is a beautiful example of Functionalist architecture, and is one of the few remaining original cinemas in the city. It screens a combination of art-house and mainstream releases, and has a friendly lobby bar. The ambience is quite cold (as you would expect from Functionalist architecture), but the late-night parties are great, with the big neon sign turning the surrounding street a surreal shade of blue. Františka křížka 15, Prague 7, www.biooko.cz

LETENSKÝ ZÁMEČEK Prague is definitely not a destination for lovers of open air, late-night drinking – most of the restaurants and bars close their gardens at 10pm. Letenský zámeček is a nice building that houses three restaurants in a surrounding park. A nearby stall sells beer all night long, so join the queue, find a place to sit on the grass, and enjoy the beautiful view from Letná Hill. One of my favourite summertime activities! Letenské sady 341, Prague 7, www.letenskyzamecek.cz

ŠMERALOVA STREET If you're after a drink, tapas or Chinese food, head to Šmeralova Street. It's packed with cafes, bars and restaurants. The pizzeria is no great shakes, but La Bodega Flamenca does good tapas, and not far from there is my favourite pub and restaurant, Fraktál. There is also a Vietnamese grocery that's open till late and a tiny and very friendly Sicilian shop selling food and drink. Šmeralova is a very popular destination for open-minded people from the whole of Prague. If you can't find a place to sit, turn into one of the side streets and try your luck there.

BARS

Streets and squares form a wonderful pattern – you can identify the older parts and more modern parts of the city.

Until very recently there were no design shops in Prague at all. Although the situation is slowly getting better, there is still no specialist bookshop or art supplier, and people like me have to get their fix in London or Berlin. On the plus side, several small shops have popped up selling designer objects by young Czech artists – so you can bypass the Moleskine and Zack staples, and go straight to the local treasures.

FUTURISTA Opened in 2007, this little shop sells products by renowned and emerging artists and designers. Allegedly 99 per cent of their stock comes from the Czech Republic. They also sell vintage chairs and lamps. Soukenická 8, Prague 1, www.futurista.cz

KUBISTA Cubist architecture is a phenomenon unique to Prague, in which architects attempted to take the ideas of Cubist art into the built environment. The Kubista shop is a nice stop for all Cubism aficionados – they offer books and postcards as well as many careful replicas of original furniture, ashtrays, candle holders and jewellery. Ovocný trh 19, Prague 1, www.kubista.cz

MODERNISTA This is a 350m^2 space in the heart of the Old Town, specialising in both classic and contemporary Czech design and decorative arts. You'll find ceramics, lighting, jewellery, contemporary glass, toys, Modernist furniture and much more. Celetná 12, Prague 1, www.modernista.cz

This scheme reflects my patterns of behaviour in the urban environment: I usually rest in the violet areas, I shop in the pink areas, and the orange areas are where I go for cultural stimulation.

HARD-DE-CORE A workshop space with a shop attached selling design items such as toys, t-shirts, tableware and jewellery by a handful of young Czech designers. There are also various craft courses on offer. Senovážné náměstí 10, Prague 1, www.harddecore.cz

LEEDA Leeda is an original Czech fashion boutique located near the National Theatre, with a distinctive collection by two fashion designers who collaborate with various artists, photographers, and most recently, the architect Jan Kaplický. Bartolomějská 1, Prague 1, www.leeda.cz

My patterns of behaviour relating to the green areas in the city.

DOX Dox is a new gallery situated in a converted old factory in Holešovice. It played a key role in promoting the area as an art hub, and is a dynamic part of the Czech contemporary art scene, hosting exhibitions, lectures and events. Its logotype was designed by the famous Czech designer, Aleš Najbrt. It also has a nice cafe with a terrace and a design shop. Osadní 34, Prague 7, www.doxprague.org

VELETRŽNÍ PALACE This Functionalist building, constructed 1925-28, hosted trade fairs until the 1950s, and was once the largest building in the world. Today it houses the extensive contemporary art collection of the National Gallery. You can see all the big names here, as well as work by top Czech artists. Try the virtual tour on the website for a taster of the fantastic shapes and lines of the white interior. Dukelských hrdinů 47, Prague 7, www.ngprague.cz

LA FABRIKA This recently renovated old factory is easy to spot by the tall brick chimney that towers over its surrounds. It's a cleverly designed, multi-functional space operating as a club, cinema, gallery and theatre. Komunardů 30, Prague 7, www.lafabrika.cz

UMĚLECKOPRŮMYSLOVÉ MUSEUM V PRAZE The Museum of Decorative Arts is a two-storey Neo-Renaissance building, exhibiting historical and contemporary crafts and applied arts. The print and image department has a great collection of Czech posters from 1850-1938, as well as a big selection of typography from Europe and Bohemia through the ages. Across the road, you'll find the impressive Rudolphinium building, which houses a music hall and the best contemporary art gallery in Prague, and around the corner is the VŠUP – the Academy of Arts Architecture and Design, which holds an open house at the end of each semester, as well as occasional exhibitions. 17 Listopadu 2, Prague 1, www.upm.cz

DESIGNBLOK OCTOBER An annual week-long event at over 100 galleries, boutiques and other venues all over the city, exhibiting new pieces from the world of design. The main attractions feature in the Designblok 'Superstudios' – the locations of which change from year to year. Buy a programme and find out what's on offer. www.designblok.cz

DESIGN SUPERMARKET DECEMBER A great place for Christmas gifts – it's a fair in which 30 or so designers (mostly from the Czech Republic) sell their jewellery, glass, fashion and other products. It's got a fantastic atmosphere. www.designsupermarket.cz

ARCHITECTURE WEEK SEPTEMBER An annual festival of architecture and interior design, featuring debates, films, lectures, presentations and exhibitions around the city. www.architectureweek.cz

UNITED ISLANDS OF PRAGUE JUNE A summer music festival located on the Prague islands featuring a mixture of local and world pop music. There's a special programme for children as well. www.unitedislands.cz

JEDEN SVĚT/ONE WORLD MARCH One World is the largest human rights film festival in Europe. Book in advance. www.oneworld.cz

FEBIOFEST MARCH-APRIL This is a large international film festival that is located in the Village Cinemas Multiplex at Anděl. I love this event – the atmosphere is great – an otherwise deserted cinema complex is suddenly packed with people discussing movies, the restaurants around offer discounts and performances for those who didn't manage to get film tickets, and the basement garage is transformed into a club. www.febiofest.cz

STROMOVKA This is one of my favourite walks in Prague. If you want a break from the traffic and crowds, take a tram to the Výstaviště stop, and walk into Stromovka Park. You can follow the tram tracks – the effect of the trams driving through the old trees is magical – especially at night. Follow the signs to the zoo. You'll pass the planetarium and the folly, crossing the Vltava on a footbridge, until you find yourself next to the Baroque park walls and the Troja Château, a grand 17th Century summer palace on the river, which holds art exhibitions for the City of Prague Gallery. Behind the Troja Château you'll find the zoo – it's a good one – I visit there several times a year. While you're there, check out the exhibition of the 2002 floods, which completely covered Stromovka, Troja Château and the lower part of the zoo. Imagine – the water level was about 6m higher than normal – many of the zoo's animals perished in the devastation. To get back, you can take the 112 bus to the nearest metro station. www.planetarium.cz, www.ghmp.cz, www.zoopraha.cz

CUBIST ARCHITECTURE Cubist architecture was a fairly brief experimental movement that explored the new shapes facades could take in reinforced concrete structures. Some of the loveliest examples of Cubist architecture are located under Vyšehrad Hill. Take a tram to Výtoň stop, and follow the tracks along the bank to a huge rock, which has a tunnel for trams and cars. On your left you'll see several Cubist villas. Pay attention to the detailing – window bars, door handles etc. If you then go back to the iron railway bridge, and turn right just before the railway line, you'll find yourself at the end of Neklanova Street, where there's an amazing corner block of flats designed in 1913, and one of the most interesting examples of Cubist architecture in Prague. From here, take the tram back to the city centre and get off at the Lazarská stop, to admire the wonderful Cubist house with an adjacent Cubist niche built over a Baroque statue. Then find the Bata shoe store in the lower part of Wenceslas Square. Just behind the shop there is a Cubist street lantern hidden in a small yard next to the church.

OLD PRAGUE To experience the narrow cobbled streets of old Prague, start your walk in the New World, the maze of beautiful alleys and medieval houses near Prague Castle and Prague Loreto. Then walk up the hill to Loreto Square (if you don't mind hordes of tourists, you can visit the Renaissance Santa Casa). Walk to Pohořelec Square. Hidden in house number eight is a staircase that will take you to the yard of the Strahov monastery, which has a very well preserved Baroque library. From here you can either go down the hill to to Malá Strana (Lesser Town) or escape to the green space of Petřín Hill. If you choose the latter, just follow the footpath that starts in front of the Museum of Czech Literature, until you reach the Petřínské Terasy pub (I can't really recommend the food, but the view is fantastic). If you are tired and want a glass of beer, try the former popular rock club Újezd (Újezd 18), which has been transformed into an unusual three-storey cafe. The Petřín itself is a great place to discover. It hides several caves, long underground passages, a fountain, rose garden and an observatory. www.loreta.cz, www.strahovskyklaster.cz, www.petrinska-rozhledna.cz , www.klubujezd.cz

The green areas are mostly on the left bank of the river, as it's much steeper than the right bank and so has seen less urban development.

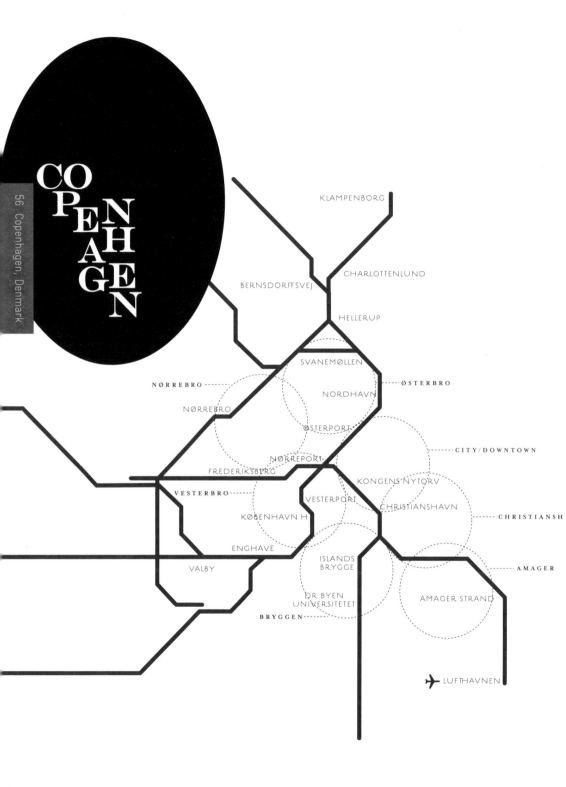

COPENHAGEN

KLAMPENBORG

CHARLOTTENLUND

BERNSDORFFSVEJ

HELLERUP

SVANEMØLLEN

NØRREBRO

NORDHAVN

ØSTERBRO

NØRREBRO

ØSTERPORT

CITY/DOWNTOWN

NØRREPORT

FREDERIKSBERG

KONGENS NYTORV

VESTERBRO

VESTERPORT

CHRISTIANSHAVN

KØBENHAVN H

CHRISTIANSH

ENGHAVE

ISLANDS
BRYGGE

VALBY

AMAGER

DR BYEN
UNIVERSITETET

AMAGER STRAND

BRYGGEN

✈ LUFTHAVNEN

LIZET HEE OLESEN & Anne Strandfelt's
COPENHAGEN

Three essential tips before travelling to Copenhagen:

1. Come here in the summer – people in Copenhagen can seem a bit introverted (goes with living in darkness for most of the year), but we live it up in the summer and become quite happy!
2. Bring money – this is one of the most expensive cities in the world.
3. Copenhagen is a bit like Berlin in the way that a lot of the cool things are not immediately apparent. Use this guide, but also ask locals for tips and check out this cool website: www.copenhagen.unlike.net

It's an easy city to get around – either on foot or using one of the free city bikes you'll see scattered around. It is divided into these main districts:

ØSTERBRO: This is the well-behaved, expensive part of the city, with a lot of young families. There's not much to see here, especially after the shops have closed and the kids have been tucked in.

NØRREBRO: Also called Nørrebronx, this used to be a working class neighbourhood, but now it's more of a melting pot, with lots of immigrants and students. It has lots of theatres, bars, restaurants and drive-by shootings. Ravnsborggade is the best street for antiques.

VESTERBRO: Another working class area/red light district. It's a very colourful part of town – you'll find seedy bars, hotels, pornshops, restaurants, happy families, drug addicts and poets. The industrial area of the 'meatpacking district' has some of the best clubs and bars in town.

CITY/DOWNTOWN: Downtown has most of the shopping; the main shopping street is called Strøget, but the interesting shops are in Krystalgade or the Pilestræde/ Grønnegade area. The City is where you'll find lots of the cultural institutions; the brand new Playhouse, the National Museum of Art etc.

CHRISTIANSHAVN/AMAGER: Amager is a small island that is home to a few interesting areas' Christianshavn is a beautiful little quarter, with houseboats on small canals and cute little cafes on cobblestone streets. It's also where you'll find Christiania – a semi-legal community that declared independence in 1971, and is still fighting the current right-wing government for its right to survive. You'll see the flag of Christiania – red with three yellow dots – on posters, t-shirts, graffiti and flags throughout the city. For Copenhageners Christiania symbolises the right to live freely without government intervention.

HOTEL FOX This was an ambitious PR stunt for the launch of the new Volkswagen Fox in 2005. Over 20 rooms were individually designed by artists, illustrators and graphic designers from around the world. The result, if now a tad faded, is an exciting myriad of wild, colourful images, with a newly opened sushi restaurant on the ground floor. It's a lifestyle hotel with an unbeatable location at affordable prices. Jarmers Plads 3, Copenhagen V, www.hotelfox.dk

HOTEL GULDSMEDEN This is a friendly eco-hotel, with three branches in the trendy district of Vesterbro. All their toiletries and foods are organic, and made especially for the hotel. Helgolandsgade 11, Vesterbrogade 107, Vesterbrogade 66, Copenhagen V, www.hotelguldsmeden.dk

PLACES TO STAY

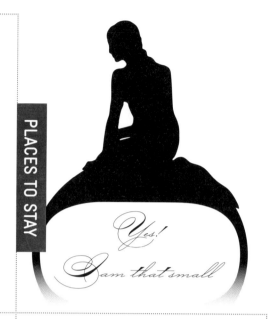

Yes!
I am that small

FISHY

DANHOSTEL Danhostel, Copenhagen City branch, is Europe's biggest designer-hostel. Rooms and common areas have been furnished by the Danish designers Gubi (whose furniture is featured in MOMA in New York). Great location just behind the Central Station and Rådhuspladsen, and with its 15 floors you get a fantastic view over the city and the opera. H.C. Andersens Blvd 50, Copenhagen V, www.danhostel.dk

WITH WATER ALL AROUND US WE HAVE NO EXCUSE NOT TO

EAT IT.

A NEW FUNKY FISHBAR, WITH REASONABLE PRICES,

WILL OPEN IN THE SUMMER OF 2009 IN THE MEATPACKING DISTRICT.

BEHIND IT IS A BUNCH OF WELL-KNOWN DANISH GOURMET PERSONALITIES,

WHO ARE TIRED OF THE FORMAL SETTINGS YOU ARE NORMALLY

FORCED TO DINE IN WHEN OPTING FOR FRESH FISH IN CPH.

HOME-GROWN WHITE WINE FROM COLD-CLIMATE GRAPES,

CULTIVATED ON A SMALL SOUTHERN ISLAND OF DENMARK WILL ALSO BE SERVED.

YUMMY!

THE SETTING WILL BE LIVELY, UNPRETENTIOUS AND BAR-LIKE.

FLÆSKETORVET 100, KØDBYEN, COPENHAGEN V

NOMA This is an absolute must if you're into gourmet food. It has been awarded two Michelin stars and nominated third best restaurant in the world. It specialises in traditional Nordic food and is definitely worth a visit! Strandgade 93, Copenhagen K, www.noma.dk

TOLDBOD BODEGA A historic restaurant where even the city's finest chefs go for the Tuesday special: Stegt flæsk med persillesovs (a traditional dish of fried pork-ribs with potatoes and parsley sauce). It is often hosted by Ivar – the kindest host in Copenhagen. He'll offer a schnapps for every dish and happily tell you amazing stories! Esplanaden 4, Copenhagen K, www.toldbod-bodega.dk

ROYAL CAFE This cafe is a girly, pastel, flowery little haven, situated inside the Royal Porcelain Shop. It's perfect for lunch, and the only place where you can get smooshies – a 'sushi' version of the Danish open sandwich. Amagertorv 6, Copenhagen K, www.theroyalcafe.dk

PASTIS Not quite like Pastis in New York, but still very worthy of a visit. Probably the best Boeuf Bearnaise in town and very pleasant service. A cosy place to spend an evening with friends. Always very crowded – even on weekdays – which is unusual for Copenhagen. Gothersgade 52, Copenhagen K, www.bistro-pastis.dk

Icecream tastes like liquorice

BREAD

A TRADITIONAL DANISH BREAKFAST IS A 'RUNDSTYKKE' FROM YOUR LOCAL BAKERY. EAT IT CUT IN HALVES WITH SALTED BUTTER.

FOR A MORE ADVANCED CARBOHYDRATE EXPERIENCE, GO TO **MICHELIN CHEF BO BECH'S BREAD-SHOP ON STORE KONGENSGADE 46** (CITY). HIS AMBITION WAS TO CREATE THE **PERFECT BREAD**. HERE YOU HAVE ONE TABLE IN THE MIDDLE OF THE OTHERWISE EMPTY SHOP, WITH A HUGE PILE OF BREAD. ONLY ONE PERFECT KIND. FRESHLY BAKED EVERY MORING FROM HIS OWN RECIPE IN A SPECIALLY IMPORTED ITALIAN OVEN. THEY ONLY ACCEPT CASH AND A LOAF IS 30 KRONER. SIMPLE!

PLACES TO EAT

KUNG FU IZIKAYA BAR A nice little unpretentious bar/restaurant located in a quiet alleyway in Vesterbro. They have an open, smoky kitchen, serving sushi and grilled sticks. It's reasonably priced with an extensive cocktail card (their ginger mojito is particularly nice). One Friday a month it holds a club night with DJs. Check for this on their website. Sundevedsgade 5, Copenhagen V, www.kungfubar.dk

VERDENS MINDSTE KAFFEBAR The name translates as 'World's Smallest Coffeeshop'. Come here for coffee and good vibes and then check out funky bookshop Thiemers, just down the street (see Shopping). Tullinsgade 1, Copenhagen V, www.myspace.com/vmbar

NIMB BAR The Nimb Bar is situated in the Tivoli Gardens in Nimb House – a newly renovated building which also houses a boutique hotel, a gourmet restaurant, a concept hotdog stand, a super-exclusive supermarket and a dairy. The Nimb Bar is simultaneously cosy and highly exclusive. It's in a room that resembles a ballroom with wall decorations made by Danish artist Cathrine Raben Davidsen. It's quite expensive; afternoon tea is about €50 and must be ordered in advance. Ask to be seated in front of the fireplace. Bernsdorffsgade 5, Copenhagen V, www.nimb.dk

KARRIERE This restaurant/bar is in the meatpacking district, across the road from the largest meat supplier in town. It's owned by artist Jeppe Hein and his sister, Lærke, and the whole space is one big art installation. The tables are designed by the artist Fos and the lamps by Olafur Eliasson. The bar is constantly, almost imperceptibly moving. The toilets are interesting – especially if you are desperate for a pee. There's a labyrinthine choice of doors, most of which lead nowhere. Flæsketorvet 57-67, Copenhagen V, www.karrierebar.com

DYREHAVEN Dyrehaven literally translates as 'Animal Garden' and is the name of a very famous deer park north of Copenhagen. As such, the walls here are decorated with deer antlers, probably left over from the previous owners, who ran the place as a traditional Bodega/Værtshus. The new owners have transformed it without losing its spirit, and it's got a relaxed and happening vibe. You can eat breakfast, a basic dinner or stay late for cocktails. It's a bit like something you might find in Berlin, and it attracts everyone from young, poor musicians to established artists and other free spirits. Sønder Blvd 72, Copenhagen V

JOLENE Next to Karriere is this hip watering hole founded by Icelandic friends Dorá and Dorá. Jolene is the 'so-now' choice – the cheeky little sister to Karriere's intellectual older brother. The crowd mostly comprises club kids, designers, artists and locals. They have some of the most popular underground DJs playing, from Trentemøller to Djuna Barnes – and occasionally they host gigs with up-and-coming rock/electro bands. Flæsketorvet 81-85, Copenhagen V, www.myspace.com/jolenebar

BOBI BAR The sweetest, cosiest little bar with an authentic interior from 1900. It's just across the road from Gyldendals Forlag (one of Denmark's oldest and largest publishing houses), and you might just run into a famous writer, as well as some of the legendary Bobi Bar regulars. Klareboderne 14, Copenhagen K

BYENS KRO A few steps down from Bobi Bar, you'll find this venue, which is the bar of choice for the Royal Academy of Art's students. Møntergade 8, Copenhagen K

ANDY'S Andy's is open after all the other bars are closed and is the final pitstop before going home or passing out. The crowd in here is as mixed as it gets – from 24-year-old Malene, who works for Louis Vuitton to 62-year-old Finn who used to be a crane operator. Gothersgade 33B, Copenhagen K

BARS

PARIS TEXAS PT is the most avant-garde fashion shop in Copenhagen, selling expensive clothing and accessories for both men and women. Givenchy, Preen, Martin Margiela, Alexander Wang, Helmut Lang, Charles Anastase etc. Pilestraede 35, Copenhagen K, www.paristexas.dk

HENRIK VIBSKOV This Danish design wunderkind, who trained at St Martins, finally opened his own shop in 2006. It also stocks a wide selection of complementary labels like Wackerhaus, Stine Goya, Cosmic Wonder and Opening Ceremony. Krystalgade 6, Copenhagen K, www.henrikvibskov.com

SHOPPING

ANDY'S BAR

TIME'S UP VINTAGE Time's Up specialises in handpicked vintage designer couture finds from Chanel, Dior, Givenchy, Cardin etc. They also carry the largest collection of vintage shoes in Copenhagen – at least 200 pairs of shoes and boots – as well as collectables and costume jewellery. Krystalgade 4, Copenhagen K, and Blaagårdsgade 2A, Copenhagen N, www.times-up.dk

NORSE PROJECTS

LOT#29 This shop sells the most beautiful, elegant jewellery by goldsmiths Line Hallberg and Jo Riis-Hansen. These two jewellers are always one step ahead, and their unique styles make their pieces individual works of art. Lot#29 also stocks offbeat pieces from Wunderkind, Etro, Missoni and Nina Ricci. Gothersgade 29, Copenhagen K, www.lot29.dk

CRÈME DE LA CRÈME A LA EDGAR This is a kids' shop, selling patchwork pillows, knitted dolls and clothing from Sonia Rykiel, Marimekko, Ivana Helsinki and the up-and-coming Danish brand, Soft Gallery – all in the most original and nostalgic 1970s interior. They also carry selected pieces for adults. Kompagnistræde 8, Copenhagen K, www.cremedelacremealaedgar.dk

THIEMERS MAGASIN This is a very special bookshop inside an old 1960s tile shop. You can enjoy fresh coffee and sit and browse a big selection of new and used books – a real home away from home. Once a month there are readings, lectures or concerts, which you can find out about by joining their mailing list (hidden somewhere on their webpage). Tullinsgade 24, Copenhagen V, www.thiemersshop.dk

NORSE PROJECTS Run by professional skateboarder Anton and V1 Gallery partner Mikkel, Norse Projects is regarded as the vanguard sneaker shop in Copenhagen, stocking Alife, Stussy, Levi's, Neighbourhood and all the other hip streetwear names. They also host occasional exhibitions with underground photographers and street artists. Pilestræde 41, Copenhagen K, www.norsestore.com

CREME DE LA CREME A LA EDGAR

Paris Texas

MINI
PHRASE BOOK

Hello!

Hej!

(Don't say this to strangers!)

Sorry!
Undskyld!

(Say this if in any kind of trouble)

Is it gonna rain all week do you think?
Kommer det til at regne hele ugen tror du?

Are all the shops closed?
Er alle butikkerne lukket?

VESTERBRO FESTIVAL JUNE Music, parties and happenings at Den Brune Kødby ('Brown Meat City') in Vesterbro. www.vesterbrofestival.dk

DISTORTION JUNE Over 60 parties over five days, spread across a few different neighbourhoods. There are three giant street parties, and a focus on new talent in music. www.cphdistortion.dk

CPH:DOX NOVEMBER Documentary film festival. www.cphdox.dk

STELLA POLARIS AUGUST Chilled-out outdoor concert with different DJs playing. www.stella-polaris.dk

VEGA MAY Music festival featuring top of the pops, underground, rock and electro. www.vega.dk

ROSKILDE FESTIVAL JULY Northern Europe's biggest music and culture festival. www.roskilde-festival.dk

V1 V1 is the enfant terrible on the Copenhagen gallery scene. It focuses on emerging talent from Denmark and abroad, and represents artists such as Dearraindrop, Futura2000, Kasper Sonne, Peter Funch and Copenhagen street art darling, HuskMitNavn (RememberMyName). Their vernissages pull in the hip fashion and street crowds, and usually end with an afterparty at Jolene, next door. Flæsketorvet 69-71, Copenhagen V, www.v1gallery.com

GALLERY NICOLAI WALLNER Nicolai Wallner breathed new life into the Danish art scene when he opened his gallery on the traditional gallery street, Bredgade. Whilst everyone else was stuck in the days of Modernism, he introduced artists like Paul McCarthy, David Shrigley, Olafur Eliasson, Douglas Gordon and Ingar Dragset, earning himself a loyal following. He later moved his gallery to Islands Brygge, and a load of other galleries followed suit. He's now set for another move – to Valby, into the old premises of Carlsberg beer. Carlsberg have moved their operations to the countryside, providing a rare opportunity to redevelop a substantial urban space. One of the proposals for this redevelopment is to turn the space into a creative hub called 'Our Town'. Fingers crossed! Njalsgade 21 , Building 15, Copenhagen S, www.nicolaiwallner.com

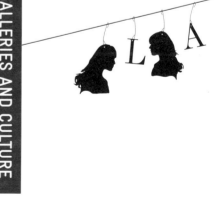

CHRISTIANIA AND ITS ARCHITECTURE Take a walk through Christiana and see the freetown's astonishing and creative architecture, all built by hand. A lot of the houses were built by the famous 'Navere' (short for Scandinavere), a special tradition of travelling workmen/carpenters from the 19th Century. For more Christiania info: www.copenhagen.unlike.net/locations/300857-Christiania

FINN JUHL'S HUS AND ORDRUPGAARD Finn Juhl was one of the pioneers of Modernist furniture in Denmark. His designs are often softer and more organic that the more renowned Arne Jacobsen. Juhl's house in Gentofte, 8km from the centre, was recently bought and turned into a museum in collaboration with Ordrupgaard (a state-owned museum with a large collection of French Impressionist art). It's now open to the public, with complete original furnishing. Ordrupgaard is also worth a visit – its new extension was designed by Zaha Hadid. While you're in Gentofte, notice the street signs. They were designed by legendary industrial designer Knud V Engelhardt. The little hearts above all the 'i's are original. Ordrupgaard, Vilvordevej 110, 2920 Charlottenlund, www.ordrupgaard.dk

COPENHAGEN WAS IN 2009 HONOURED

"BEST CITY TO BE A CYCLIST IN"

BY TREEHUGGER.COM

FOR BEAUTIFULLY HANDBUILT DANISH BICYCLES, VISIT:
RECYKEL.DK, TULLINSGADE 10, COPENHAGEN V

5A 5A is a bus route. Get on at Nørrebro station (the drive-by shooting district) and enjoy the ride through the inner city until you reach Amager. When you get to Amagerbrogade (the main street), notice the shop signage overload. 'Big is beautiful' and 'the more the merrier' are the slogans to die by around here. There are noble old butchers' signs, discount immigrant-run candy shops, perfectly preserved dry cleaners from the 1970s, and some specialist shops dealing in theatrical make-up and crystal glass. A lesson in everyday living.

COPENHAGEN HARBOUR Copenhagen has a large harbour, and the most interesting part of it is the bit near the beautiful Knippelsbro bridge, which connects the inner city with the island of Christianshavn and Amager. There are a couple of interesting buildings that are worth looking at. Firstly the Royal Danish Library, partly located in the famous 'Black Diamond' building. Down the road is the Danish National Bank, designed by Arne Jacobsen. Make sure you look at the door front and custom-made bronze signage.

welcome
to

TAL
LINN

VLADIMIR & MAXIM LOGINOV'S TALLINN

The name 'Tallinn' translates as 'Danish town' – which is odd, because there's nothing inherently Danish about it – except that the Danish at some point conquered Estonia, as did many northern European powers over the ages. It's one of the smaller capitals in Europe (less than half a million people), and it sits on the southern coast of the Gulf of Finland, just 70km from Helsinki. The sea is as much part of the town as the streets and buildings – even when you can't see it, you can always sense it. It's hard for us to comprehend how people can live in cities without the sea.

Tourism-wise, the sea is too cold to be a major factor, so Tallin is mostly famous for its Old Town and its beautiful blondes (unless you're Finnish, in which case Tallinn is famous for cheap goods). The Old Town is where most of the attractions – galleries, shops, restaurants, etc. can be found. Built around the cathedral hill (called Toompea), it's filled with ancient buildings and winding cobbled streets. Surrounding it are several medieval towers connected by an ancient, partially ruined wall. It's beautiful, especially in the Christmas period, when the streets look like a fairytale illustration. The Old Town is home to a small number of wealthy people. Most people can't afford to live there, and are based outside in the slightly monotonous, Soviet-style periphery. As it's quite a small city, even from the furthest reaches, it's only a 20 minute walk into the centre of town. If you live here it's almost impossible to walk down the street without bumping into someone you know. To say 'hello' just go 'tere'. People will automatically appreciate that you are a considerate, friendly tourist.

It's hard to pinpoint our favourite place in the city. You'll just have to come here, walk through the Viru Gate and let the Old Town itself be your guide. If, for whatever reason, you get bored of the Old Town, there's always Birgitta Monastery. Situated by the sea, it's especially beautiful at night. You're not really supposed to go in after hours, but don't let that stop you. Just go around the fence and you'll find a perfect place to sneak in (ideally with one of those beautiful blondes we mentioned).

KOLM ÕDE (THE THREE SISTERS)

A luxury boutique hotel based in an impressive trio of medieval merchants' houses. It's won lots of awards and accolades. In fact, the Queen of England chose to stay here on a recent visit – and if it's good enough for her.... Pikk 71 / Tolli 2, www.threesistershotel.com

HOTEL G9

This is a cheap option for the low-budget traveller. It's a small-ish hotel on the third floor of a building on the student campus, ten minutes' walk from the town centre. Gonsiori 9, www.hotelg9.ee

RADISSON BLU HOTEL TALLINN

One of the tallest buildings in town. On the top floor there's a cafe with an open terrace, where you can enjoy fresh air and panoramic views of the town while drinking coffee. It's international standard luxury, and most of the presidents, sportsmen and pop stars visiting the capital stay at this hotel (although not the Queen it turns out). Rävala pst 3, www.tallinn.radissonsas.com

PLACES TO STAY

VÕITLEV SÕNA

In the Soviet era, this place was a popular bookshop. Today it's a cafe/nightclub serving European and Indian cuisine. Stylish interior and nice music. Parnu mnt 2

OLDE HANSA

Traditional Estonian cuisine served in a medieval merchant's house. The prices bite a little, but it shouldn't stop you from tasting the meat of a bear or a moose. Vana-Turg 1, www.oldehansa.com

C'EST LA VIE

French-style cafe-restaurant with a nice 1930s style interior. The food isn't bad either. A good place to sit with a cup of coffee, watching people passing by. Suur-Karja 5, www.cestlavie.ee

KLOOSTRI AIT

A big restaurant in an old medieval granary serving delicious food at reasonable prices. There's a huge open fireplace and live music at weekends. Vene 14, www.kloostriait.ee

NOKU

One of the cosiest and hippest places in town, serving tasty food at moderate prices. It's a favourite hangout of the town's creative folk. Don't be fooled by the unmarked door. Pikk 5

TROIKA

A Russian tavern/restaurant on two levels. They hold regular live gigs, and in the basement restaurant they serve vodka, pancakes with caviar and borsch. It's impossible to leave this place feeling hungry. Note the way they pour the vodka. Raekojaplats 15, www.troika.ee

PLACES TO EAT

HELL HUNT This is the oldest pub in Tallinn (it's not some kind of biker bar – the name translates as 'The Gentle Wolf'). Proper food and pleasant service. It's always busy, but you can usually find a free table. In the summer you can enjoy your pint on an open terrace. Pikk 39, www.hellhunt.ee

NIMETA BAAR If you want to get with the ex-pats, 'The Bar With No Name' is the place to go. Pretty much all foreigners in Tallinn end up here, drinking cheap ale and watching the never-ending football on the screens. Suur-Karja 4, www.nimetabaar.ee

REVAL CAFE This is more of a restaurant than a cafe, with candlelight creating a warm, romantic atmosphere. It's a place to spend a night drinking wine, deep in conversation with your friends. Müürivahe 14, www.revalcafe.ee

MATILDA CAFE Pop into this cafe on your way down from Toompea on 'short leg street'. It's a real childhood candy store with a Viennese interior and pleasant service. The pavlova tart is a must. Lühike jalg 4, www.matilda.ee

MAIASMOKK CAFE This nice old cafe has been open since 1864, and is an architectural landmark, with amazing pre-war décor and lots of mirrors. It's famous for its marzipan – don't miss out. Pikk 16

BARS

NU NORDIK If you are looking for fresh, contemporary products by local designers, this little shop is the place to go. They stock everything from clothes to table lamps. Vabaduse väljak 8, www.nunordik.ee

RAAMATUKOI This shop sells vintage books and postcards. It's a great place to rummage through. We always dig up something amazing that brings back memories of our childhood. Voorimehe 9, www.raamatukoi.ee

VIRU GATE MARKET All along the Old Town wall by Viru Gate, little old ladies sell traditional knitted jumpers with funny patterns and woollen socks and hats. At least it will keep you warm in the winter! Mütivahe 17

HOOCHI MAMA Fashion boutique selling clothes and accessories, many of which are exclusive or limited edition. Vana-Posti 2

BALTI JAAM Behind the train station is one of the biggest markets in Tallinn. It's quite an extraordinary place. Endless counters sell cheap clothes, food, carpets, books and anything else you can think of. There are lots of cheap antique shops in the area too. It's like going back in time by about 15 years. Kopli 1

SHOPPING

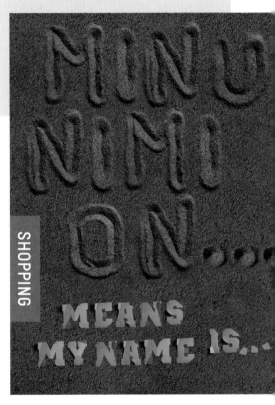

CENTRAL MARKET This is the main food market, and is the place to go for fresh meat, fruit and vegetables. Great if you're organising a picnic. Take tram 2 and get off at the Keskturg stop. Keldrimae 9

CHRISTMAS MARKET Every December, the Christmas Market sets up in the main square of the Old Town. It's a nice place to hang out, drink some mulled wine under the Christmas tree, listen to music and buy some silly stuff that you'll never use. Raekojaplats

KUMU The Art Museum of Estonia is housed in an 18th Century palace in the beautiful Kadriorg Park. It has a collection of medieval European and Russian art, and more contemporary Estonian pieces, but it's more interesting for its architecture than its exhibitions. Weizenbergi 34, www.ekm.ee

SOO-SOO This shop/gallery stocks designer furniture and accessories and also hosts exhibitions of photography, graphic design and art. Soo 4, www.soosoo.ee

DRAAKONI GALERII This gallery displays works of Estonia's leading contemporary artists. It's housed in a beautiful old building in the city centre, and you can buy some of the works in the gallery shop. Pikk 18, www.eaa.ee/draakon

SÕPRUS A grand old Soviet-style cinema built in the 1950s, with massive columns guarding its entrance. It used to have two screens, but now there's only one, mainly showing art-house movies. Vana-Posti 8, www.kino.eew

KINOMAJA A small cosy cinema for the real movie fans, run by the Estonian Filmmakers Union. It screens art-house movies, documentaries and locally produced films. There are evenings and weekly events that are dedicated to films from one country or region, and they sometimes have exhibitions in the lobby. Uus 3, www.kinomaja.ee

GALLERIES AND CULTURE

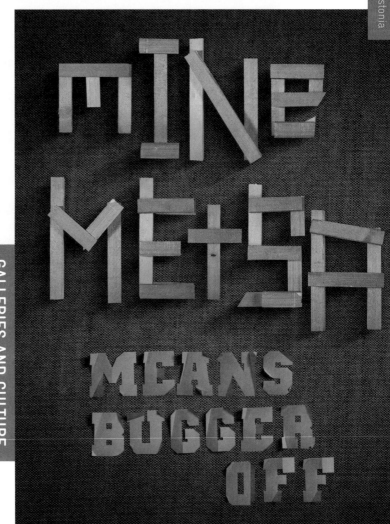

TOOMPEA (UPPER TOWN) The Upper Town is built on a hill about 30m above the rest of the city, and is a must-see for any visitor. Climb Pikk Jab, and you'll find yourself in Castle Square, with Toompea Castle, which now houses the Estonian Parliament, on one side, and the Russian Orthodox Alexander Nevsky Cathedral on the other. Winding streets and cafes surround the square, and there are great views from the observation decks at the Old Town. By night this part of Tallinn is just magical.

MAARJAMÄE WAR MEMORIAL After regaining independence in 1991, the first thing Estonians did was remove all traces of Soviet rule. This is one of the few Soviet structures left standing. It's a half-abandoned concrete construction built in 1960 in memory of the Russians who died in the war (a similar memorial can be found in virtually every ex-Soviet city). It consists of a four-sided spire, surrounded by concrete and iron figures, and avenues cut into the grassy hillside. It's right alongside the highway to Pirita Beach, and there's something eerily mystical about it. An ideal place to have a minute with yourself and the sea.

ROTERMANNI QUARTER The Rotermanni Quarter is sometimes called the second Old Town of Tallinn. It's an industrial area, with architecture from the 19th and early 20th Centuries, located between the Old Town, Viru and the port. For a long time it was pretty much derelict, but is now being energetically redeveloped by some of the best architects in the country, with each building totally unique. It's been pedestrianised and has some of the most prestigious shops in town, but is still in the process of being reconstructed, so lots of building sites around. It's only a five-minute walk from here to the Estonian Architectural Museum. www.rotermannikvartal.ee

LASNAMÄE There's something magnetic about the suburbs of Tallinn, where almost a quarter of the town's population lives. The endless cloned Soviet-era concrete blocks were originally built for Russian workers, who were employed at the various factories and industrial plants in the city. It still has a big Russian population living there, but as it is (for obvious reasons) a cheap place to live, it also houses a broad mix of other people. There's no green here, just the monotony of concrete, and there are various drug problems and crime issues in some parts.

SONG AND DANCE CELEBRATION JULY Every four years, around 100,000 people from all over Estonia gather at Lauluvaljak for The Song and Dance Celebration. Dressed in traditional costumes, this massive crowd creates arguably the biggest choir in the world symbolising true national unity.

ÕLLESUMMER JULY This beer festival takes place every year at the beginning of July. All beer festivals are probably the same, which doesn't make this one less fun. Lots of beer, sausages with cabbage and many swaying customers. www.ollesummer.ee

PÖFF TALLINN BLACK NIGHTS FILM FESTIVAL NOVEMBER Every winter in Tallinn starts with a cinematic orgy. One of the biggest film festivals in the Baltic states, featuring the creme de la creme of the modern cinema. www.poff.ee

Ylppä Hynkäs'
Helsinki.

Until 1809, Sweden and Finland were one state. When Russia defeated Sweden in the Finnish War, Finland was given domestic autonomy and its capital was moved from Turku (close to Sweden) to Helsinki. In the building boom following its new status as a capital, the central area of the city was reconstructed in a Neo-classical style reminiscent of St Petersburg. Many of these buildings still stand. The rest of the architecture is a bit of a mixture. It was bombed heavily during the Second World War, and experienced a period of fast expansion in the 1970s. This means there is a lot of relatively contemporary, functional architecture. However, in and amongst this, there is a lot of older stuff as well, including some beautiful Art Nouveau buildings (such as the railway station, designed by Eliel Saarinen), some areas with original wooden houses that have been carefully preserved, and of course some truly spectacular architecture designed by Alvar Aalto.

Helsinki manages to be both cosmopolitan and maintain a small-town feel. It is located in the south of the country over several islands in the Gulf of Finland. The inner city is based on the southern peninsula, and the traditional heart of the city is Senate Square (the one that looks like St Petersburg). Connecting to this square are the shopping streets of Aleksanterinkatu (or Aleksi for short) and Esplanadi (or Espa). A few yards down the hill and along the bustling waterfront lies the Kauppatori – the square market. Only 1km away from the city centre, but separated by the Siltasaarensalmi Strait, lies the district of Kallio. Traditionally a working class area, it is now home to a vibrant mix of workers, students, immigrants and young professionals. It is the most densely populated area of the city, and has lots of great bars and restaurants (you'll notice it features a lot in my listings).

Helsinki is warmer than you would expect for this latitude (-5°C in the winter and 20°C in the summer). Nonetheless, the days in winter are short, and the time to visit is summer, when outdoor bars and cafes bring the city alive. Having said that, in winter you can cross-country ski from the city centre all the way out to the forests and skate on the lakes. And you don't need to worry about getting your hands on a warm drink – the Finns are apparently the most caffeinated people in the world (averaging nine cups of coffee a day), so cafes are a dime a dozen!

HOSTEL EROTTAJANPUISTO This hostel is clean, comfortable and central – located on Uudenmaankatu, right in the heart of downtown. A good, cosy budget option. Uudenmaankatu 9, 00120 Helsinki, www.erottajanpuisto.com

HOTELLI TORNI This hotel (which translates as 'Tower Hotel'), is owned by the biggest chain in Finland, Sokos. It's easy to spot – it's a 14-storey building in the centre, and it's been done up in three different styles – Art Deco, Art Nouveau and Functionalism. It also has an interesting history, as it was used to hide spies during the two world wars, and afterwards was the base for the Allied Control Commission, to ensure Finland's compliance with the Moscow Peace Treaty. It's worth staying here for the 14th floor bar if nothing else (see bars). Yrjönkatu 26, 00100 Helsinki, www.sokoshotels.fi

KLAUS KURKI HOTEL This is something of a concept hotel with rooms that are classed from 'passion' (standard) to 'envy' (luxury). Weird. But it's reasonably priced for what it is. It's quite lively, well located and does a great breakfast. Bulevardi 2, 00120 Helsinki, www.klauskhotel.com

HOTEL KAMP If you've got the cash, this is the luxury option. It's in a 19th Century building, which has been accurately restored with replica drapery, chandeliers etc. Expect some 21st Century perks such as heated divans! Pohjoisesplanadi 29, 00100 Helsinki, www.hotelkamp.com

PLACES TO EAT

KOSMOS Kosmos was founded in 1924, and has been in the same family ever since. It retains a lot of its original charm, but has some very elegant contemporary touches, and throughout its history has hosted virtually the entire Finnish cultural and political elite. The cuisine is primarily modern Finnish, with some influences from Russian, Swedish and French cookery. Ingredients are locally sourced. Kalevankatu 3, 00100 Helsinki, www.ravintolakosmos.fi

SOUL KITCHEN As you might have gathered from the name, this place is inspired by the American South. Much of its menu is deep fried or barbecued with rich spices and tastes (gumbo features, of course). The music is deep and mellow, the service fast, straightforward and warm, and the prices very reasonable. It's also got loads of vegetarian options – which is a bonus for me at least! Fleminginkatu 26, 00510 Helsinki, www.soulkitchen.fi

SEA HORSE This restaurant is also known by the name 'Sikala', which translates as pigsty. It's quite a bizarre nickname, as the place is anything but! It's situated in an old Jugendhaus, and although it's a la carte, the food and especially the lunches are perfectly affordable (lunch won't come to more than €13). I really like this place, because even though it attracts its fair share of famous artists and the like, everyone is treated equally – warmly and with no pressure. It's just outside the city centre, reachable by tram. Kapteeninkatu 11, 00140 Helsinki, www.seahorse.fi

MY CUP OF T

LUFT Situated right next to Soul Kitchen (see places to eat) this is a traditional hangout for students and artists in the Kallio area. It's cheaper than more central places, and on most evenings there's a DJ playing. The cafe doubles up as a gallery space, and there's a large selection of magazines you can flip through. I like the chilled-out vibe here. You can just come and go as you are. Aleksis Kiven Katu 30, 00510 Helsinki

CORONA BAR AND CAFE MOSCOW These are two bars set up by quirky filmmakers, Aki and Mika Kaurismäki, in a converted old cinema. Corona Bar has nine pool tables, draws in young artists and pool players, and has a raw urban atmosphere – which you'll either love or hate. Cafe Moscow is all done up like an Eastern bloc drinking den – with heavy curtains, and deliberately shabby furniture. Even the staff are brusque in an Eastern European sort of way. In the same building there are other bars and a small cinema. Eerikinkatu 11, 00100 Helsinki, www.andorra.fi

CAFE TIN TIN TANGO Situated next to the Töölö market, this is more than just a cafe/bar – it's also a sauna and laundry service. It's named after the cartoon character, and it's got a very French feel, serving filled baguettes and salads with Edith Piaf in the background. There's a glass booth for smokers, with a view of the market. You rent the sauna out by the hour, and you need to reserve it at least one day before. Töölöntorinkatu 7, 00260 Helsinki

BARS

HIUTALEBAARI There are two branches of this bar, both of which are funky and friendly, with big windows and good music. Every night they have well-known Finnish DJs playing, and it attracts a youngish (under 35) trendy crowd. They can get busy! Annankatu 4, 00120 Helsinki, Porthaninkatu 9, 00530 Helsinki

ATELJEE BAR On the 14th floor of Hotel Torni, you'll find this small bar with a good cocktail list and a fantastic view of the city. In fact the best view is from the women's toilet. The entire city is under your feet. Yrjönkatu 26, 00100 Helsinki, www.ateljeebar.fi

MARIMEKKO Marimekko is the Finnish company established by Armi Ratia and her husband Viljo in the 1950s. They started by asking some graphic designers to apply their talents to textiles, and then made simple dresses to showcase the bold results. They were made famous by Jackie Onassis in the 1960s, and had a resurgence in the late 70s/early 80s when the bold floral Unikko design came out. Marimekko formed a big part of my childhood. We were four kids, who throughout the 70s were entirely dressed in Marimekko striped unisex t-shirts. I can still hear my mother's voice saying "they're expensive but good quality". She was right. The colours kept their brightness wash after wash. We had Marimekko pyjamas, curtains, tablecloths, sheets, bags, jackets and hats. Last summer I found a black and white dress in the loft of our summer house. It fitted me perfectly. I got so many people asking me where it was from – a 35-year-old vintage Marimekko – naturally! The Marimekko shop is an absolute must when visiting Helsinki. Pohjoisesplanadi 2 and 31, 00100 Helsinki, www.marimekko.com

LUX This is a small shop specialising in clothes and accessories by Finnish designers (although they also stock international labels). The rough, hand-drawn typography of their branding works really well. Last time I walked by there I saw a great winter coat by Finnish designer Polla Jam, called 'Laulupuu' (Song Tree), made in a beautiful summery printed canvas. It was so nice I drew a picture of it! Uudenmaankatu 26 00120, Helsinki, www.lux-shop.fi

HELSINKI 10 A very cool shop selling clothes, books, art and records, with a kind of independent, rock-and-roll, street attitude. They also stock vintage clothes and even have a bar. The prices vary dramatically and it's a popular shop for young trendies. Eerikinkatu 3, 00100 Helsinki, www.helsinki10.fi

PENNY LANE BOUTIQUE An interesting vintage shop. It's quite small, but split over two levels with shoes, accessories and casual clothes on street level, and very feminine dresses from the 1930s, 40s and 50s upstairs. It's definitely got its own style. Runeberginkatu 37, 00100 Helsinki

TOMORROW'S ANTIQUE A homeware shop selling both antique and contemporary designer furniture, lighting and glass. There's a lot of mid-century stuff with an emphasis on Finnish and Scandinavian heritage, including pieces by Alvar Aalto and Ilmari Tapiovaara. Even if you don't buy anything it's worth the trip – it's like a museum of northern European design. Runeberginkatu 35, 00100 Helsinki

LEVYKAUPPA ÄX (RECORD SHOP ÄX) A large record shop specialising in Finnish and international underground music – they've got a great selection of heavy rock amongst all the other stuff. They also have an online shop. Arkadiankatu 14, 00100 Helsinki, www.levykauppax.fi

MUSEUM OF CONTEMPORARY ART KIASMA The Kiasma building was designed by American architect Steven Holl. There was a lot of controversy surrounding the design – complaints that it's too big, too different, too ugly, and infringes upon the famous statue of the Finnish war hero C G Mannerheim. I, however, love this museum. I've seen some exhibitions here that have really made an impact, including one of cards by the American art critic Kim Levin, as well as the big ARS 2006, which I went to with my daughters. I believe that Mannerheim would have liked this museum, its cafe, its shop and its visitors. It's a great adventure in its own way. Mannerheiminaukio 2, 00100 Helsinki, www.kiasma.fi

ALKOVI This gallery is just one 18m long window in bustling Kallio, with exhibitions on display 24 hours a day. It's a kind of urban art laboratory where you can stumble upon amazing works by accident. Alkovi's curation has recently been taken over by Kiasma. Helsinginkatu 19, 00510 Helsinki

HUUTO This is where I come to find experimental art, performances, and crossover projects. Operating in two addresses, it was founded by a group of renegade artists, and is run by an artists' collective on a voluntary basis. Laivurinkati 43, 00150 Helsinki, and Uudenmaankatu 35, 00120 Helsinki, www.galleriahuuto.net

NAPA This is the gallery of Napa publishing house, which specialises in graphic novels. It was established by two comic artists, Jenni Rope and Jussi Karjalainen Jr, and represents talented young Finnish illustrators. One wall has changing exhibitions, and the other stocks their books. You can also leaf through the portfolios of featured illustrators. Eerikinkatu 18, 00100 Helsinki, www.napabooks.com

GALLERIES AND CULTURE

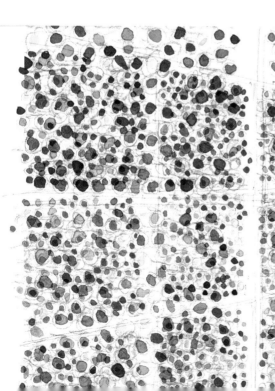

YRJÖNKADUN UIMAHALLI This is a public bath with one pool, two saunas and a cafe. It has separate times for men and women, for the primary reason that most people prefer to swim in the nude (although you can wear a swimsuit if you want). It's in a beautiful 1920s building in the middle of downtown, with all original fittings, and has a calm, serene atmosphere. Yrjönkatu 21, 00100 Helsinki

TORKKELIMÄKI This area is part of the district of Kallio. It was built in classical style between 1926-28, and it's a kind of garden city, with small communal gardens and parks between the buildings. The streets are narrow and labyrinthine, which means you can view the buildings and surroundings from lots of different angles. It's easily accessible from the centre on foot, by tram or by subway.

THE NIGHT OF THE ARTS, HELSINKI FESTIVAL AUGUST The annual arts festival presents programmes in all the art forms. On one night during the festival, bookshops, galleries, libraries and other venues around the city host art events (some free and some not) until the wee hours. The atmosphere is electric – on a beautiful summer's night, the mix of people enjoying art integrated into urban life is truly compelling. www.helsinginjuhlaviikot.fi

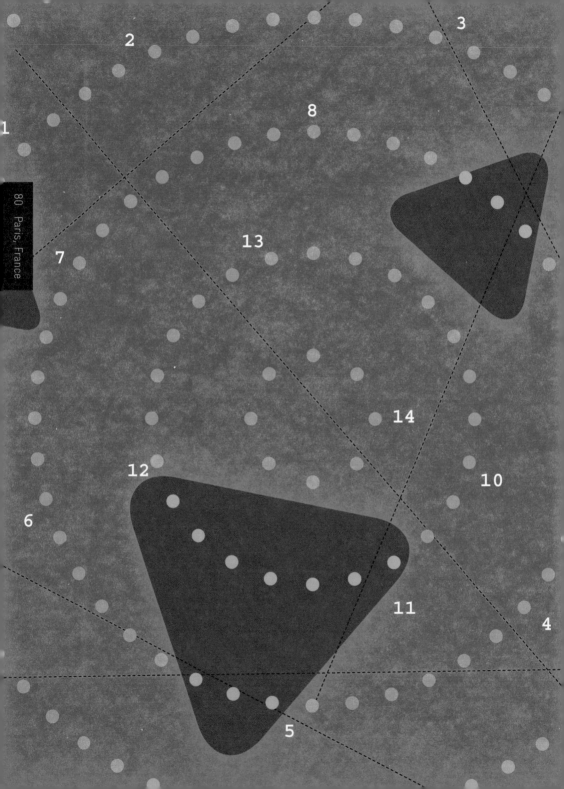

ELAMINE MAECHA'S PARIS

There are many stereotypes that spring to mind when people think of Paris: it's romantic, it's chic, it's rude, it's arrogant, it's beautiful.... There is an element of truth and an element of untruth in all these descriptions, so let's start with the facts: it's a reasonably large city with over two million inhabitants, it's the most visited city in the world, and it's divided in two by the river Seine. The city centre is on the right bank, and is comprised of elegant 18th Century buildings. The left bank is a mix of tangled medieval alleyways and 19th Century boulevards.

Paris is divided into 20 districts, arranged in a snail shape – the 'escargot'. It's taken me three years to understand this metaphor, and to realise how the city spirals out from its centre. For a visitor, the classic 'heart' of Paris is in the old districts (arrondissements) 1,2 and 3 – where most of the renowned monuments and big galleries can be found. Le Marais, one of my favourite areas in the city, can be found in arrondissements 3 and 4. I can spend hours walking around the shops here, stopping for coffee at any number of cool cafe/bars, and checking out the latest exhibition at the Pompidou Centre. However, you should also explore the bit of the city that is further out and less well known, but which is fast becoming a rival to the centre in terms of its artistic inhabitants and funky vibe. Arrondissements 18, 19 and 20 are inhabited by a mix of immigrants and what's known as 'bobos' (bourgeois bohème) – architects, lawyers, designers and artists, who have moved there, outpriced by the property in the so-called 'intellectual quarters', such as Saint-Germain-des-Prés and Odéon. I live in the 18th district – not just because it's cheap, but because its diverse population is a natural breeding ground for creativity. Indeed, one of the things I like most about Paris is the different faces and colours you see here. Populations from Africa, Vietnam and Latin America keep the city fresh, vibrant and open to change.

In terms of getting round the city, the metro system is very good, and the taxi system much less so. Also, in an effort to reduce pollution and improve facilities, the mayor of Paris has introduced a successful network of public bicycles that you can rent from stations scattered around the city, and is considering adapting the same system for cars. If you do decide to drive, beware – congestion can be terrible, especially during school holidays.

HOTEL DU PETIT MOULIN This is one of my favourite hotels in the city (although I've never actually stayed here – apart from actually living in the city, it's somewhat beyond my budget!) It's a four-star hotel in a converted 17th Century bakery, which was completely renovated with an interior design by Christian Lacroix. It's ideally located in the heart of La Marais. 29/31 Rue du Poitou, 75003 Paris, www.hotelpetitmoulinparis.com

HOTEL SEZZ This beautiful boutique hotel is right on the Seine, not far from the Eiffel Tower. The facade is totally classical, but inside it's a mixture of elegant contemporary and classical design. I come here for drinks sometimes and to admire the materials and colours of the décor. 6 Avenue Fremiet, 75016 Paris, www.hotelsezz.com

HOTEL OPERA LAFAYETTE Although the design and architecture of this place is nothing to write home about, its location is ideal, right in the centre, close to the Grand Opera, Sacré Cœur and good shops. The staff are very friendly and go to some lengths to make you feel at home. 80 Rue Lafayette, 75009 Paris, www.paris-hotel-operalafayette.com

HOTEL DES GRANDS HOMMES A really great little hotel right next to the Pantheon, around the corner from bustling Rue Mouffetard. The rooms are small but nice with very intense wallpaper, and eccentrically classical decor. 17 Place du Pantheon, 75005 Paris, www.hoteldesgrandshommes.com

PLACES TO STAY

LES GALOPINS This place is practically my second home – I come here twice a week. It's near Bastille in the 11th arrondissement, with nice retro décor, and serves great local cuisine at reasonable prices. 11 Rue des Taillandiers, 75011 Paris

LE GEORGES / AU CENTRE G. POMPIDOU
Situated at the top of the Centre Pompidou, I recommend this place for its architecture and the view. The food is good – although not the best in Paris. It's overwhelming after an exhibition. I love it. 19 Rue Beaubourg, 75004 Paris

APOLLO This is a surprising, romantic little place inside the Denfert Rochereau RER train station (the entrance is outside on the left). It's got nice décor, a modern menu and funky clientele. I come here when I want a cosy, special meal with a friend. 3 Place Denfert Rochereau, 75014 Paris

LA MAISON BLANCHE Located on the seventh floor of the Art Deco Theatre des Champs-Elysées, this restaurant serves truly delicious Southern French cuisine. It's beautifully designed by a former member of Philippe Starck's studio, and is one of the best places to watch the sun set over the Seine. 15 Avenue Montaigne, 75008 Paris, www.maison-blanche.fr

LE WINCH Just near Montmarte, this seafood restaurant has a great view and a lovely atmosphere. It serves specialties from Bretagne in the north-west of France that are delicious, but not great for the waistband – you have to like butter! 44 Rue Damrémont, 75018 Paris

L'AFFRIANDE Located at Batignolles, not far from my place. This is the kind of restaurant you can go to every day – inexpensive and very friendly. If it's not to your liking, there are loads of other cute restaurants in the neighbourhood. 39 Rue Truffaut, 75017 Paris

FONTAINE FIACRE I like this place for its interior design – which is industrial but warm at the same time. The food is traditional and reasonably priced (you can get a set lunch menu for €15), and it's also available for hire. 8 Rue Hippolyte Lebas, 75009 Paris, www.fontainefiacre.com

GAYA RIVE GAUCHE This seafood restaurant is located in St-Germain-des-Prés, one of the chicest neighbourhoods in the city. It's run by top chef Pierre Gagnaire, and is beautifully designed with a great wine list. It's expensive, but has cheaper options for those less financially endowed. After one drink you'll start to feel that it's worth every penny...! 44 Rue du Bac, 75007 Paris

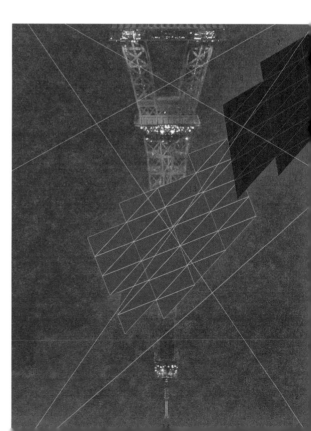

CAFE DE L'INDUSTRIE One of the coolest places to go for a drink with a friend before a night out. The atmosphere is very special – old industrial design adorned with vintage posters and African masks. They serve decent bistro food as well. 17 Rue Saint-Sabin, 75011 Paris, www.cafedelindustrie.com

CLUB LE DJOON Over the past few years, the area around the Grande Bibliothèque François Mittérand has exploded with bars, clubs and restaurants floating on the river. This place is a restaurant during the day and evening, and at night it becomes a bar/lounge/club. It's a big space spread over two levels. It reminds me of clubs in New York. 22 Blvd Vincent Auriol, 75013 Paris, www.djoon.fr

MOOD The movie *In the Mood for Love* was inspired by this trendy place. It's on the wonderful Champs Élysées, and is one of the 'places to be seen'. Designed by Didier Gomez in Asian style, its got three floors, over which are spread a bar, a lounge and a restaurant serving excellent but pricey food. The lighting changes according to the time of day – I like its zen vibe. 114 Avenue des Champs Elysées, 75008 Paris, www. mood-paris.fr

CAFE BACI I don't come here often, but it is a nice Italian place, with quite good interior design (think leather stools and Baroque chandeliers) creating an intimate, fun atmosphere. 36 Rue de Turenne, 75003 Paris, www.cafebaci.fr

L'HÔTEL KUBE A bar made entirely of ice that has proved a big hit with Parisians. It serves vodka and cocktails, with a DJ playing electronica. You have to book in advance, and you're only allowed to spend 15 minutes in there (believe me that's quite enough). Passage Ruelle, 75018 Paris

AU GÉNÉRAL LAFAYETTE A typical French brasserie/bar in the 9th arrondissement, it can be quite noisy sometimes, but usually it's pretty tolerable. I go there with clients or partners. 52 Rue La Fayette, 75009 Paris

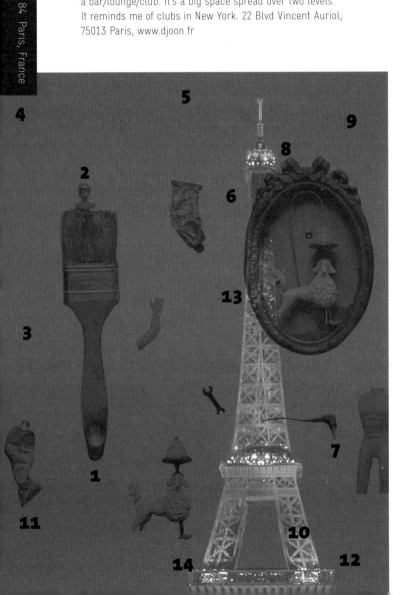

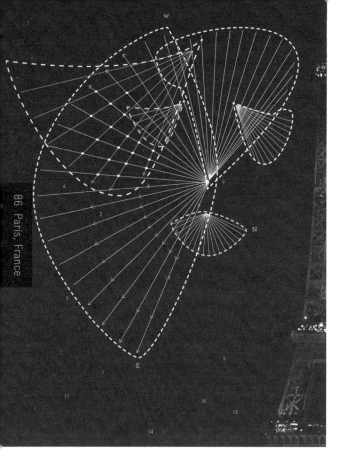

GÉRARD DURAND If, like me, you have something of a socks fetish, this is the place to indulge. It's a traditional old Parisian shop in the 7th, selling tights, stockings, gloves and other elegant accessories for the glamorous Parisian. 75 Rue du Bac, 75007 Paris, www.accessoires-mode.com

LAVINIA A fantastic wine shop in the 1st that is a must for any connoisseur. The staff are very knowledgeable and helpful. 3 Blvd de la Madeleine, 75001 Paris

GRIBOUILLAGES If you want your child to look like a stylish Parisian, this shop in the heart of Sèvres is the place to go. It stocks high-end clothing and artisan/designer toys and also runs craft workshops some afternoons. 85 Rue Mademoiselle, 75015 Paris, www.gribouillages.typepad.fr

CITADIUM Über-cool urban and streetwear emporium spread out over a massive space that feels like a stadium. They sell rare denim brands and shoes, and there's a cafe too. On Saturday afternoons a DJ plays while you shop. 50-56 Rue Caumartin, 75009 Paris, www.citadium.fr

GALERIE DANSK A beautiful vintage (mid-century) furniture shop, specialising in Danish design. It is immaculately laid out and great to just look around. 31 Rue Charlot, 75003 Paris, www.galeriedansk.com

LIBRAIRIE LA HUNE This bookshop is in the heart of Saint-Germain-des-Près, in the 5th. It's got a rich history, and since its establishment in 1949, figures such as Max Ernst, Henri Michaux and André Breton have all been regulars. 170 Blvd St-Germain, 75006 Paris

ARTAZART A bookstore/design shop with a great selection of graphic design titles. A good place for presents. 83 Quai de Valmy, 75010 Paris, www.artazart.com

PUCES PORTE DE VANVES FLEA MARKET This is basically a car boot sale in the 14th. It's much smaller and less overwhelming than the famous antiques market in Porte de Clignancourt, with around 300 sellers selling old linens, Hermès scarves, toys, ephemera, Art Deco jewellery, perfume bottles etc. Many antiques dealers go there, so get there really early if you want the good stuff. And be prepared to haggle – they will rob you blind if you let them. Avenue Georges-Lafenestre, 75014 Paris

MARCHÉ BOURSE This is an open-air farmers' market in the 2nd, selling high quality foodstuffs with a nice trendy vibe. Open on Tuesdays and Fridays. Place de La Bourse, 75002 Paris

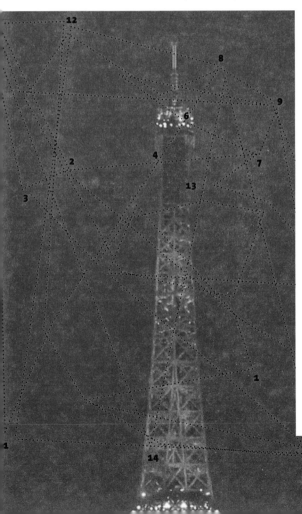

PALAIS DE TOKYO Right next to the Musée d'Art Moderne, the Palais de Tokyo is an experimental, unorthodox gallery with no permanent collection – just ever-changing temporary installations and exhibitions. The space was a derelict Art Deco building that was renovated by architects Anne Lacaton and Jean-Philippe Vassal, who stripped it right down in such a way that it resembles a construction site – all exposed concrete and piping. It has a good shop and a cafe, and don't miss the vernissages on the first Thursday of the month. Oh – and it stays open until midnight. 13 Avenue du Président-Wilson, 75016 Paris, www.palaisdetokyo.com

FONDATION CARTIER Similarly to the Pompidou Centre, the architecture of Fondation Cartier is integral to its contents. Designed by Jean Nouvel, the foundation promotes contemporary art, and merges into its surroundings, not far from the Luxembourg Gardens. It has some good exhibitions – such as a recent one of photography by William Eggleston. 261 Blvd Raspail, 75014 Paris, www.fondation.cartier.com

GALERIE MICHEL REIN One of the only places where you can see young emerging artists hanging alongside established names in the same space. 42 Rue de Turenne, 75003 Paris, www.michelrein.com

GALERIE MAGDA DANYSZ This place is extremely visually interesting. The audience is young and trendy, so 'bobo', I love it. 78 Rue Amelot, 75011 Paris, www.magda-gallery.com

ESPACE TOPOGRAPHIE DE L'ART A strange and beautiful gallery in La Marais, right near the Picasso Museum. It's in an old warehouse space that hasn't been modernised at all and hosts some great exhibitions. I remember Maria-Carmen Perlingeiro, one of the best exhibitions of 2008. 15 Rue de Thorignhy, 75003 Paris, www.topographiedelart.com

GALERIE ANATOME For me, this is just the best place in Paris to see a graphic design exhibition. From Wim Crouwel to Peter Knapp, a lot of excellent designers have exhibited here. Marie-Anne, the art director, is one of the friendliest hosts in Paris. 38 Rue Sedaine, 75011 Paris, www.galerie-anatome.com

LE LABORATOIRE An interesting and surprising gallery a few minutes from the Louvre. Its concept is the intersection of art and science. I like their new identity – even though my studio lost the competition. 4 Rue du Bouloi, 75001 Paris, www.lelaboratoire.org

HAUSSMANN ARCHITECTURE Much of the Paris we know today was built by Baron von Haussmann in the 19th Century with a lot of support from Napoleon. Straight avenues and big, uniform buildings are characteristics of the Haussmann style. The area of Opera is a good example, with its cafes, terraces and boutiques on either side of the grand streets. Boulevard Haussmann is another one. It runs from the 8th to the 9th arrondissements, and is a wide, tree-lined boulevard. Walking along it you get a sense of the grandeur that made Paris the epitome of European luxury in the days of the second French empire.

LE MARAIS Le Marais (the name literally translates as 'the marsh') is in the 3rd and 4th arrondissements on the Right Bank. It's a great area to walk around at any time of day or night with beautiful buildings, a rich cultural and artistic heritage and fantastic shops, cafes and bars. Unlike a lot of places in Paris, the streets are narrow and cobbled, and the architecture is amongst the oldest in the city, with some timbered buildings dating to the 14th Century. Before the Second World War it used to be the heart of a thriving Jewish community, and after the war it was left to deteriorate. In the 1980s, a big renovation project breathed new life into the area, and the shops,

galleries and restaurants drew in an eclectic crowd of fashion designers, artists and young professionals. It later became a hub of the gay community. Even though it's a lot less alternative than it once was, it's still got a buzz about it today. Lots of fun.

CANAL SAINT-MARTIN The Canal Saint-Martin is a 4.5km long canal that cuts through north-east Paris, connecting the Seine to the Canal de l'Ourcq. It was built in the days of Napoleon as a means of getting goods into the city, but is now a popular place to walk, with a number of nice parks and good restaurants and bars along it. Although parts of it are underground, it can still offer a welcome respite from the city (Paris is not known for its green spaces), and it's a particularly nice route for a bike ride. Pick it up a few blocks east of Place de la Republique and follow it north.

BERCY VILLAGE This can be a nice thing to do for a few hours. It's a pedestrianised area of small wine warehouses that were renovated into posh cafes and shops in the 12th arrondissement next to the Parc de Bercy and the Seine. Again – it can be a nice little oasis from the bustle of the city, and often has outdoor performances or activities going on. Rue François Truffaut, 75012 Paris, www.bercyvillage.com

LE CORBUSIER'S PARIS Paris is home to several important Modernist buildings by the infamous Le Corbusier. Not all of them are open to the public, but even if you're just looking from outside, they're still amazing.
VILLA LA ROCHE 8-10, Square du Docteur Blanche, 75016 Paris
PAVILLION SUISSE 7 Blvd Jourdan, 75014 Paris
VILLA SAVOYE 82 Rue de Villiers, 78300 Poissy (just outside Paris - easily reachable by RER)
IMMEUBLE MOLITOR 24 Rue Nungesser et Coli, 75016 Paris

WALKS AND ARCHITECTURE

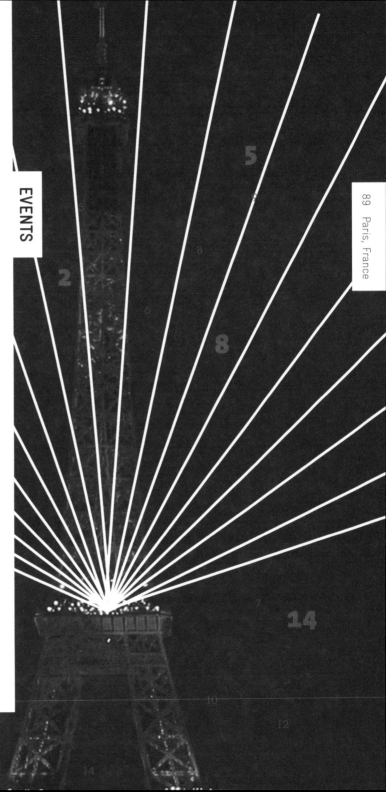

GRAPHISME EN REVUE

A bi-monthly event that opens up a platform for discussion and debate around specific areas of graphic design (in French of course). Pompidou Centre, Place George Pompidou, 75004 Paris, www.centrepompidou.fr

FÊTE DE LA MUSIQUE JUNE Every year on the 21st June, amateur and professional musicians hit the streets (and every available venue in the city) playing everything from jazz to hip hop to electronica – for free.

LES PLUS BEAUX LIVRES FRANÇAIS

An annual book design competition at the Galerie Anatome (see Galleries), which pits the best of French designers against one another. 38 Rue Sedaine, 75011 Paris, www.galerie-anatome.com

PALAIS DE TOKYO CONFERENCES

The graphic design association hosts a series of conferences about book design at Palais de Tokyo. 13 Avenue du Président-Wilson, 75016 Paris, www.palaisdetokyo.com

INTERNATIONAL POSTER

COMPETITION For the past 16 years, La Galeru – a gallery in a shoe repair shop in the Paris suburb of Fontenay-sous-Bois – has been holding a competition called 'graphisme dans la rue' (graphics in the street). It invites graphic artists to present large-format posters on the theme of 'the city' to be exhibited on billboards throughout the town. 20 Rue Dalayrac, 94120 Fontenay-sous-Bois, www.lagaleru.org

CHRISTIANE WEISMÜLLER'S
BERLIN

Berlin is a city that is tricky to define geographically. After the Second World War, the Allies divided it into four sectors, but in 1961, as a result of widening political differences, the communist East German government (GDR) built the Berlin Wall, and for 28 years it was a city divided. When the wall came down in 1989, the architectural legacies of the two regimes were clear to see. In place of the buildings that had been bombed in the war, distinct architectural styles were instated. Karl-Marx-Allee, which used to be the central boulevard of East Berlin, was lined with massive communist architecture, and entire residential areas were built up with tall Plattenbau buildings. The West, on the other hand, shows the architectural influences of the Modernist architects – Gropius, Le Corbusier, Niemeyer and Aalto. All in all, the architectural style is quite varied: you can see buildings from many different historical periods (starting from medieval times), within the centre of Berlin. The general architectural style is of low, ornate constructions, usually four or five stories high, built around the turn of the century, lining wide, spacious streets.

Berlin is the capital of Germany and the largest city, with a population of 3.4 million. It has an excellent public transport network, making it easy to get around. There are S-Bahn trains, underground trains, trams and buses. I particularly like exploring the city by bike – and with a good network of cycle lanes, this is easy to do.

There is no single heart to the city. The area around Ku'damm in the Charlottenburg district used to be the city centre of West Berlin, and Alexanderplatz in Mitte was the centre of East Berlin. However, there are 12 different districts to the city and each one has within it one or more neighbourhoods (called a 'Kiez'). Each of these Kiezes has its own centre, usually with cafes, restaurants, bars, parks, market places and other social spaces. It is therefore hard to pin down a single overall character to the city, but easy to see the various vibes that are going on in each area.

YES-RESIDENZ Whenever I feel like camping but don't want all the inconveniences (cold feet, mosquito bites), I book myself and three friends into the Yes-Residenz. A tent sits right in the middle of the main room, with proper beds inside and photographic forest themed wallpaper on the walls. The location is unbeatably central, the prices are fair and even include a welcome drink at the equally charming Yes-Bar (see Bars). Fehrbellinerstraße 83, 10119 Berlin, www.yes-berlin.de

PENSION LIEBLING This is the more down-to-earth alternative, based near Helmholtzplatz in Prenzlauer Berg: There are three very reasonably priced apartments of different sizes available, all with cool interiors. Here, too, the owners run a bar with the same name. I live close to Helmholtzplatz, and Cafe Liebling is one of my favourite places to drink (see Bars). Various addresses, www.pension-liebling.de

MINILOFT This is a 100-year-old building that was recently converted into award-winning, self-contained apartments. Prices range from €85-130 per night, and it's located a stone's throw from the Central Station. Hessische Straße 5, 10115 Berlin, www.miniloft.com

Q! HOTEL Designed by Brad Pitt's favourite architects, Graft, this award-winning luxury hotel has a striking design palette of dark wood and warm red, and uses rounded shapes that create an elegant but space-age kind of look. The attention to detail is impressive – in some rooms the bed and bathtub are made with one piece of wood, and there is real sand in the sauna. Located in Charlottenburg, just off Kurfürstendamm with its high-end fashion stores. Knesebeckstraße 67, 10623 Berlin, www.loock-hotels.com

PLACES TO STAY

CHEZ GINO I discovered this place by accident a few years ago and it quickly became one of my favourites. The interior is a brilliant mix of rustic furniture and charming/cool details – a photographic forest wallpaper covers the back wall, which in combination with the white tablecloths and old-fashioned lighting gives this place a cosy yet trendy feel. It serves German food and Alsatian-style pizza. Booking essential! The owners also run a bar just around the corner, which is well worth visiting afterwards. Sorauer Straße 31, 10997 Berlin, www.sanremo-upflamoer.de

SOLAR This is a perfect spot for visitors. It's on the 17th floor of a 1970s block, and offers an amazing view of the city. I haven't actually been to the restaurant – only to the bar, which is even higher up – but I've heard it's very good. Go there just before sunset and watch the lights coming on. It's absolutely stunning. Stresemannstraße 76, 10963 Berlin, www.solarberlin.com

NOLA'S AM WEINBERG Serving excellent Swiss food, this restaurant is situated at the top of the Weinbergspark in Mitte. It has a spacious terrace, but don't miss out on the authentic Swiss interior – with antlers on the walls and impressive lampshades. Veteranenstraße 9, 10119 Berlin, www.nola.de

CAFE AM NEUEN SEE A cafe in Tiergarten Park; if you go there on a nice sunny day you can sit outside in the beer garden and watch couples paddling across the lake – extremely romantic! Lichtensteinallee 2, 10787 Berlin

THE GORGONZOLA CLUB A very charming Italian restaurant in the Kottbusser Tor area, serving pizza and pasta in a beautiful wooden interior. It's hidden in a small side street where you'll also find a very good art-house cinema. The Würgeengel bar is next door, serving good gin and tonic. The Möbel Olfe bar is at the end of this street – another cool place with gay parties on Thursdays. Dresdener Straße 121, 10999 Berlin, www.gorgonzolaclub.de

PLACES TO EAT

MONARCH I personally love going out in the area around Kottbusser Tor. The Monarch is a quirky bar on top of a supermarket. The entrance is well hidden (an unimpressive glass door to a run-down stairwell), but once inside the bar, the huge glass windows offer you an excellent view of the U1 underground train which actually goes overground in Kreuzberg. I love sitting on the windowsill, watching the trains on the outside or the mixed crowd on the inside. They occasionally have famous DJs playing on Wednesdays. Skalitzerstraße 134, 10999 Berlin

ICK KOOF MIR DAVE LOMBARDO WENN ICK REICH BIN This is certainly the bar with the best name – roughly translating as "The day I get rich I'll buy myself Dave Lombardo". The place itself isn't bad either – the hip Mitte and Prenzlauer Berg crowd comes here for breakfast in the morning or for drinks and Franconian snacks in the evening. Lots of other nice, cool bars nearby. Zionskirchstraße 34, 10119 Berlin

CAFE LIEBLING This is actually both a cafe and a bar, and I go there just as often for coffee and cake as for a glass of wine. The dominating colour here is white, and I would assume the dominating profession among the guests is designer. Raumerstraße 36A, 10435 Berlin, www.cafe-liebling.de

HEINZ MINKI If you get off at Schlesisches Tor station in Kreuzberg and then walk down Schlesische Straße, you will find this picturesque brick building. If you go in summer you must sit in the beer garden, where the coloured fairy lights, ornamental chairs and candles make it a totally romantic space. I love it. Vor dem Schlesischen Tor 3, 10997 Berlin, www.heinzminki.de

FREISCHWIMMER Only a few metres away from Heinz Minki, this bar is a simple canopied pier on the edge of the canal. Vor dem Schlesischen Tor 2, 10997 Berlin, www.freischwimmer-berlin.de

YES A small, charming bar opposite the water tower in Prenzlauer Berg. Julian, the friendly owner, also runs the Yes-Residenz (see Places to Stay) and always aims to please. Smoking is allowed here. Knaackstraße 14, 10405 Berlin, www.yesberlin.de

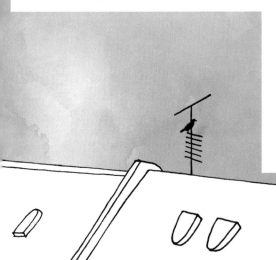

DO YOU READ ME?! This new shop mostly sells magazines from around the world, and is in the gallery district of Berlin-Mitte, only a few steps away from one of my favourite cafes, Strandbad Mitte (which is perfect for breakfast on a sunny Saturday morning). Auguststraße 28, 10117 Berlin, www.doyoureadme.de

PRO QM This is my favourite shop for design books, also located in Berlin-Mitte. It offers a wide selection of art, architecture and design books, and the staff are always helpful. Almstadtstraße 48-50, 10119 Berlin, www.pro-qm.de

SUPALIFE KIOSK I discovered this place just recently when walking past Helmhotzplatz; they sell a fine selection of design books and magazines as well as one-off screenprints, handmade puppets and notebooks. Raumerstraße 40, 10437 Berlin, www.supalife.de

MIKRO A dangerous place for people like me, who buy nice stationery just for the sake of it. This tiny shop sells paper objects from around the world – letters from greyboard, wrapping paper from the 50s and Japanese paper balloons shaped like fish. The friendly and patient shop owner, Lisa Kaechele, is a designer herself and is always there to help. Lychener Straße 51, 10437 Berlin, www.mikro-berlin.de

BERLINOMAT This spacious shop is located on Frankfurter Allee in Friedrichshain, and only sells products and fashion design by Berliners. You can order pretty much everything from their website. Frankfurter Allee 89, 10247 Berlin, www.berlinomat.com

MAMSELL For really nice chocolate, go to this shop. They have an excellent selection, plus a back room sells all sorts of beautiful little objects – screenprinted kitchen towels, vases with tiny typography on them and candles in the shape of gnomes. Goltzstraße 48, 10781 Berlin, www.mamsellberlin.de

MODULOR This is my favourite art supply shop. It stocks all kinds of art materials, like special paper, card, even wood, everything needed for model making, paint, sketchbooks, etc. Gneisenaustraße 43-45, 10961 Berlin, www.modulor.de

TÜRKENMARKT AM MAYBACHUFER This is the Turkish Market that takes place every Tuesday and Friday on the border of Kreuzberg and Neukölln districts, right on the edge of the canal. I usually come here just to look at the colourful stalls, but it is obviously great for buying Turkish vegetables, pastries and fabric. The surrounding area has become very trendy, so there are lots of nice cafes and little shops around. Kottbusser Brücke/Maybachufer, 12047 Berlin, www.tuerkenmarkt.de

SAMMLUNG BOROS I haven't been to this exceptional space yet but I've heard it's really amazing: Christian Boros started his own design company in 1990 and has been collecting art pretty much since then. He recently converted an old bunker close to the Deutsches Theater into an ultra-modern living space at the top and a gallery space down below. To visit you need to book a guided tour. Reinhardtstraße 20, 10117 Berlin, www.sammlung-boros.de

KINO INTERNATIONAL This cinema has been left untouched from GDR days, with an impressive, spacious interior, a wood-panelled lobby, typical GDR furniture and amazing chandeliers. Rankestraße 31, 10789 Berlin, www.yorck.de

C/O BERLIN Based in the former Royal Post Office (Postfuhramt), this GDR building was sympathetically converted into a gallery space in 2000. It's still pretty run down and has a slightly brooding aura – perfect for the photography exhibitions that it regularly hosts. Oranienburger Straße/Tucholskystraße, 10117 Berlin, www.co-berlin.com

CONTEMPORARY FINE ARTS GALLERY This is another cool art space, which has in the past exhibited the likes of Daniel Richter, Jonathan Meese, Georg Baselitz and Juergen Teller. Am Kupfergraben 10, 10117 Berlin, www.cfa-berlin.com

MÄRCHENHÜTTE Only open during winter months, this is such a charming institution that I have to mention it. It's an old barn, which apparently was dismantled in a forest somewhere in Poland, and brought to Berlin, where it was reconstructed as a theatre. The interior is very rustic with creaking wooden benches, a fireplace and a simple stage at the front. Watch fairytale performances while drinking mulled wine and cake – the perfect thing to do around Christmas. www.maerchenhuette.de

RADIALSYSTEM V Situated on the bank of the river Spree, somewhere between Friedrichshain, Mitte and Kreuzberg, an old pumping station has been recently converted into a new space for the arts in Berlin. In the same way as the building's architecture brings together old and contemporary elements, the programme combines traditional concepts with contemporary ones. If you go there in summer, you can sit on the terrace by the water, have a drink and watch the ducks. Holzmarktstraße 33, 10243 Berlin, www.radialsystem.de

HANSAVIERTEL Hansaviertel sits on the edge of Tiergarten Park. The area was heavily bombed during the war, and so was a convenient site for the International Building Exhibition of 1957 – the Interbau. Architects like Alvar Aalto, Egon Eiermann, Walter Gropius and Oscar Niemeyer contributed to this exhibition, and today the whole ensemble is protected as a historic monument. Various tours are on offer – Gerhild Komander is one provider. www.gerhildkomander.de

THE SPREEWEG WALK A walk along the Spree River will take you past lots of interesting sights: Bellevue Palace, residence of the German President, the Bundeskanzleramt (Chancellor's office), the House of World Cultures (a beautiful building from the 1960s, which was America's contribution to the Interbau exhibiton), the newly built Central Station and a bit further away, the Museum Island. A good starting point is Hansaplatz in the Hansaviertel area.

BERLIN WALL CIRCUIT You can walk or cycle around the perimeter of the Berlin Wall – which encompassed all of West Berlin. If you do the whole thing, it works out at around 160km – so you might want to rent a bike.

BERLIN UNDERWORLD The Berliner Unterwelten Association offers guided tours around underground sites, which are normally not open to the public. Most tours explore bunker complexes or civilian shelters from the Second World War and the Cold War. www.berliner-unterwelten.de

LANDWEHR CANAL Another beautiful walk runs along the Landwehr Canal. The section I like best starts near Prinzenstraße Station in Kreuzberg. The footpath runs past a bank where people gather in the summer to sunbathe and have a picnic. After you pass the Urban Hospital, you'll find the Graefekiez area on your right – lots of sweet cafes and little shops can be found here. Reederei Riedel offers boat trips along the canal and the Spree River. www.reederei-riedel.de

SWIMMING BATHS AND SAUNAS I am not a keen swimmer but there are two swimming baths I really like. The first is called BADESCHIFF, an open-air pool on a boat that is permanently anchored in the river Spree. In winter, they transform it into a swimming sauna. Even better is the STADTBAD NEUKÖLLN – a listed Neo-classical building which opened in 1914. The architecture evokes the thermal baths of ancient Greece with amazing mosaics and columns. There are two pools and very good sauna facilities.

WALKS AND ARCHITECTURE

Dimitris Kardiskos' Athens

The crazy Athenian adventure is the story of a city that became a village that became a city again. From its salubrious beginnings as the heart of an ancient civilisation, it was rampaged, looted and raped over the course of history, and entered the 20th Century as a town of 10,000 inhabitants. After the Second World War, there was a massive surge in population and the demand for new housing spawned endless apartment blocks, designed and planned with virtually no regulation. By the mid-1970s, Athens was already the little monster it is today. A sea of concrete has spread from its centre towards the suburbs, and become home to almost four million people. There are very few parks, and the majority of the city is ugly, harsh and lacking in any greater plan. However, it is a city of small secrets – the right corner, rooftop taverna, view from Lycabettus hill and trip down to the unfrequented beach half an hour's drive from the centre, can all reveal Athens' hidden charms.

As a tourist, it's important to know where to go to find these charms. Athens has many neighbourhoods, each with its own distinct feel: Posh (sometimes pseudo-posh) Kolonaki is full of designer boutiques and trendy types drinking cappuccinos all day. Exarhia is the student/intellectual/troubled area – often a focus for clashes between protesters and police. Plaka is the ancient part of town built on the northern slope of the Acropolis – full of Byzantine churches, romantic promenades and tacky tourist shops. Gazi and Kerameikos are areas that were formerly neglected, and are currently being revived, leading to a slew of new restaurants, bars and exhibition spaces popping up – along with a glittering new metro station. Psyrri, on the other hand, was once the 'bar area' of town, but is now slowly degenerating.

In all, Athens is a strange city. It's a crazy amalgamation of architectural styles and cultures; a city of cold winters and blazing hot summers, pollution and clear blue skies, tense days in traffic and long leisurely summer nights drinking outdoors. A place where chaos meets order and east meets west.

Design-wise Athens has been stuck in the dark ages for the past century. With the exception of the occasional star (check out Vakirtzis, K&K and Dimitris Arvanitis), it's been a fairly bleak picture. In recent years, however, a new generation of London-educated designers has breathed life into the city, and suddenly there are galleries, bookshops and a bright new future.

PERISCOPE HOTEL A brilliantly designed boutique hotel in Kolonaki, with interesting typography, eclectic furniture, a fantastic mini-suite with a jacuzzi overlooking the city, and a periscope with a camera attached spying on the city and projecting what it sees in real time in the hotel lobby. 22 Charitos Street, 10675 Athens, www.periscope.athenshotels.it

FRESH HOTEL A small gem of a design hotel in the once hip but now run-down area of Psyrri. Standing among derelict buildings, this colourful hotel has carefully placed typography, funky, minimal architecture and a roof bar with a pool, great cocktails and an amazing view of the concrete monster and the Acropolis. 26 Sofokleous Street, 10552 Athens, www.freshhotel.gr

HOTEL CECIL A good budget option in Monastiraki, a stone's throw from Plaka and the Acropolis. It's in a nicely renovated Neo-classical building. 39 Athinas Street, 10554 Athens, www.cecil.gr

IL POSTINO A small, great value Italian trattoria with friendly staff and a warm ambience, in a lively area bordering Kolonaki and Exarhia. They serve great pasta in a room plastered with a colourful collage of Italian memorabilia. Griveon 3, 10680 Athens

CHEZ LUCIEN Lucien, a Frenchman, prepares delicious steaks, which you can enjoy in a small, packed, sui-generis space that's a bit reminiscent of a Spanish cantina, and where chairs and tables are bolted upside down to the ceiling. 32 Troon, 11851 Athens

KOUTOUKI This is included in this list for the very fact that it's not designed at all. It's a totally unhip, old-school Greek taverna, tucked away under a bridge at the foot of Philipappou Hill in Petralona. But it serves amazing home-cooked food at cheap prices, with a relaxed vibe, far from the trendy crowds. It has a makeshift roof terrace, and on summer nights, with the Acropolis glowing just above the treetops, it can be quite magical. 9 Lakiou Street, 11851 Athens

TIKI BAR Next to the new Acropolis Museum in the Makrygianni District, this place is a tribute to all things Polynesian. Kitsch, retro beach scenes adorn the walls, and Tiki sculptures, low lighting and exotic cocktails add to the ambience. The people who run this place love 1960s lounge music, but on some nights they host mod/ska parties, with visiting DJs and live acts. 15 Falirou Street, 11742 Athens, www.tikiathens.com

NIXON A cool place to come for a beer around the big bar or on one of the leather sofas. A 1960s chandelier presides over the place, and Nixon paraphernalia cover the walls. It also has a full-size private cinema. 61B Agisilaou Street, 10435 Athens, www.nixon.gr

K44 A two-storey, concreted warehouse space in Gazi, full of vintage furniture and dogs wandering about. It's a bar, a studio and an exhibition space all in one – and is an artsy and humorous bohemian underground hangout. 44 Kostantinoupoleous Street, 10676 Athens, www.k44.gr

ANTHROPOS Small, dark, creepy and fun, this improvised bar/hangout place has an old piano, a wooden gymnastics horse, black lights and a DJ mixing music on a laptop somewhere among the audience. It's the kind of place that makes weird cool – you can kneel on the floor pretending to be a chicken without anyone looking twice. The building is completely inconspicuous – just a small old shop-front with no obvious signage or marking. If you peer through the window you can just catch a glimpse of the bar. It's indicative that I tried to find out the official address, and couldn't find it anywhere! Corner of Megalou Alexandrou and Giatrakou Street (a pedestrianised alley)

BARS

SHOPPING

PIRAEUS FLEA MARKET Monastiraki is the big touristy flea market, but Piraeus Flea Market is more interesting (although grottier). It's right next to the metro station, and takes up the streets parallel to the train lines with stalls and small shops selling antiques, jewellery and everything else. A second, new market has also popped up in Piraeus, on Schistou Avenue. This is a very strange place – an avenue cut into the rock wedged between industrial wastelands and a cemetery. It's got a real third world vibe about it. You can buy anything from second-hand goods, to animals, bikes – and even cars. Both are only open on Sundays. Plateia Ippodamias and Schistou Avenue

KOAN This small and eclectic art bookstore in Kolonaki is also the Taschen boutique in Athens. Great books on design, architecture and the arts and a bohemian feel. 64 Skoufa, 10680 Athens

LYSSIPOS The small basement showroom-cum-studio of Mr Christou, a wonderful, old self-taught sculptor from the Epirus region, is well worth a visit. His ad hoc creations are full of folklore näiveté and beauty at the same time. 6 Veikou Street, 11742 Athens

MYRAN A wonderful gallery/shop run by a Swedish guy called Martin Olofsson. He presents and sells the best of Scandinavian design – it's the only place like this in the country. 8 Fokilidou Street, 10673 Athens, www.myran.gr

OASIS This place sells unique 1950s furniture and has a distinctly Kolonaki-chic flea market vibe. You can find some amazing lamps here. Dimokritou Street corner of Anagnostopoulou Street, 10673 Athens

ELINA LEMPESI The sui-generis fashion designer creates wonderful limited edition dresses, and has a small shop in Kolonaki. 13 Iraklitou, 11528 Athens

KORRES This is an up-market cosmetics company that uses natural products, and has great graphic and packaging design. They have shops all over the world, but are originally from Athens. 8 Ivikou, 11635 Athens, www.korres.com

Q-BOX A small eclectic space that provides a refreshing change from the usual shop-like commercial gallery space. It hosts international, well-researched projects, primarily by emerging artists, and also manages a residency for artists and curators, that takes place on the gallery's premises on the Island of Kea. It's situated in the central food market. 10 Armodiou, 1st Floor, Varvakios Agora, 10552 Athens, www.qbox.gr

AMP A new gallery space that challenges the boundaries of the so-called 'white cube'. It mainly represents artists from New York (although it does have artists from other places too), and has really brought a new, American factor into the Athens art scene. It's in a converted old Neo-classical building in the centre. 26 Epikourou and 4 Korinis, 10553 Athens, www.a-m-p.gr

THE NEW BENAKI MUSUEM This is a new branch of an older, more traditional museum (the Benaki Museum in Kolonaki). It has an amazing (and vast) architectural space, and features carefully selected seasonal exhibitions that can be quite bold and exciting. 130 Pireos Street, 10552 Athens, www.benaki.gr

THE EPIGRAPHICAL MUSEUM Obscured by the nearby National Archaeological Museum, this small museum boasts an amazing collection of about 13,000 stone inscriptions, which cover the period from early historical times to the late Roman period. It goes without saying that it's especially interesting in a typographical sense. 1 Tositsa Street, 10682 Athens

THE BREEDER Partly because of the amazing architecture of the space, designed by famous architect Zambikos, and partly because of the fresh curation of the duo behind the place, The Breeder is a modern art space in Athens to look out for. 45 Iasonos Street, 10436 Athens, www.thebreedersystem.com

THE BLUE BUILDING Built in the inter-war period, this was the first proper apartment building in Athens, and is a Modernist masterpiece by visionary architect Koulis Panagiotakos. The lobbies, doors and staircases are fantastic, and it even has a recreation/party area on the roof, with amazing views of the city. When Le Corbusier visited it, he wrote in the entrance, 'C'est tres beau'. 61 Arachovis Street, 10681 Athens

LYCABETTUS AND THE FIX These are two pieces of 1950s Modernism by the great and yet sadly overlooked architect Takis Zenetos. Lycabettus is an open-air theatre that's still in use, and The Fix is a tour-de-force, which was once a brewery and is now being converted into a modern art museum. Lycabettus Hill and Syngrou Avenue corner Frantsi Street, 11745 Athens, respectively

ELECTRIC COMPANY SUBSTATIONS The substations of the old electric company are dotted throughout the city. They are neglected architectural masterpieces of industrial charm. Many of them have contemporary interpretations of the themes of the ancient temples, and some have really nice industrial stencils. Keep an eye out for them as you're walking around.

THE GERMAN CEMETERY Situated just outside the city on Mount Dionysos, this is worth a visit if you're in town for a bit longer. It's built on a mountain slope, surrounded by forest, and is a uniquely serene corner of the world, with some great contemporary architecture and planning.

ST NICHOLAS AT VOULIAGMENI BAY A very weird chapel built on the rock out of a hotch-potch of found elements. It's a peculiar little architectural monster – like an improvised Gaudi or something. It stands enigmatically above the waves, and has a strange, romantic feel.

FALIRO Take a walk along the newly rejuvenated seaside promenade, 15 minutes outside central Athens. You can drive or take the new tram from Syntagma Square. It can be a lovely thing to do on a Saturday afternoon – you can have a swim in the sea (which is pretty clean), eat an ice cream or even challenge the locals at the giant open-air chessboard.

WALKS AND ARCHITECTURE

EVENTS

ATHENS FESTIVAL JUNE-AUGUST This lasts all summer long and boasts an impressive line-up of world class acts. The city's most impressive venues embrace international performers of music, dance and theatre, and it's a great way to see sights like the ancient Roman open-air theatre of Herodus Atticus used as they were originally intended to be. www.greekfestival.gr

FÊTE DE LA MUSIQUE 18-21 JUNE This is the Athenian version of the festival that started in France offering free concerts by amateur and professional musicians at venues across the city. It can be a very rich event with great musicians from all around the world.

DESIGN WALK FEBRUARY For three days in winter, the design agencies in Psyrri hold open studios. There are events and talks aimed at opening up discussion around design. www.designwalk.gr

DANUBE

BUDA

MARGIT ISLAND

PEST

DAVID BARATH'S BUDAPEST

What I like about Budapest is its variety. You can find everything here, from fashionable design restaurants to shabby, airless bars. A bit arty Berlin, a bit elegant Paris. I love its ambiguity.

Budapest is situated on both sides of the River Danube – the Buda side is on a hill and Pest is on a plain. In past times, Buda was where the kings and queens lived, while Pest was home to their servants. In later days, factories were built on the Pest side, because its flatness and proximity to the railways and river made transport easy. Today Buda is still much richer, more elegant and snobbish than Pest. But Pest is really where it's at – with most of the clubs, restaurants, shops and galleries. This is where I live and work, so I might be a little biased – but just the fact that I can get into town without waiting in a traffic jam for half an hour sells it to me!

Visitors to Budapest are often struck by the eclecticism of its architecture. Contemporary, Neo-classical, Art Nouveau and inter-war architecture stand side by side. Very little of it has been renovated, giving the city a shabby but romantic atmosphere. Some areas to look out for are: Kazinczy utca (district 7) - the old Jewish area; Napraforgo utca (district 2), which has some great examples of Bauhaus architecture; Andrassi utca (district 6) has some beautiful old villas; and Nagymező utca and Király utca have a buzzing nightlife with great 'ruin bars' - semi-derelict places that look like squats – such as Kumplung, Szimpla Kert, Mumus or Csendes. They close down as the buildings are renovated and pop up elsewhere.

One thing you must try while you're in Budapest is the Turkish baths. The city has many thermal springs, and in the days of Ottoman rule, many baths were built, some of which still stand. They're open throughout the year, but it's especially recommended in winter – sitting in the hot water, with steam all around you, breathing in the ice cold air is an unforgettable experience.

Just one last word about the locals – people can seem negative and pessimistic at first glance, but sit with them over a glass of Unicum or Palinka, and they'll open up eventually. Some words in Hungarian: egeszsegedre (eges-sheggedre) means 'cheers' and köszönöm (kosonom) means 'thank you' – drop them into conversation and you will surely raise a smile.

GRESHAM If you really want to feel WOW! you should stay in the Four Seasons Hotel Gresham Palace. Situated in a wonderfully renovated Art Nouveau building, the rooms face the Chain Bridge and the Castle – it is really breathtaking (and the prices are too). Roosevelt tér 5-6, 1051 Budapest, www.fourseasons.com/budapest

LÁNCHÍD 19 The first design hotel in Budapest is on the other side of the Chain Bridge – so you can wake up to the view of Pest from your bed. It's decked out in design furniture, but it's the façade that really makes it special. Created by local artist collective Szovetseg 39, the decorated glass panels move in response to the weather, chronicling the eco-system of the Danube. It's an artwork in itself. Lanchid 19-21, 1013 Budapest, www.lanchid19hotel.hu

ATRIUM Cheap and chic with fresh, colourful and comfortable design. Stay here if you want to be centrally located, but be careful walking around this neighbourhood after dark. Csokonai 14, 1081 Budapest, www.atriumhotelbudapest.com

ZICHY Situated at the former residence of a famous noble, Count Nandor Zichy, this newly opened hotel is probably the most architecturally authentic, with impressively renovated Neo-classical interiors. Lőrinc pap tér 2, 1088 Budapest, www.hotel-palazzo-zichy.hu

GERLÓCZY A small hotel above a fantastic restaurant, run by Tamas T Nagy, who also owns a great cheese store and butchers. It's done up in French-style, elegant and sophisticated. V. Gerlóczy utca 1, 1052 Budapest, www.gerloczy.hu

PRINCESS APARTMENT If you're after a really cheap option, this is my top tip. It's in a wonderful street next to the Bazilika in a lovely garden, and has space for ten people. Hercegprimas utca 2, 1051 Budapest, www.apartmentsinbudapest.hu

PLACES TO EAT

PLACES TO STAY

KLASSZ The name means 'cool' and it really is. It's situated on posh Andrássy Street, but it's got no pretensions – nice wallpaper, comfortable seats, exposed pipes and very simple delicious food. You can't reserve a table, but you can happily pass the time at the bar. Andrassy utca 41, 1061 Budapest, www.klassz.eu

GERLÓCZY French elegance with good authentic food (ie. lots of fat, onion and paprika). Live music in the evenings makes it even nicer, but I especially recommend it for breakfast. V. Gerlóczy utca 1, 1052 Budapest, www.gerloczy.hu

CAFE KÖR If you really want to eat authentic Hungarian food with international style, this is the place to go. The venue is nothing interesting, just a small hole with lots of old chairs, but the food is really special. Small wonder this is the favourite of all the expats! Sas utca 17, 1051 Budapest, www.cafekor.com

DONATELLA'S KITCHEN Wonderful design and authentic Italian food, under the surveillance of a Michelin-starred chef. Hang out with the rich and famous – and book in advance. Kiraly utca 30-32, 1061 Budapest

MENZA This place has been the most fashionable restaurant in town for seven years now. Situated on bustling Liszt Ferenc Square, it is often impossible to book a table, although the place itself is quite big. The reasons: food is good, portions are huge, staff are friendly, prices are reasonable and the decor is nice. Try the beef soup, especially if you're suffering from a hangover. Liszt Ferenc ter 2, 1061 Budapest, www.menza.co.hu

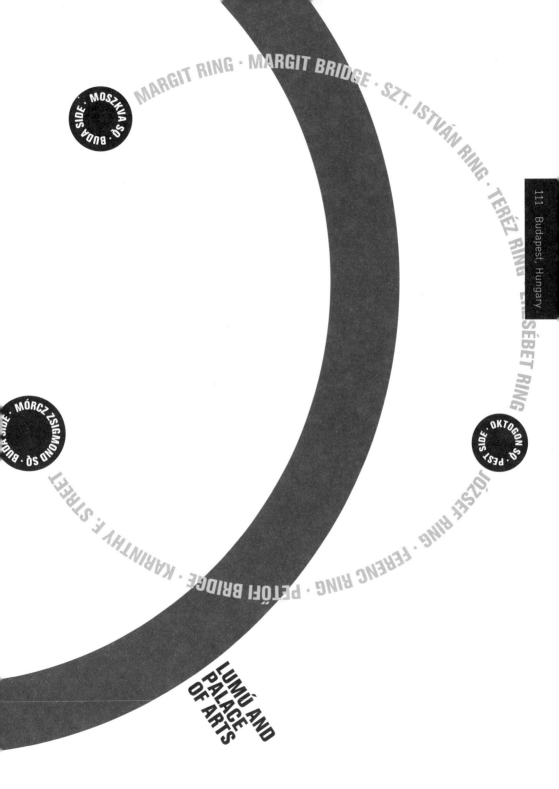

MARGIT RING · MARGIT BRIDGE · SZT. ISTVÁN RING · TERÉZ RING · ERSÉBET RING

BUDA SIDE · MOSZKVA SQ.

BUDA SIDE · MÓRCZ ZSIGMOND SQ.

PEST SIDE · OKTOGON SQ.

JÓZSEF RING · FERENC RING · PETŐFI BRIDGE · KARINTHY F. STREET

LUMÚ AND
PALACE
OF ARTS

I don't really like posh clubs, I prefer small, simple bars with nice music and staff. If you're into high-end clubs, check out Negro or BOB (both on the Bazilika Square in district 5) or look online for Creol, Symbol, Deryne, Mini or Kyoto.

SANDOKAN LISBOA A tiny, friendly pub with a nice terrace behind the Opera. Hajós utca 23, 1065 Budapest, www.sandokanlisboa.hu

MŰVÉSZ Literally meaning 'artist', this old fashioned 19th Century cafe has recently been done up, and is the perfect place for a latte before, or a drink after visiting the opera, which is just opposite. Andrassy utca 29, 1062 Budapest

SZIMPLA KERT You've probably heard about the 'ruin bars' in Budapest – unreconstructed dives that look like squats. This is the first and still the most popular of them all. It takes up an entire building in the Jewish district and is filled with students, artists, table football and cheap drinks. In the summer it also has an open-air cinema. Kazinczy utca 14, 1075 Budapest, www.szimpla.hu

GÖDÖR KLUB If you like just sitting around and meeting people, this is a good place to come. They have a huge terrace in the middle of the city, so it's especially nice in summer. Erzsébet tér, 1051 Budapest, www.godorklub.hu

JELEN BISZTRO AND CORVINTETO Jelen is a place for jazz lovers. Simple and shabby, with flea market furniture, jazz posters and lots of smoke, it is situated on the ground floor of an old warehouse, and accessed from the right side of the building. Upstairs in the same building but accessed from the left side, you'll find Corvinteto, a dance club that hosts lots of live gigs. On the rooftop, there's a lovely bar (and fresh air – finally!) Blaha Lujza tér 1-2, 1085 Budapest, www.jelenbisztro. blogspot.com and www.corvinteto.hu

DOMBY BAR This tiny place is only about drinks – they offer a huge variety of them. Extra-small, extra-elegant, extra-professional, extra-sophisticated. Anker koz 3, 1061 Budapest, www.bar-domby.hu

BARS

SUBVIBE I love street style and all the subculture that goes around bicycles, skateboarding and street art, so my favourite shop is Subvibe in prestigious Váci Street. They sell old-school brands like Paul Frank and Adidas, while in the outlet just two blocks away you can find all kinds of shoes and streetwear. Váci utca 40, 1056 Budapest, www.myspace.com/subvibe

FORMA Whenever there is a birthday in my family I always buy presents at Forma. A small shop stocking a huge variety of funny or simply beautiful design objects, many by Hungarian designers. Ferenciek tere 4 (in the arcade), 1053 Budapest, www.forma.co.hu

RETROCK AND RETROCK DELUXE
Retrock is an anti-fashion store selling second-hand and handmade items – t-shirts designed by students, earrings shaped like LPs – that kind of thing – popular among poor students. Retrock Deluxe is an upmarket version, selling more sophisticated designer items – appealing to young arty professionals. Henszlmann Imre utca 1, 1053 Budapest, www.retrock.com

SUGAR! Once upon a time there was a little girl who grew up in a dynasty of pastry-makers. She always dreamed about opening her very own confectioners, and when she grew up she realised her dream by opening this spectacular shop with colourful Kartell lamps, bar stools that look like lollipops and cakes that look like fairytales. It's a bit far from the centre but easily accessible by tube line 3. The little girl is already working on her second shop in the centre of the city.... Petofi utca 35, 1042 Budapest, www.sugarshop.hu

BUDA SIDE IS ON THE HILLS, IT HAS LOT OF TREES AND PARKS

G13 ART GALLERY I designed the identity of this gallery. It focuses on modern artists from Brassaï to Vasarely, and also represents contemporary Hungarian photographers and painters. It's also worth a visit because of its prestigious location in a series of recently renovated courtyards. Király utca 13, 1075 Budapest, www.g13.hu

LUDWIG MÚZEUM A contemporary art museum, situated on two levels of the Palace of Arts. It holds works by the likes of Andy Warhol, Jasper Johns and Claes Oldenberg, as well as Hungarian artists. The building itself is pretty spectacular. Komor Marcell utca 1, 1095 Budapest, www.lumu.hu

TRAFÓ A centre of contemporary arts with a good programme of contemporary theatre and dance performances. There's also a club in the basement that hosts live gigs. Check their website first. Lillom utca 41, 1094 Budapest, www.trafo.hu

MŰCSARNOK This palace of contemporary arts is situated on Heroes Square, facing the Museum of Fine Arts. It generally hosts big travelling exhibitions, and has a very good bookshop too. Hosok ter, 1238 Budapest, www.mucsarnok.hu

KARTON GALÉRIA A private gallery specialising in caricatures and comics – mainly Hungarian. It has some good books and posters for sale. Alkotmány utca 18, 1054 Budapest, www.karton.hu

BOULEVARD ÉS BREZSNYEV A tiny gallery showcasing emerging young artists. Almost every week there is a vernissage, a party or a ping-pong match, drawing in hundreds of people. The art is fresh and often provocative. 39 and 46 Király utca, 1074 Budapest, www.bbgaleria.creo.hu

HŐSÖK TERE · HEROES SQUARE

SZÉP-MŰVÉSZETI MUSEUM OF FINE ARTS

HŐSÖK TERE

MŰCSARNOK MUSEUM OF CONTEMPORARY

THE STATUE OF LIBERTY ON THE GELLERT HILL/BUDA SIDE

MUSEUM OF APPLIED ARTS

The exhibitions here can be old-fashioned, and the staff are so mean-tempered (in a very Hungarian way), but the building is really breathtaking. Art Nouveau mixed with oriental elements – the trademark of Hungarian architect Ödön Lechner. Üllői utca 33-37, 1450 Budapest, www.imm.hu

WALK THROUGH DISTRICT 6

Stroll along Andrassy Street till you get to Heroes Square. The twin museums of Mucsarnok and the Museum of Fine Arts face each other across the space. Then turn right and come back towards the city on Városliget Fasor. This is the most beautiful part of Budapest, and there are so many different architectural styles on offer. Check out Terror Haza (Museum of Terror) at number 60 – the imaginatively renovated headquarters of the communist political police. On Dózsa György út, you will find two wonderful modern buildings; number 84 is a great example of soz-real (Socialist Realism) architecture, that was typical of the Socialist era. Its neighbour is the HQ of ING Bank – a hyper-modern, floating glass structure designed by Dutch architect Erick van Egeraat.

WALKS AND ARCHITECTURE

SZIGET FESTIVAL AUGUST One of the biggest week-long music and cultural festivals in Europe, with impressive international line-ups. www.sziget.hu

WAMP Try to visit Budapest on one of the weekends when Wamp takes place – a design market where you can find funky shoes, bags, scarves, jewellery and toys, many of which are unique pieces made by the individual designers. Gödör Klub, Erzsébet ter, 1051 Budapest, www.wamp.hu

EVENTS

URBAN MAY FESTIVAL MAY-JUNE Interesting urban and cultural events mainly taking place along the banks of the Danube. www.urbitalis.hu

NOTE. Railways constructed under Tramways
& Light Railways (Ireland) Acts ... shown thus
Railways under construction ....
Coach Routes ....
Joint Lines

Scale — Ten Statute Miles to One Inch

NORTH

Keen to Left
Carnagway

REFERENCE
A ... ndalk, Newry & Greenore.
B ... Cork, & Muskerry.
C ... Cork, Blackrock & Passage.
D ... Giant's Causeway & Portrush.
        (Electric)
E ... Dublin & Lucan Tramway.

noelle cooper's Dublin

Although I was brought up in Kildare, the horsey capital of Ireland, I have spent most of my adult life living, studying and working in Dublin.

Ireland is self-titled 'the land of saints and scholars', and it seems our literary reputation has come at the expense of any real visual or design tradition. Most of our architectural heritage has been borrowed from our closest neighbours and historically there is very little understanding or appreciation of design. However, in more recent times, through the efforts of a number of small groups, design in Ireland, and particularly in Dublin, has started to find its feet. There are three colleges in Dublin offering degrees in Visual Communication, and events and forums like SweetTalk and CreativeIreland have given us a focal point away from the stuffy and exclusive industry-based associations. This change has also been reflected in a shift towards smaller creative studios.

With a population of half a million, Dublin is big enough to keep you busy, but small enough to retain a sense of community. You can practically walk to anywhere in the city centre in half an hour, which is handy as we lack an integrated transport system. Buses are a cheap way around but they can be difficult to figure out and the services are sporadic at best. Design consultants Image Now are doing a good job of updating Dublin Bus's signage and timetabling but it'll take time to be fully implemented. There is a very limited train service called the DART, which is cool if you want to visit the beach in Malahide in the north or Bray in the south (the journey to Bray is quite nice with a large part of it hugging the coastline). The Luas light rail service is another way to get around the inner city, but it's not finished – so none of the lines actually meet up yet!

Dublin is split down the middle by the river Liffey, the Northside being a bit more colourful than the posher Southside. As you would expect, most of the fun can be had in the centre of town, but spots a little further out like Camden Street, Stoneybatter and Rathmines are also worth a visit if you're here for a few days. As the stereotype goes, a large part of city life revolves around the pub, but there is plenty to do in between scoops.

AVALON HOUSE HOSTEL Dublin's only eco-friendly budget hostel close to the heart of the city. The property is listed as a building of 'outstanding architectural merit', and has quite an artistic philosophy, occasionally hosting photography competitions for its guests. 55 Aungier St, Dublin 2, www.avalon-house.ie

THE MORRISON Probably Dublin's trendiest boutique hotel. Very centrally located, across the river from Temple Bar, which despite its reputation for drunken stag and hen parties, actually has quite a few good galleries. The interior was designed by John Rocha and is super-cool with a warm friendly atmosphere. Ormond Quay, Dublin 1, www.morrisonhotel.ie

THE CLARENCE This hotel was bought and restored by Bono in 1992, and is now one of Dublin's most luxurious hotels. The Octagon Bar makes really great cocktails, and there used to be a great club in the basement, which no longer exists, but rumours suggest it may rise again. 6-8 Wellington Quay, Dublin 2, www.theclarence.ie

STAY DUBLIN This company provides high quality and reasonably priced apartment accommodation in the heart of the city. I haven't stayed here personally but I have used the same company for accommodation in Amsterdam and it was really pleasant and spacious. Various addresses, www.staydublin.com

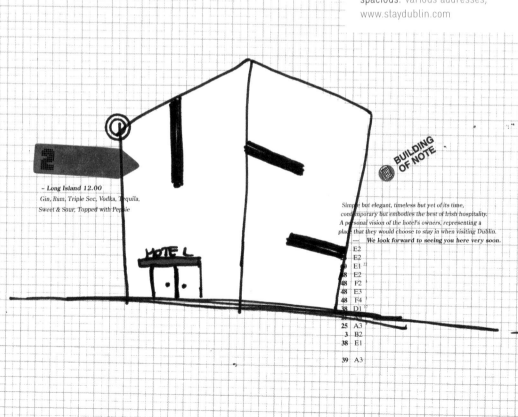

- Long Island 12.00
Gin, Rum, Triple Sec, Vodka, Tequila, Sweet & Sour, Topped with Pepsie

BUILDING OF NOTE

Simple but elegant, timeless but yet of its time, contemporary but embodies the best of Irish hospitality. A personal vision of the hotel's owners, representing a place that they would choose to stay in when visiting Dublin.
— **We look forward to seeing you here very soon.**

	E2
	E2
	E1
	E2
8	F2
48	E3
48	F4
38	D1
25	A3
3	B2
38	E1
39	A3

Pinville Burger — Bun (Top), Beef, Fresh Salsa, Avocado & Bun (Bottom)
Accompanied by Sweet Potato Fries
and a side of Good Tunes.

SIMON'S PLACE This should be the first cafe stop on your list. It's great for tea and toast at around 10am, when everyone else is at work. You can plan the rest of your visit by reading the copious number of posters and flyers that plaster the walls. It's like a virtual event guide! 22 South Great Georges Street, Dublin 2

JO'BURGER You may have to take a bus or taxi to experience this gem of a burger joint, but I can promise you it's well worth it. This is the tastiest organic burger experience I've ever had. The interior is small and noisy, with a casual, house-party atmosphere and walls adorned with graffiti and street art. A nightly DJ spins an eclectic mix of tunes. 137 Rathmines Road, Dublin 6, www.joburger.ie

ODESSA This place might seem intimidatingly cool, but once you make it through the entrance, you'll see that it's stylish but comfy, and the food is reasonably priced – great for a weekend brunch or in the evenings try the 'fivers' dishes. If you're nice to your fellow diners you might get invited upstairs to the members club, which has three levels and a roof terrace smoking area. 14 Dame Court, Dublin 2, www.odessa.ie

THE WINDING STAIR This is a buzzing little restaurant on the Northside, overlooking the Ha'Penny Bridge, serving simple, modern, organic Irish food. Sitting above the quirky bookshop of the same name (see Shopping), it's been a favourite spot for writers, musicians and artists since the 1970s. 40 Ormond Quay, Dublin 1, www.winding-stair.com

SHEBEEN CHIC I love the laid-back atmosphere of this alternative take on a 'dirty old man's pub'. All the furniture is reclaimed – each chair is unique, every lampshade is crooked, the tables are scuffed, the chandeliers are cracked, and crap pictures are hung sideways or upside down. The vibe is young and funky and the food isn't bad either! 4 Georges Street, Dublin 2

THE CAKE CAFE This is a beautiful haven of cakey-sweetness nestled at the back of a paper shop called Daintree. The whole building is eco-friendly, and the cafe uses recycled napkins and mismatched old crockery. It's small and fills up quickly, but there's a covered terrace and hot water bottles if it gets nippy – or you could just grab a dainty box of tiny cupcakes to take away. 62 Pleasants Place, Dublin 8, www.thecakecafe.ie

He... Hamak
Jan... ...res
Ste... ...fore
Ein...
Eel...
Sic...
I-Li...
Ce...
Tim... ...ren
Ma... Cattelan
Jake ... Dinos Chapman
...
Rachael Whiteread
Barbara Kruger
Gavin Turk
Tom Friedman
Paul McCarthy
Matthew Ronay
Tunga
Yayoi Kusama
The Hilton Brothers
Peggy Stephaich Guinness
DEAF
Kenny Scharf
Mike Bouchet
Helen Chadwick
John Kenny

DICE BAR This is my favourite place on a Friday night – a gritty New York street vibe bar that takes over the street with an electric atmosphere. A live DJ plays everything from Johnny Cash to early Prodigy, and come midnight you'll be tempted to dance on the tables. It draws in designers and couriers, and can get packed. If it does (ie. the bikes are stacked three high outside), pop round the corner to Jack Ryan's for a more relaxed pint. 79 Queen Street, Dublin 7

THE BERNARD SHAW A music bar with occasional exhibitions from emerging designers and artists. You can't miss this place, as it's wedged between graffiti covered hoardings near the canal. The owners also run a club on the Northside called Twisted Pepper, so they get some good DJs and bands in. Check the website for information. 11–12 South Richmond Street, Dublin 2, www.bodytonicmusic.com

THE SECRET BAR This place is hidden away on the top of the French restaurant l'Gueuleton, and as there's no name on the door it's hard to tell if you're in the right place. When you enter, you're greeted with a surprisingly large space, lightbox art, high stools along the bar and walls, and snug areas for private comfort. Out the back is a decent-sized beer garden. It feels like a welcome break from the bustle of the city. 1 Fade Street, Dublin 2

MULLIGANS Personally, I'm not so keen on the old 'black stuff', but if Guinness is your tipple, this is the place to come. With tobacco-stained ceilings, a great pint of Guinness (or so I hear) and a friendly, sociable atmosphere, this is the definitive old Irish pub. Especially crowded on Fridays after work. 8 Poolbeg Street, Dublin 2

SOUTH WILLIAM This 'urban lounge' is a tiny bit pretentious, but it does serve up some funky tunes, the best mojitos in town and delicious pies (the bacon and cabbage is to die for!) The interior is small and narrow, but there's a good size dance floor so you can break out your latest moves. 52 South William Street, Dublin 2, www.southwilliam.ie

BARS

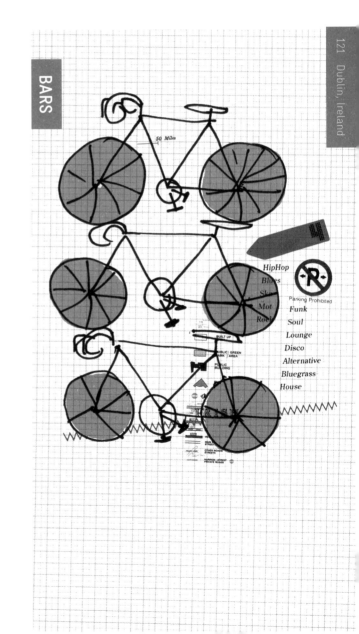

THE WINDING STAIR Step in off the busy quays and it's like stepping back in time. This tiny place is one of the best bookshops in Dublin, stocking everything from fantasy fiction to design and architecture. There's a comfy leather chair for you to sit and browse the goods, and occasionally the owner plays music on an ancient turntable in the corner. It often hosts artistic events; exhibitions, cookery classes, play readings and other intriguing happenings. 40 Ormond Quay, Dublin 1, www.winding-stair.com

THE LOFT MARKET On the top floor of the Powerscourt Centre on South William Street is a stylish and crafty weekend market. It has a bright, airy New York loft vibe, with stalls run by Irish fashion and jewellery designers, photographers, illustrators etc. They also occasionally host exhibitions and workshops. 59 South William Street, Dublin 2

CIRCUS Also based in the Powerscourt Centre, this is a high-end fashion shop by day and a creative exhibition space by night. Dangling from the old-style fashion rails hang obscure labels that you won't recognise but will definitely want. It's also the only place in Dublin to stock *Monoculture Magazine*. Bring your credit card. 59 South William Street, Dublin 2

G1 SKATE A small skater-owned store, little known outside the skate fraternity. The tiny stairwell entrance doesn't inspire you with much confidence, but when you enter you're hit with the colour, type and illustration of the boards that cover the walls. The staff are very friendly and helpful – and very very passionate about skateboarding. Make sure to say hello to Anto – the paper guy at the entrance downstairs – he'll give you other directions and general insider info. 55 O'Connell Street Lower, Dublin 1, www.g1skatesupply.net

THE BERNARD SHAW CAR BOOT SALE This is one of the coolest car boot sales I've ever been to. It's not too well known, and it really is worth a visit, so make sure to check their Facebook site for dates. While it's relatively small, it's packed with treats and wacky wonderful bits and pieces, plus cupcakes, homemade lemonade and falafels. 12 South Richmond Street, Dublin 2, www.bodytonicmusic.com/bshaw

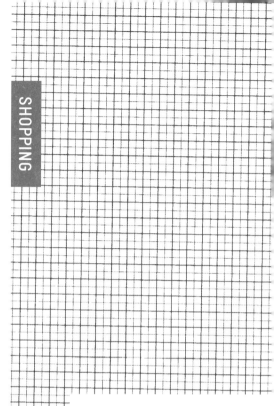

BEWLEYS CAFE & THEATRE This is a unique little theatre venue on top of the old Bewleys Cafe. The small room is beautifully lit by tiny flickering tea lights, and holds about 50 bodies – so get there early or you won't be let in! It's so small and intimate you'll feel like part of the show. If you haven't had time to eat, don't worry, they serve delicious food from the restaurant directly to your table. 78 Grafton Street, Dublin 2, www.bewleyscafetheatre.com

MONSTER TRUCK At the bottom of the not-so-pretty Francis Street is this small, unusually shaped art space. It's basically a creative co-operative, where people can experiment and present their work. It's known for its frequent launch nights, when Francis Street becomes flooded with warm wine and creative energy. Watch out for the buses! 73 Francis Street, Dublin 8, www.monstertruck.ie

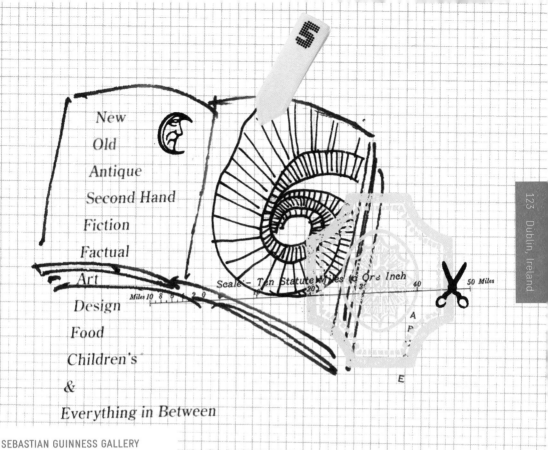

New
Old
Antique
Second Hand
Fiction
Factual
Art
Design
Food
Children's
&
Everything in Between

Scale - Ten Statute Miles to One Inch

Miles 10 8 6 4 2 0

20   30   40   50 Miles

SEBASTIAN GUINNESS GALLERY (SGG) This is a relatively new gallery owned by Sebastian Guinness (yes he is one of THE Guinnesses). You can expect established international artists like Damien Hirst and Andy Warhol alongside newer emerging artists. It's well worth a visit – even if you can't afford to buy the work. 18 Eustace Street, Dublin 2, www.sebastianguinnessgallery.com

THE FACTORY SPACE Established Dublin design agency Design Factory have opened up a gallery space in their studio to showcase the best in graphic art. If you're lucky you might get a sneaky look at the design studio itself. 100 Capel Street, Dublin 1, www.thefactoryspace.ie

THE NATIONAL PRINT MUSEUM This is a bit out of the way, but worth the 20 minute walk. It's in the old Garrison Chapel of Beggars Bush Barracks, and it's home to an incredible collection of artifacts from the Irish printing industry. It runs a variety of workshops, such as a letterpress day I took part in. It was a great experience – with just three to a class, we each had a corner of the workshop to ourselves, a really passionate teacher and tons of old type at our disposal. Beggars Bush Barracks, Haddington Road, Dublin 4, www.nationalprintmuseum.ie

NCAD GALLERY This is a new gallery in the National College of Art and Design. I haven't yet visited, but I'm sure it will be cool, as the graduate shows are always worth a look. 100 Thomas Street, Dublin 8, www.ncad.ie

LIGHTHOUSE CINEMA This is a small four-screen cultural cinema in Smithfield, showing independent, foreign-language, art-house and classic films. It's great because there are never really any queues and there's no pressure to buy a bucket of popcorn and three litres of cola! Market Square, Dublin 7, www.lighthousecinema.ie

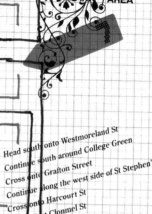

SECRET GARDEN

Miles 10 8 6 4 2 0

PUBLIC GREEN PARK AREA

Head south onto Westmoreland St
Continue south around College Green
Cross onto Grafton Street
Continue along the west side of St Stephen's Green
Cross onto Harcourt St
Turn left at Clonmel St
Enjoy the Peace & Quiet

EVENTS

DARKLIGHT FILM FESTIVAL
OCTOBER A weekend film
and animation festival, which
explores a mix of art, film and
technology. www.darklight.ie

SYNTH EASTWOOD MAY This is
a Dublin based music, art and
technology group. It's got a gig-
like atmosphere that presents
work from around the world.
www.syntheastwood.com

VISIT APRIL A free annual event
where artists' studios across
the city are open to the public.
It offers a great insight into the
variety of contemporary work
taking place in printmaking,
painting, drawing, glassmaking,
ceramics, video and photography.
www.visitstudios.com

OPEN HOUSE OCTOBER This is a
great way to see the architecture
of the city from the classic
to the contemporary. For one
weekend, buildings, spaces and
houses of architectural merit
open their doors to the public.
www.architecturefoundation.ie

Wim Crouwel
Michael C. Place
Adrian Shaughnessy
Richard Gilligan
Stefan Sagmeister
Ben Drury
Hort
Airside
Jon Burgerman
SEA
Timothy Saccenti
Mark Blamire
Michael Gillette
Glen E. Friedman
Playbeast
Swifty
Pete Fowler
Designers Republic
Trevor Jackson

WALKS AND ARCHITECTURE

THE IVEAGH GARDENS This has been called 'Dublin's Secret Garden' and when you step in you'll see why – it's slap bang in the middle of the city, but very much away from the hustle and bustle. There's a maze, a rosarium and a fountain. It's so calm and tranquil, you can lose yourself in a world of your own. In the summer it hosts the SpiegelTent – a mini music festival. Clonmel Street, Dublin 2

GEORGE'S STREET ARCADE A beautiful, Victorian, purpose-built market that still serves the Southside shopping scene. It's got a great mix of everything, from costume jewellery to fortune telling, music and art books, fine wine and coffee. Among the many trendy shops and stalls in this arcade you'll find Simon's Cafe (see Places to Eat). Georges Street, Dublin 2, www.georgesstreetarcade.ie

MOVIES ON THE SQUARE JUNE A highlight of the summer is watching a movie at the only purpose-built open-air cinema in the country. It's the perfect way to unwind with friends on a summer evening, if we ever get one. Meeting House Square, Dublin 2

DEAF (DUBLIN ELECTRONIC ARTS FESTIVAL) OCTOBER Taking place in a range of venues across the city this is a celebration of music and art with electronic music workshops and performances by Irish and international acts. www.deafireland.com

SWEETTALK This is an excellent monthly event in a cinema-like venue, where acclaimed local and international designers and creatives showcase and discuss their work. It's very inspiring, and has had a real impact on me and other young designers I know. www.candycollective.com

LUCA PASQUALIN'S TRIESTE

However you get there, car, plane or train, the sight of Trieste will make you catch your breath. The first thing you'll notice is the sea that stretches out to the horizon. The second thing that stands out is the geography. Trieste lies around two bays – the Bay of Trieste to the north and the Bay of Muggia to the south, with a promontory separating the two. The sunset there is one of the best I have ever seen.

Most of the things to do are found in the centre, which is on the promontory. It's quite steep and many of the older residents (there are lots of elderly people in Trieste) therefore rely on the buses to get around. You can also walk or cycle (although this can be difficult on the steep hill). If you travel there in winter you might experience the 'Bora' – the cold wind that reaches up to 150km/h. If you're lucky enough to have it at your back, try walking around the city – it's a great experience – but be careful not to fly away!

Trieste is very close to the Slovenian border, and it was one of the most prosperous ports of the Austro-Hungarian empire. Walking around Trieste is like travelling back in time to the days of Habsburg Vienna – with coffee shops and traditional taverns that haven't changed at all since that time. I adore the Citta Vecchia (Old City), situated behind Piazza Unita. During the day it's got some great shopping and if you go there at night it's just magical. The colours and the smells make it feel like a completely different city. Walk through to San Gusto, where you can look down at the city from a totally different perspective – it's like a little model or a game that you can change with a flick of your wrist.

PLACES TO STAY

URBAN HOTEL DESIGN This isn't the cheapest place to stay but it's a great hotel for those who appreciate classic design. Androna Chiusa 4, www.urbanhotel.it

L'ALBERO NASCOSTO Situated in an ancient building, this hotel has studio apartments and a handful of really nice rooms. It has a very warm and cosy atmosphere. Via Felice Venezian 18, www.alberonascosto.it

B&B AL PONTEROSSO AND B&B I MORETTI These are two basic but nice little B&Bs for those on a budget. Piazza Ponterosso 3, www.alponterosso.it, and Piazza Venezia 1, respectively

PLACES TO EAT

L'ISTRIANO The best fish restaurant in Trieste, but it doesn't come cheap. Call ahead to book, as it fills up fast. Riva Grumula 6

OSTERIA DA MARINO I love this place. It's the first place I take visitors to. Good wine, nice service, delicious food, fair prices. What more could you ask for? 5 Via Del Ponte, www.osteriadamarino.com

BUFFET SIORA ROSA An authentic, cheap buffet with 1970s décor. This is the best place in Trieste to eat typical food. Get there early – they close at 9pm. Piazza Hortis 3

PEPI SCIAVO An old-style buffet serving traditional Triestin cuisine. Via Cassa di Risparmio 3

PIZZERIA NAPA If you like pizza, this is the place to go. Seriously. It's the best. Original 1970s furniture makes it taste even better. Via Caccia 3

BARS

OSMIZZA This place is totally punk. Don't be scared of the people you find there, as they tell you of their adventures at sea. They're only the drunk pirates of the new millennium. Via Torretta 1

CAFFÈ SAN MARCO Go there with a newspaper or a book (you don't need to read it). Order a coffee, relax, and breathe in the atmosphere that hasn't changed for centuries. Via Cesare Battisti 18

LA BOMBONIERA I come here almost every morning for my favourite brioches. It is the last Liberty confectioners in the city, and it hasn't changed since 1850, still serving typical Austro-Hungarian cakes. Via XXX Ottobre 3

NAIMA A nice place to chill out for a couple of hours with a cup of tea. Check out the photography exhibitions and enjoy the jazz playing in the background. At nights you can sometimes find local DJs playing. Via Rossetti 6

TETRIS This is my favourite place to listen to new bands. It's a nice, friendly place for impromptu concerts, with the added bonus of a cheap bar. Via Della Rotonda 3, www.myspace.com/gruppotetris

ETNOBLOG This is a hub of alternative culture. I come here for the Balkanic concerts, but check out the website – there are always interesting music events going on. Via Madonna del Mare 3, www.etnoblog.org

KNULP An exhibition space, internet point, bookshop and bar. You can easily while away the hours here. Check out their tasty multi-ethnic food too. Via Madonna del Mare 7

LA BOTTEGA DEL NONNO You can lose yourself in this ancient bookshop, selling precious old and first edition Italian books. Take a tissue with you, because there's also a vast amount of dust. Via Felice Veneziano 20

RIGATTERIA You'll find this antiques shop in the old Jewish area. All around there are other second-hand book and furniture shops. Via Malcanton 12

STILE MISTO Nice design shop with an interesting selection of books. Via San Michele 9

AMSTICI SHOWROOM This is the creative laboratory of two girls, Alessandra and Tullia. Working with discarded furniture, clothes and any other lost or forgotten objects they can get their hands on, they tinker and tweak, giving things a new lease of life by turning them into new and unique design objects. Via Della Cereria 5, www.amstici-showroom.it

NO SOLO LIBRI A really good comics bookshop. Piazza Barbacan 1A

SPAZIO 11B This is the most beautiful clothes shop in Trieste, it has fantastic design pieces. Via Santa Caterina 11B

PODRECCA If you are a vintage enthusiast, try this homeware shop. It's another typical Triestin place – nothing has changed there for decades. Via Mazzini 42A

ANTIQUES MARKET Every third Sunday of the month there's a flea market in the Jewish area behind Piazza Unità, where you'll find most of the antiques shops even when the market isn't on.

SHOPPING

GALLERIES AND CULTURE

GALLERIA TORBANDENA A contemporary art gallery showing Italian and international artists. It's in a beautiful location and the vernissages are lots of fun. Via di Torbandena 1B, www.torbandena.com

TEATRO MIELA A theatre/exhibition space dedicated to Miela Reina, a famous Triestin artist. It hosts various cultural events and often has really interesting concerts. Piazza Duca Degli Abruzzi 3, www.miela.it

STAZIONE ROGERS I really, really like this space, which is in an oil station that has been converted by architect Richard Rogers. It hosts art, architecture, music, video and design events, and is well worth a look. Riva Grumula 12, www.stazionerogers.eu

EVENTS

ELECTROBLOG SEPTEMBER This is an electronic music and digital arts festival run by Etnoblog (see Bars). Much of it is free entry. www.electroblog.net

TRIESTE FILM FESTIVAL JANUARY A nice little festival that features a lot of cinema from Central and Eastern European countries. www.triestefilmfestival.it

BARCOLANA REGATTA OCTOBER Barcolana is an annual sailing race in the Gulf of Trieste. www.barcolana.it

SCIENCE+FICTION NOVEMBER A multimedia event specialising in fantasy, horror and science fiction. www.scienceplusfiction.org

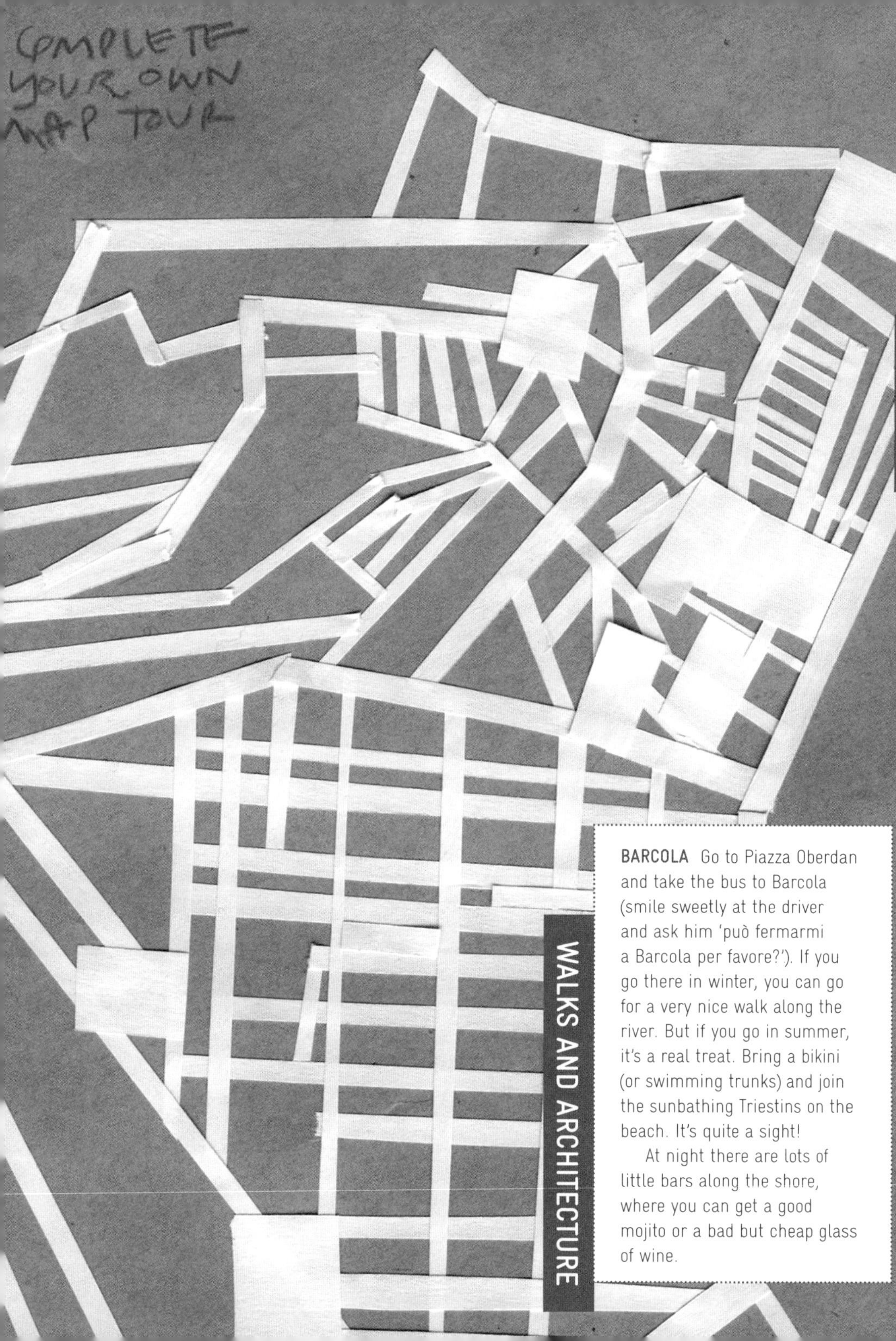

COMPLETE
YOUR OWN
MAP TOUR

WALKS AND ARCHITECTURE

BARCOLA Go to Piazza Oberdan
and take the bus to Barcola
(smile sweetly at the driver
and ask him 'può fermarmi
a Barcola per favore?'). If you
go there in winter, you can go
for a very nice walk along the
river. But if you go in summer,
it's a real treat. Bring a bikini
(or swimming trunks) and join
the sunbathing Triestins on the
beach. It's quite a sight!

At night there are lots of
little bars along the shore,
where you can get a good
mojito or a bad but cheap glass
of wine.

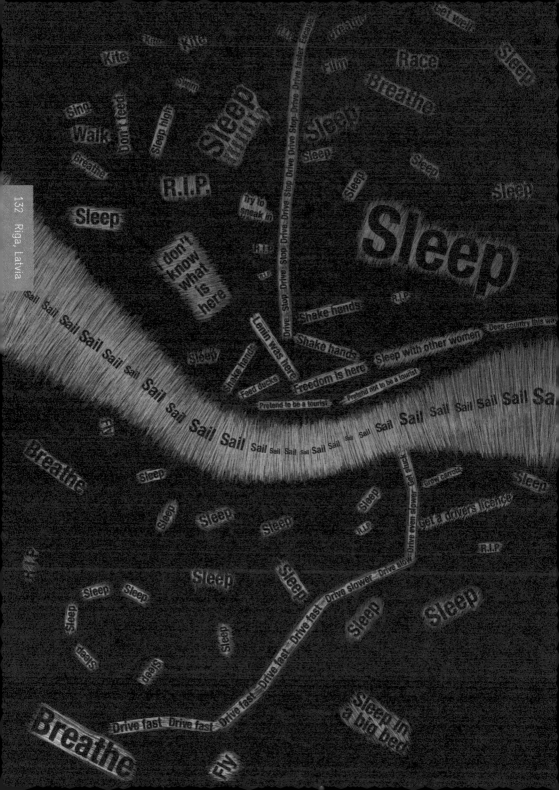

Arvids Baranovs' RIGA

Riga is the largest city in the Baltic states. It is situated on the Baltic Coast, and is split in two by the river Daugava. If you include its suburbs, it counts for around 720,000 people – almost half of the entire population of Latvia. Only around 40 per cent of the city's residents are native Latvians. The rest are Russian with a few other nationalities thrown in. Riga consists of six administrative regions, but locals like to divide it into the left and right banks of the river, and then into several micro regions. The left bank is green and leafy and is known as Pārdaugava, which means 'across the river Daugava'. This is where I spent my teenage years, in a district called Agenskalns – full of little winding streets and old houses. It's only a short walk to the Old Town, but the countryside is also easily accessible, and it's still my favourite district in Riga.

The centre lies on the right bank, with the Old Town in the heart of it, nestled against a canal. To the south stands the central market, which you'll recognise by the vast German zeppelin hangars. Next to the market, a chain of old warehouses is being transformed into an art and culture centre, and right behind it is the area known as the 'Moscow Suburb', which used to be a Jewish ghetto during the Second World War, and still maintains its pre-war aura. The north of the city is where you'll find a lot of the Art Nouveau architecture that Riga is famous for, as well as the neighbourhoods of Andrejsala and Eksportosta, known jointly as 'Riga Port City' – another up-and-coming culture and business area in the docklands.

Riga is not a designer's Mecca by any stretch of the imagination, but I find it very inspiring nonetheless. It exhibits a convergence of pre-war elegance, Soviet ghosts and youthful modernism, and it has a rawness to it that is very graphic in a certain special way. I like to hop on my bike and pedal through all the districts with my camera, capturing the rhythm of the Soviet blocks, the concrete and the greenery, the dereliction and the development. It's all those things that are not necessarily pretty that make it interesting. Escape the main tourist routes and use the tram, trolley or bus to explore the city beneath.

HOTEL BERGS One of Riga's top boutique hotels located in a posh pedestrianised area in the centre of town. It's in an Art Nouveau building and has been done up with 38 individually designed suites and a slightly African vibe. Elizabetes Street 83/85, 1050 Riga, www.hotelbergs.lv

EUROPA CITY HOTEL Although it's set a bit away from the city centre, this three-star 1960s-style hotel has a nice roof terrace where on Thursdays, Fridays and Saturdays live jazz events take place. Brivibas Street 199C, 1039 Riga, www.groupeuropa.com

VILMĀJA This basic but nice three-star hotel is in the quiet neigbourhood of Pārdaugava. Nearby are two islands – Lucavsala and Zaķusala. The first one houses the popular mini-gardens owned by the people living in the big grey Soviet blocks known as the 'sleeping districts'. The second one has a rocket-like TV tower on it. Both are worth visiting. Ilmājas Street 12, 1004 Riga, www.vilmaja.lv

RIGA OLD TOWN HOSTEL Get yourself a good night's sleep on the cheap. A good starting point for your trips on foot through the city, with a decent pub attached. Vaļņu Street 43, Riga 1050, www.rigaoldtownhostel.lv

BUFETE (CANTEEN) A Soviet-style workman's canteen in the basement of a river barge that has been converted into offices and event spaces. Although the boat has been done up, they have preserved the original fittings of the navigators' canteen, and if the weather's nice you can sit on the deck and admire the Daugava. Peldošā Darbnīca 659, 1045 Riga, www.peldosadarbnica.lv

ĶIPLOKU KROGS (GARLIC PUB) Latvians eat a lot of garlic – it's hot and it smells, but it does keep you healthy. Every single dish in this cosy and atmospheric place has garlic in it. Including the desserts. Jekaba Street 3/5, 1050 Riga, www.kiplokukrogs.lv

VINCENTS Home to one of Latvia's renowned chefs, Martins Ritins, this is an upmarket joint where all the great and the good go to eat delicious 'slow cooked' food. Elizabetes Street 19, 1010 Riga, www.restorans.lv

RĀMA This is one of my favourites. A vegetarian restaurant inside the Hare Krishna Centre. Delicious. Barona Street 56, 1011 Riga, www.krishna.lv

HOSPITĀLIS This unique design restaurant was developed with the help of the Museum of Medical History and various hospitals in Riga. It is sterile, sleek, modern and white, with Soviet medical apparatus lining the walls, and screens showing medicine-related episodes from movies. If you want the full experience you can become a 'patient' and eat in an operating theatre using surgical instruments. Stabu Street 14, 1011 Riga, www.hospitalis.lv

BARS

GOIJA TEA ROOM One of my favourite places. I love sipping their masterfully prepared herbal tea, listening to down-tempo music, playing boardgames or just resting on the colourful pillows or in the winter garden. Strelnieku Street 1A, 1010 Riga, www.tea-room.lv

LENINGRAD A crazy cafe in the Old Town where art students and masters, musicians and actors hang out to drink and listen to live music. Kalēju 54, 1050 Riga, www.leningrad.lv

GAUJA This small bar is basically set inside a typical 1970s Soviet living room. It's the real thing – no imitation – with original furniture, records and magazines. Terbatas Street 56, 1001 Riga, www.gauja.je

META-KAFE A minimalist cafe in a former tennis clubhouse, where folks from nearby advertising agencies go for lunch. In the evenings it turns into a groovy bar playing funk, soul, house and hip-hop. I often come here to meet friends or to chat to the owner, who is a fellow designer. Kronvalda Bulvāris 2B, 1010 Riga, www.metakafe.lv

ANDALŪZIJAS SUNS A pub by the side of Bergs Bazaar (see Shopping), where an ever-changing exhibition of posters by Latvian and foreign graphic designers and artists is on display. Elizabetes Street 83/85, 1050 Riga, www.andaluzijassuns.lv

SHOPPING

ZNAK WALLPAPERS A shop stocking imaginative artisan wallpapers designed by the best and brightest young Latvian artists. Kalnciema Street 33, 1046 Riga, www.znak-life.com

CENTRAL MARKET Experience the original scent and flavour of Latvian food, seasonings and little things you'd never find in a supermarket. Leave the fish pavilion for last. Careful of pickpockets! Nēģu Street 7, 1050 Riga, www.centraltirgus.lv

MARKET LATGALĪTE The not-so-traditional flea market where you can find all kinds of Soviet memorabilia. If you're searching for something specific, just ask someone — they'll get it for you. Corner of Gogola and Dzirnavu Streets, 1050 Riga

BERGS BAZAAR A 19th Century pedestrianised complex of boutique-y shops and restaurants. A craft and farmers' market takes place every second and fourth Saturday of the month, featuring food from Latvia's top chefs. Bergs Bazaar, 1050 Riga, www.bergabazars.lv

UPE A music retail and publishing house that specialises in Latvian folk and world music, as well as authentic musical instruments, gifts and toys. Vaļņu 26, 1050 Riga, www.upe.lv

LERELINI The last original linen factory, which sells textiles that are famous for their lifelong durability and reasonable prices. Brivibas Street 196, 1012 Riga, www.larelini.lv

ISTABA A trendy gallery where each month, the proprietor invites artists to create items on a particular theme. There's a shop where you can buy jewellery, design objects and books, and on the first floor there's a cafe where the chef makes food according to how much you want to pay and what kind of food you want. Barona Street 31A, 1011 Riga

ARSENĀLS An exhibition hall that operates out of an early 19th Century customs warehouse and features work by modern Latvian artists. Every year, Latvian Art Academy graduates take part in a workshop and form an exhibiton on a particular theme. K Valdemara Street 10A, 1010 Riga, www.vmm.lv/en/arsenals

MUSEUM OF DECORATIVE ARTS AND DESIGN This place specialises in Latvian decorative and applied arts dating back to the late 19th Century. Of special interest is the collection of industrial design objects by Latvian designers. Skārņu Street 10/20, 1050 Riga, www.dlmm.lv

RIGA ART SPACE A contemporary art space with regularly changing exhibitions. Kungu Street 3 (below Town Hall Square), 1050 Riga, www.artspace.riga.lv

RIXC A centre for new media that encourages collaboration between the media and the arts. There's a busy events calendar, and a media lab where artists and designers can share ideas. 11 Novembra Krastmala 35-201, 1050 Riga, www.rixc.lv

NOASS An exhibition space and cultural centre set on a barge across the river from the Old Town with an alternative vibe. Especially of interest for video and performance artists. AB Dambis 2, 1048 Riga, www.noass.lv

MOSCOW SUBURBS This is an atmospheric part of town, where the Jewish ghetto used to lie. Tumble down wooden houses and cobbled streets, along with several deserted parks and gardens that were built on top of cemeteries give it a slightly spooky vibe. There are very few tourists here, and the area can be a bit dangerous. www.maskfor.lv

COMMUNITIES Riga houses a number of 'sleeping districts' – neighbourhoods made up of Soviet apartment blocks that are lined up in a special way so that they would dampen a nuclear blast. It's always a challenge to navigate the strange layouts. Take a bus and notice how far these suburbs are from the city centre.

ART NOUVEAU DISTRICT Riga is renowned for its Art Nouveau buildings, so this is very touristy. Look out for the buildings that haven't been restored, and check out their beautiful detailing. www.artnouveau.lv

RIGA'S BREAKWATERS In the harbour of Riga, where the Daugava meets Riga's Gulf, there are two long breakwaters (or moles) – one on the left bank – Mangalsala Mols – and Bolderajas Mols on the right bank (slightly easier to reach by bus). On both trips you can walk on a white sand beach. Go there at sunset and watch the ships. It's an unusual urban experience!

E.A.T. RIGA This is an alternative tour provider that takes visitors around the hidden gems of the city on foot and by bike. They'll take you to all the above places and more, avoiding all the tourist traps, and are worth signing up with for an informative and fun guided tour. www.eatriga.lv

UŽUPISP

OLD TOWN HEART ♡

SEREIKIŠKIŲ PARK

'SMC

GEDIMINO AV. →

When I think about my hometown of Vilnius the images that spring to mind are of red roofs, narrow cobbled streets, green spaces, dark bread, singing, and above all, a cosy, friendly atmosphere. It's a small European capital and it doesn't take long to get to know it and feel part of it.

I won't bore you with all the cheesy tales about the iron wolf's prophesy, or why Vilnius is built on two rivers. Suffice it to say, it's very old, a bit pagan and quite beautiful. The river Neris runs through the middle of it. On one bank you'll find the quaint Old Town, packed with Baroque architecture, and a sprinkling of architectural souvenirs from its more recent Soviet past. This is where a lot of the action happens, and it's particularly bustling in summer. On the other side of the river is the new business district with its giant Europa Tower and shiny modern skyscrapers. To the east of the Old Town over the smaller river Vilnele, lies Uzupis, the bohemian quarter. It declared independence from Lithuania in 1998 and now has its own president and pacifist constitution, which declares that all animals, birds and humans are equal, as well as that 'man is free to be idle'. As you might imagine, it's pretty chilled out. Have a beer at a local cafe, and check out the native artists.

There are lots of green spaces around the city (actually almost 70 per cent of the city is green space). Some of the parks still have old Soviet-style rollercoasters in working condition, and the green bridge that crosses the Neris has huge sculptures of Soviet revolutionaries on both sides of it. Other slightly bizarre sculptures dotted round the city include one of the children's doctor, Schabad, and a bust of Frank Zappa.

The time to come is really the summer. I wish we had better weather, but in winter temperatures range from -5°C to 8°C, so it's pretty bitter. In the summer it's in the mid-20s, and the city really becomes colourful and alive with outdoor restaurants and events, and a buzzing nightlife. To get around the city, you're best off on foot – especially if you're staying centrally. You can use public transport, such as trolleys and buses, but taxis are also very cheap. If you rent a car, make sure not to drive it in the city around five or six o'clock – it gets very congested! Also, although you can rent bikes, I'm afraid Vilnius is not a very cycle-friendly city, with very few cycle paths.

PLACES TO EAT

PLACES TO STAY

BLUSYNE This tiny restaurant/wine bar is named after the owner's dog, Bluse (which means flea), who can be spotted roaming freely around the place. It serves great wine and fresh original cuisine in a cosy intimate atmosphere. Savičiaus Street 5, www.blusyne.lt

ZOE'S BAR AND GRILL This is the steakhouse of choice for locals, famed for its tasty grills, Scandinavian interiors and smiley staff. Odminių 3, www.zoesbargrill.com

OLD MARKET This is my top recommendation – a friendly, mid-range B&B with six rooms stylishly done up with market themes (flower, fish, animal, chocolate, flowers and flea market). It's centrally located in an early 20th Century building in the Old Town, and their breakfast is all organic, sourced from the local market. Pylimo Street 57, www.oldmarket.lt

SKONIS IR KVAPAS Its name translates as 'taste and smell' and it serves great tea and coffee, as well as a nice light selection of food. It's a romantic, cosy space, and it often gets packed. The interior is done in Latino colonial style, and salsa music is often played in the background. It's a good place for a date or a girly catch-up. Traku Street 8

LITINTERP GUESTHOUSE VILNIUS This is not a bad choice either. It has less character, but it's very reasonably priced and perfectly comfortable, with a good breakfast. It's also friendly and centrally located. Bernardinų Street 7-2, www.litinterp.com

NERINGA This is a legendary restaurant from Soviet days, when it was used as a hangout for artists and members of the intelligentsia. It's a classic atmosphere with live piano music, and that old-school elegance of 1970s-80s Vilnius. If you go you must try the Kiev cutlets. An all-time favourite. Gedimino Avenue 23, www.restoranasneringa.lt

HOTEL TILTO Finally, if your wallet will stretch a bit further, try this hotel for some quality relaxation. It's near the cathedral and the main shopping street, Gedimino, but in a peaceful location. The rooms are very nicely designed – bright and clean with exposed brick, and they have a jacuzzi and sauna. Tilto Street 8, www.hoteltilto.com

ITALISKA KEPYKLELE A real Italian bakery selling freshly baked pastries and delicious bread. Domininkonu 16

WOO This bar/cafe/club is one of the best all-rounders. It serves tasty oriental food during the day, and at night it's a funky bar where you can drink, chat, dance and listen to DJs strut their stuff. They also often have small art exhibitions on show. Vilniaus Street 22, www.woo.lt

IN VINO If you love wine, this is the place for you. The people are friendly, and it's a very down-to-earth place (unlike a lot of wine bars). In summer it becomes a very nice lounge-style place with live music in the courtyard. It does get crowded! Ausros Vartu 7, www.invino.lt

HAVANA SOCIAL CLUB A restaurant, bar and club in one with lots of live music and DJs, plus a nice lounge and terrace. It's done up in a 1940s Havana style that manages not to be too kitsch and contrived. Šermukšniu Street 4A, www.havanasocialclub.lt

GRAVITY If you want to get down, this is the city's hottest dance club. It's stylishly done up with lots of leather and funky lighting, features top local DJs and attracts a young, trendy crowd. It's a bit pricey though. Jasinskio Street 16, www.clubgravity.lt

ALUMNATO The Alumnato courtyard is part of Vilnius University, which was founded in 1579, and is of architectural interest in itself. In summer, the Italian cafe there hosts open air DJ sets – very groovy. Alumnato Courtyard

CAFE DE PARIS A small bar near the French Cultural Centre that hosts DJ sets most nights, and live acts on Saturday nights. It has a funky interior and a laid back atmosphere. Oddly enough if you come here on a Sunday morning in summer there's a little food market selling organic cheeses and veggies. Didžioji 1, www.cafedeparis.lt

CAC KAVINE A legendary cafe housed in the CAC (Contemporary Art Centre), where artistic folk meet for coffee or a beer. DJs occasionally play here, and there's a very cool courtyard in the summer. Vokieciu 2, www.cac.lt

HUMANITAS The art, design and photography bookshop. If you're here for a longer period, they'll order in any specific request you might have. Dominikonų 5, www.humanitas.lt

AUKSO AVIS Lithuania has a long history of textile manufacture and design, and this shop is one of many that specialise in local craftsmanship. They sell jewellery and accessories made by Lithuanian textile artists, and have a gallery downstairs. Savičiaus 10

GEDMINO 9 Fashionistas should check out the top floor of the new Gedmino 9 shopping centre, where the National Gallery of Fashion and Design displays the work of the top Lithuanian designers. Gedmino Street 9, www.gedmino9.lt

AKADEMIJOS GALERIJA You can admire and buy the work of students from the National Academy of Arts – paintings, graphics, ceramics and jewellery are all on offer. Pilies 44/2

SHOPPING

DAIKTU VIESBUTIS (CAC SHOP) This is a must. The shop for the Contemporary Art Centre stocks all sorts of design objects as well as a big range of one-offs by Lithuanian designers. Ševčenkos Street 16A, www.cacshop.lt

VELTINIO NAMAI This shop is a good example of how traditional handicrafts can evolve into a desirable modern commodity. It specialises in wool and felt – selling both materials and crafted creations. It also runs courses and workshops, and the staff will helpfully advise you on any felting techniques you may be interested in. Žemaitijos Street 11, www.veltinio-namai.lt

FLEA MARKET There is a flea market on Saturdays from early morning until noon where you can buy second-hand furniture, old-school Soviet objects, books, coins, ceramics, badges, and pretty much anything else you can think of. Tauras Hill

TYMO MARKET For tasty, organic local produce, check out this market which is held every Thursday in Uzupis. Uzupio

CAC The Contemporary Art Centre is the first place to go. It's a huge space (2,400m²) – the biggest in the Baltics, and certainly the most important art venue in Vilnius. It features serious exhibitions of Fluxus, conceptual art, installations and other contemporary art. They also have impressive archives you can access and they host lecture series and informal artist talks – as well as featuring the great cafe and shop that I already mentioned. Vokieciu 2, www.cac.lt

TULIPS&ROSES A fresh space for international artists to exhibit in. The owners take a conceptual approach to curation, and the shows tend to be quirky and refreshing. Gaono 10, www.tulipsandroses.lt

UZUPIO GALERA Known locally as UMI, this is a quirky place with an interesting history and a welcoming atmosphere, right on the river Vilnele. Artists from Uzupis are usually exhibited here, and in the summer, the exhibition space spills outside. Uzupio 2, www.umi.lt

VARTAI GALLERY This gallery was founded in 1991, and focuses on contemporary Lithuanian and international art. It balances between modern classics and new mixed-media pieces, with an emphasis on Neo-romanticism, Surrealism and naïve art. Vilniaus 39, www.galerijavartai.lt

KAIREDESINE Graphic art is something that is very integral to Lithuanian mentality. This small graphic art gallery is part of a centre for graphic arts, which incorporates a printing house. It sets out to promote experimental graphic art, and to provide the circumstances in which artists can produce it. Definitely worth a visit. 1st floor, Latako Street 3, www.graphic.lt

MENO AVILYS MEDIATEKA Meno Avilys is a media education centre that promotes cinema and visual medias in schools and to the public. As part of their programme they have opened a mediateka – a club/library where you can read about or watch films for free. They have quite a big archive of Jonas Mekas films – a successful Lithuanian auteur, now living and working in New York. Vilniaus 39, www.menoavilys.org

KULTFLUX This is a small gallery/cultural space that juts out into the river Neris. It focuses on urban, design and visual arts, and invites people to re-examine the role of the river in the city. It hosts alternative art exhibitions, music sessions, design workshops and even a crafty flea market in the summer. The Neris embankment near the Mindaugas Bridge and the Energy Museum, www.kultflux.lt

ST CATHERINE'S CHURCH This church is one of the finest examples of 17th Century Baroque architecture in the city. In the high season it's open for various concerts and events – world music, classical, jazz or contemporary choreography. Vilniaus 30

UZUPIS WALK Start at the bank of the river Vilnele, and walk along it, across the park. Cross the bridge, and you'll see Uzupis Street. Since the 17th Century, this has been the district of craftsmen – especially weavers, and to this day it is the area for artists and craftspeople. One square up, you'll find the statue of the Angel, who symbolises the artistic freedom of the semi-independent district. This statue replaced one of an egg, which stood here until 2001. While walking through the suburb, look into the courtyards to get a real sense of the place. You'll notice that some of the buildings have been carefully restored while others remain virtually derelict. For the goth inside you, check out the Bernadino cemetery while you're there – the oldest one in the city. If it's a sunny day, go to Barbacan Place and sit on the grass with all the young people, and admire a stunning view of the old city.

EVENTS

KINAS PO ATVIRU DANGUMI JUNE An annual open-air film festival organised by Meno Avylis. A big screen is set up in the courtyard of Vasaros Teras (the House of Teachers), and you can watch Eastern European films from places like Georgia or the Ukraine free of charge. People come to drink and chat and it's got a creative, relaxing atmosphere.

VASAROS KIEMELIS JULY Another open-air film festival that screens a free movie every Wednesday, attracting peole of all ages. Bring drinks and a picnic and enjoy the movie.

KULTFLUX SUMMER This cultural platform that I mentioned before holds various events and parties in the high season, including some great music gigs. It's always free of charge. www.kultflux.lt

Marco Godinho's LUXEMBOURG

Luxembourg City, the capital of the Grand Duchy of Luxembourg, is a picturesque town. It is placed at the point where the rivers Alzette and Pétrusse meet, and the city centre is built on the cliffs around the rivers' gorges, with bridges and viaducts connecting its various parts.

It is small in population (only 90,000) but rich in culture and history – and also generally rich. The city is one of the banking capitals of Europe, as well as an administrative centre for the EU. This has attracted residents from over 162 nations, making up around half its population. Although it is known as a fiscal paradise, you should be a little bit careful, as not everyone in the city is as wealthy as one would think. However, on the whole its multicultural identity makes it a friendly place to visit, and it's easy to feel at home here.

The city is divided into 24 quarters that correspond to the major neighbourhoods. The most interesting ones are as follows: The Grund area – which is the old downtown, has small, labyrinthine streets and a bustling nightlife. Clausen and Pfaffenthal is where you'll find local bars and restaurants. La Gare is the most popular and multicultural, and Bonnevoie is the biggest neighbourhood, right next to the train station, with a mixed population. Kirchberg is the new part of the city, built on the plateau to the north-east of the city centre, and home to the various EU institutions. Le Centre is very clean and well arranged, and if you want a taste of the wealth that Luxembourg is famous for, visit Belair – the most expensive area, which is also home to the national stadium, Stade Josy Barthel – named after Luxembourg's one and only Olympic gold winner (Helsinki 1952).

Luxembourg is historically known as the 'Gibraltar of the North' for its many fortifications, walls and gates, and these fortifications, as well as many beautiful old buildings, have been carefully preserved and restored through the years. More recent architecture includes the Kueb, built by Pierre Bohler in the 1970s (now a European conference centre), and the remarkable Philharmonie, by Christian de Portzamparc, constructed using 823 steel columns.

It's an easy city to get around. Almost everything is within walking distance, but there are also buses, and a new bicycle rental scheme called 'Vel'oh!'. However you choose to do it, go and explore this dense and varied town – which can be provincial but boasts ever more cosmopolitan aspects.

LUXEMBOURG CITY HOSTEL

This hostel is in a prime location in the valley of Alzette, only 500m away from the bars, restaurants and cafes of Grund and Clausen, and features fantastic views. It's been recently done up, and has private rooms as well as dorms. 2 Rue du Fort Olisy, www.youthostels.lu

SOFITEL LUXEMBOURG LE GRAND DUCAL

This five-star hotel is done in colourful futurist décor with all the high-tech commodities. The top floor houses a new restaurant run by Michelin starred chef Antoine Westermann. If your pocket won't stretch to a meal, have a drink at the bar and admire the view. 40 Boulevard d'Avranches, www.sofitel.com

PLACES TO STAY

HOTEL LES JARDINS DU PRÉSIDENT (CLAUSEN)

A charming, intimate hotel in the heart of the Old City. It has seven rooms designed by Georges Blanc and Bernard l'Oiseau, in an ornate, romantic style. The area is buzzing with cafes and bars – especially at weekends. 2 Place Sainte Cunégonde, www.president.lu

PARC BEAUX-ARTS HOTEL

A small, friendly hotel, also very centrally located. Clean and comfortable, with nice minimal design. By all accounts they serve a fantastic breakfast. 1 Rue Sigefroi, www.parcbeauxarts.lu

COME PRIMA Another Italian that I think is really charming. It's done up nicely, with exposed stone walls, mosaics and an open kitchen. It has one of the best seafood lasagnas I've ever tasted and very good house wines. 32 Rue de l'Eau

CHIGGERI RESTO-CAFE This restaurant is in an old converted mansion, and is spread over three floors connected by a beautiful original spiral staircase. Downstairs, there's a contemporary cafe/bar serving 30 types of beer, and upstairs there's a nice restaurant with a great view of the Alzette Valley, serving Mediterranean dishes. When the weather's good you can sit outside on the lovely terrace. 15 Rue du Nord, www.chiggeri.lu

CIRCOLO CURIEL (ALSO CALLED KOMMUNISTEN) A nice Italian family restaurant in a venue that was once used as a meeting house for Italian communists. Friendly staff serve great pasta in a warm, rustic ambiance. The homemade tiramisu is a must. 107 Route d'Esch

LAGURA (LIMPERSBERG) A sleek restaurant serving both world cuisine and Italian food. My favourite is the pork in caramelised ginger. Nothing beats this followed by their great cheese selection, accompanied by a Muscat from Beaumes de Venise. 18 Avenue de Faiencerie, www.lagura.lu

PLACES TO EAT

INTERVIEW Situated in the centre, next to the post office, this New York-style bar has been pulling in the punters since the 1980s. It has a warm, relaxed vibe that appeals to everyone from bankers, to artists and students. They serve an excellent cappuccino during the day, and a nice cold beer at night. Upstairs there's a vegetarian restaurant. 21 Rue Aldringen

D:QLIQ This is one of the most interesting places in Luxembourg. Downstairs there's a lively bar that often features DJs and live acts, and upstairs there's a more peaceful space overlooking the Grund, where you can sit and chat. It's a very friendly atmosphere, and it attracts open-minded people of all ages and nationalities. 17 Rue du St Esprit, www.dqliq.com

BARS

URBAN I like coming here during the week to drink an aperitif with friends before dinner. It's centrally located with funky, minimalist décor, and offers a great atmosphere day and night. It's multi-lingual and multi-cultural – attracting a lot of English speakers. 2 Rue de la Boucherie, www.urban.lu

MUDAM BOUTIQUE This is the shop of the new contemporary art museum and its contents have been carefully curated by Maurizio Galante and Tal Lancman. Unique jewellery, innovative tools, beautiful books and chic trinkets – it's a poetic inventory, chosen with care and love. 3 Park Dräi Eechelen, www.mudam.lu

SHOPPING

FRUIT AND VEGETABLE MARKET Every Wednesday and Saturday mornings until 1pm, the Place Guillaume II (Centre) is transformed into a marketplace offering spices, fresh fruits, vegetables, cheese, plants and flowers. Fantastic, flavoursome produce. Place Guillaume II

MARX This bar is a popular place with good service and decently priced drinks. It gets crowded, but in the summer there's an outdoor space you can escape to. It attracts the EU/professional crowd – it's very international. 42-44 Rue de Hollerich, www.marx-bar.lu

KULTURFABRIK This is a cultural centre that provides a space and a platform for alternative and emerging talent in film, music, theatre and performance art. You can sometimes catch local acts such as Raftside, Sug(r)cane, Metro, Francesco or Tristano Schlimé (check them out on Myspace). It is connected to another four similar venues across Europe. 116 Rue de Luxembourg, www.kulturfabrik.lu

CAFE DES TRAMWAYS A small neighbourhood bar that stays open late and serves excellent coffee. Friendly, with a chilled out atmosphere. 79 Avenue Pasteur

DEN ATELIER A live music club in a former Renault truck garage in the lively suburb of Hollerich, commonly called 'Downtown'. It's an intimate, friendly space that attracts some impressive international acts. 54 Rue de Hollerich (200m from the railway station), www.atelier.lu

FELLNER ART BOOKS Located directly next to the Grand Ducal Palace, this bookshop has a great range of new and rare art and design books. The owner is very friendly and can help you source whatever you're after. True happiness! 4 Rue de l'Eau, www.fellnerbooks.com

FLEA MARKET Every second and fourth Saturday of the month, there's a flea market in Place des Armes. It's lively and relatively classy. Place des Armes

KIOSK The Kiosk is a former newsstand that has been transformed into a micro-space, in which young artists are invited by Aica (the international association of art critics) to create a site-specific project in the centre of the city. Place de Bruxelles, www.aica-luxembourg.lu

CASINO LUXEMBOURG Casino Luxembourg was the first contemporary art centre in the city, opened in 1995 in an old 19th Century casino. It has great exhibitions, archives and workshops, and it is an important educational centre for the arts. 41 Rue Notre Dame, www.casino-luxembourg.lu

MUDAM LUXEMBOURG Opened in 2006, Mudam (Musée d'Art Moderne Grand-Duc Jean), was designed by architect Ieoh Ming Pei, who grafted the building onto the original 19th Century fortress walls of the historical Fort Thüngen in Kirchberg. Since its opening, Mudam's collection has become better and better, linking the international scene with local emerging artists. Every Wednesday from 6 until 8pm there is a free concert at the cafe. It's an excellent place to escape everyday life or just to have one's mind opened to new inspirations. 3 Park Dräi Eechelen, www.mudam.lu

GALLERIES AND CULTURE

CINE UTOPIA A friendly, intimate cinema that specialises in indie films. 16 Avenue de Faïencerie, www.utopolis.lu

CINEMATHEQUE This is where all the local cinema buffs can be found. It has great programming, screening up to 16 different films a week ranging from classics, to indies, to short film programmes. It has one of the largest film archives in Europe, and you can admire the collection of original movie posters all around the foyer. 10 Rue Eugène Ruppert

GRAND THÉATRE DE LUXEMBOURG A great theatre that features work by established and emerging directors from around the world. It's an exceptional place for such a small country. The building was designed by architect Alain Bourbonnais in the 1960s. 1 Rond-Point Schuman, www.theatres.lu

PHILARMONIE This remarkable building by Christian de Portzamparc was opened in 2005, and is a huge oval structure with a colonnade screen of steel columns. It is illuminated according to which kind of concert is on that day – from jazz to classical orchestras and soloists. 1 Place de l'Europe, www.philharmonie.lu

WALKS AND ARCHITECTURE

CLAUSEN, GRUND AND PFAFFENTHAL Take a long walk through the valley of the Alzette, and the small streets of Clausen, Grund and Pfaffenthal, where you can enjoy the beautiful views, and taste one of the local beers (Simon, Battin, Bofferding, Mousel, Henri Funck or Okult) or a national wine of the Moselle Valley (Auxerrois, Pinot Noir, Elbling, Riesling, Rivaner or the Gewürztraminer). The Pétrusse Valley is an oasis of peace and calm, and features a permanent sculpture installation by Daniel Buren, entitled *From One Circle to Another: landscape borrowed.*

CHEMIN DE LA CORNICHE The Chemin de la Corniche is known as 'Europe's most beautiful balcony'. Walk along the pedestrian promenade until you reach the Plateau de St Esprit. Have a look at the casements – a warren of ten miles of tunnels cut through the rock – and then take the Vauban and the Wenzel circular walk over the plateaus to arrive at the Plateau du Rham. The Pont Grand-Duchesse Charlotte – the red bridge between Glacis and Kirchberg – looks very surreal from here.

KIRCHBERG The Kirchberg is also a good place to walk, especially around the gardens behind Mudam. At the Boulevard J K Kennedy, you'll find the Richard Serra sculpture *Exchange*, and further along the *Grand Fleur Qui Marche*, by Fernand Léger. You can go swimming at the largest sports venue in the city, D'Coque, or you can try Badanstalt on Rue de Bains, a smaller pool and sauna in the heart of the city. While you're there, have a cocktail at the luxurious old-style bar in the Grand Hotel Cravat, which looks over the Gëlle Fra War Memorial and the Notre-Dame Cathedral.

GARE Cross the city to walk along the Grand Rue, through Boulevard Royal and across the Pont Adolphe in the direction of the main train station. You'll reach the popular area of Gare. Check out the Villa Clivio, a lovely Art Nouveau building from 1908.

EVENTS

ART WORKSHOP AU CASINO LUXEMBOURG JULY The Art Workshop at the Casino Luxembourg is an annual event that lasts two weeks. It provides an opportunity for young artists from around the world to take part in seminars and lectures and work together on specific themes, culminating in a group show. www.artworkshop.lu

SCHUEBERFOUER AUGUST – SEPTEMBER A crazy fairground with mad rides and a ferris wheel that offers great views of the city. Try the fritür – the fair's fried fish speciality. www.funfair.lu

L'ÉIMAISCHEN APRIL A local tradition on Easter Monday is to buy a bird whistle (called 'pëckvillchen') at Marché-aux-Poissons in the Ville Haute quarter. They come in all shapes and sizes, and are mostly made of pottery or glass.

CHRISTMAS MARKET DECEMBER The Place d'Armes hosts a Christmas market with a nice atmosphere. Try the gromperekichelcher (potato fritter), the Drëpp (local schnapps), the stollen and the bouneschlupp (a national dish of soup with French beans).

marsamxett harbour
marsamxett harbour
marsamxett harbour
marsamxett harbour
marsamxett harbour
marsamxett harbour
marsamxett harbour
marsamxett harbour
marsamxett harbour
marsamxett harbour
marsamxett harbour
mxett harbour

marsamxett harbour
marsamxett harbour
samxett harbour
rsamxett harbour

marsamxett harbour
marsamxett harbour

marsamxett harbour
rsamxett harbour

marsamxett harbour
marsamxett harbour

samxett harbour
mxsett harbour

grand harbour
grand harbour
grand harbour
grand harbour
grand harbour
grand harb
grand harbour

grand ha
grand harbour

grand harbour

grand harbour
grand harbour

grand har

grand harbour
grand harbour

grand harb
grand harbour

grand harbour

Pierre Portelli's VALLETTA

Valletta takes its name from its founder, the Grandmaster of the Order of St John, Jean Parisot de la Valette, who sought to establish the connection of the Knights of the Order to the island. However, we locals all refer to Valletta as 'Il Belt' – the city. It's a fortress town flanked by two natural harbours – Marsamxett and the Grand Harbour – and is essentially a port town. It was one of the first cities to be laid out in grid-form in the 16th Century, and many of the buildings built under the Hospitallers from this period still survive.

It's a city that shouts Baroque at the top of its voice. Lord Byron called it 'a city of bells, steps and smells', and Benjamin Disraeli described it as 'a city of palaces built by gentlemen for gentlemen'. It really is a piece of living history – beautifully ornate palaces, knights' auberges and churches can be found everywhere you turn, and the fortified city walls overlook the Mediterranean Sea. It's the smallest European capital (with a population of under 7,000) – and the Valletta peninsula is only a couple of kilometres in length, so it's easy to walk about – although as it's built on a ridge, with narrow streets and stairs leading up and down the steep hills, it can be quite tiring. As you walk around you'll see lots of saints tucked into niches in the walls – St Dominic, St Paul, St Augustian, Our lady of the Carmelite and many others. These generally denote the different sectors of the city and their respective patron saints.

Valletta becomes subdued in the evenings. In the 1960s, jazz bars filled the city, particularly on Strait Street, catering to the sailors coming in from the port. However, for the last 30 years, Strait Street has been pretty dead. This is now changing, and thanks to a younger generation injecting fresh life into all aspects of city life, it's slowly waking up, with new wine bars and restaurants popping up left, right and centre. Young architects and designers are taking up the challenge of injecting contemporary elements into the city, whilst at the same time respecting the legacy of the past. The waterfront is a good example of this – a series of warehouses dating back to the Knights of St John have been restored and transformed into bars, restaurants, bookshops and more, but their fundamental nature has been left intact. There seems to be a fresh breeze blowing round the city... roaming the streets of Valletta I can feel it.

PLACES TO STAY

VALLETTA G-HOUSE A magnificent self-catering apartment in a 16th Century townhouse that has been restored with meticulous attention to detail. This is luxury accommodation in the heart of the city – good for a romantic break. 10 Mikiel Anton Vassalli Street, www.vallettahouse.com

MANOEL THEATRE APARTMENTS These contemporary apartments are great as long as you don't mind the sound of church bells (although if you have a problem with church bells, Malta might not be the city for you anyway...). They're very reasonably priced, plus they're part of the National Theatre complex and actually share the backstage entrance. 87 Old Mint Street, www.teatrumanoel.com

THE BRITISH HOTEL If interior design is no object, try this two-star hotel, which is one of the oldest in Valletta. It's like travelling back in time to the 1970s, and I have to say, the views from their terrace of the Grand Harbour are fantastic. 40 Battery Street, www.britishhotel.com

222 This is a pretty cool new concept space. It offers a three-in-one experience – dining, music and culture. It's not cheap, but the décor is worth experiencing and yes yes, the food is good too. It gets quite packed at the weekends, so best to make a reservation. 222 Great Siege Road, www.two-twentytwo.com

MALATA A restaurant that has survived the test of time... It has been around forever, and still has its original signage outside. It's now a cosy restaurant with a varied menu run by a French chef. A bit pricey, but worth it. St Georges Palace Square, www.malatamalta.com

COCKNEY'S If you find yourself walking down towards Marsamxett Harbour, a stop at Cockney's for lunch or dinner should not be missed. Once a simple fishermen's bar, it's now a restaurant specialising in fresh fish and pasta dishes. You can eat al fresco, enjoy the view across the harbour and then maybe get the ferry over to the neighbouring town of Sliema across the harbour. Marsamxett Wharf

CAFE JUBILEE This is my favourite place in town. It's a cafe/bistro with excellent food and a good wine list. Keep your fingers crossed that there's a table available – it gets particularly packed after theatre performances, attracting a mixed crowd of young and old. Sometimes they play music too loudly, but they don't seem to mind if you ask them to turn it down. 6 Library Street, www.cafejubilee.com

PLACES TO EAT

GAMBRINUS BAR This is more of a haunt for the locals, but hey, why not blend in. It's a small corner tea and coffee bar with original 1970s kitsch décor and excellent 'pastizzi' – a local puff pastry snack filled with either peas or cottage cheese.
9 Triq Zakkarija

SAN PAOLO NAUFRAGO BAR Many bars in Valletta carry the name of the area's patron saint. This one translates as St Paul's Shipwreck Bar, and – surprise surprise – is in the St Pauls part of the city. I have many fond memories of teenage years misspent here. Like Gambrius, this is a locals' bar, and if you go in for a coffee or a drink, you'll be made very welcome. 10A Santa Lucia Street

BRIDGE BAR If you visit during the hot summer months, then the Bridge Bar is the place to go on a Friday night. You can lounge on cushions on the outside steps, sipping a glass of wine and watching the jazz performances that take place on the adjacent steel bridge. Victoria Gate

OLLIE'S LAST PUB This pub has been recently renamed in honour of Oliver Reed, who passed away here while filming *Gladiator*. It may sound morbid, but they do serve a good pint. Many British tourists come looking for this pub.
136 Archbishop Street

TRABUXU WINE BAR Pronounced 'tra-bu-shoo', this is one of the first wine bars in Valletta to revive Strait Street. It's in a stepped part of the street, so no cars can drive through, meaning that the crowd that gathers after the theatre or an exhibition opening often spills out onto the street. 1 Strait Street

CHIAROSCURO CELLARS Essentially a wine bar, this venue also hosts alternative art events, jazz nights and film screenings. The seating is a bit limited, so you may have to stand. 44 Strait Street

The shopping in Malta has changed a lot since I was young. As in many European cities today, the big names and chains are putting the smaller, local shops out of business. There are still a few standing worth visiting:

VEE GEE BEE This art shop/gallery right next to the city gate was once an ironmongers, and today has a great stock of art materials. It recently opened a small gallery space upstairs. 309 Republic Street, www.vgb.com.mt

GILDERS SHOP This artisan's studio mainly makes ecclesiastical pieces, as well as 'Tal-Lira' – the traditional Maltese clock with a painted face and gold-leaf casing. Thsuma House, 302 St Paul Street.

NO 68 There aren't that many galleries in Valletta, and there's no National Museum of Contemporary Art, so this old four-storey house, which has been restored to its original condition, is a much-needed breath of fresh air. It provides a space for new artists in all media to exhibit their work. I curated a show here recently called *Square*, in which all the works were square. 68 Lucy Street, www.68lucystreet.com

ST JAMES CAVALIER CENTRE FOR CREATIVITY
Cavaliers, raised gun platforms that could neutralise ground attacks, were an integral part of the walled fortifications of Valletta. This cavalier is one of the oldest buildings in Malta. Today it has been transformed into a centre for creativity with various exhibition and performance spaces, a cinema, a music room, and a cafe/restaurant that, according to my daughter, serves a heavenly cheesecake. Pjazza Kastilja, www.sjcav.org

THE LOGGIA AT THE NATIONAL MUSEUM OF FINE ARTS
A quaint sort of space in the central courtyard of the beautiful Baroque building that houses the National Arts Collection. It is open for exhibition proposals by both foreign and local contemporary artists, and while you're there, why not have a look at the Mattia Preti collection upstairs. What do you mean 'who is Mattia Preti?'!!!! South Street, www.maltaart.com

GALEA'S ART STUDIO SHOP This shop has been around for as long as I can remember. I got my first inks here and I can vividly remember Chev Galea sitting in a corner, working on his watercolour maritime painting. Today his son has taken over, and stocks a wide range of watercolour paper, paints and the rest. 70 South Street, www.galeartmalta.com

VALLETTA CARNIVAL FEBRUARY
For three days in February, the city becomes alive with brightly coloured floats, fancy dress and some wild nightlife in the Paceville club area.

SUMMER ARTS FESTIVAL JULY Malta's summer arts festival is a collection of exhibitions and performances that take place at venues across Valletta. www.maltaartsfestival.com

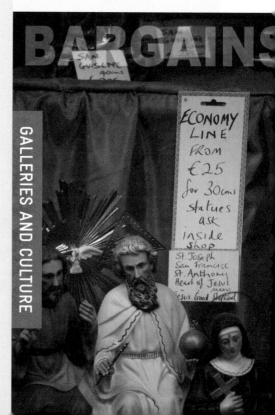

BASTION WALK A walk around the bastions of the city is a must – although if you're here in the summer, make sure to wear a hat, as the sun really can beat down. Follow the ramparts and the fortified walls. The ring road overlooking both harbours offers an inspiring view, especially on the Grand Harbour side. This area is called St Barbara's Bastions, and is one of the most desirable neighbourhoods in Valletta – oh how I envy those who live there! If you can't face walking in the heat you can also take a horse-drawn cab. It's a touristy option, but can be quite pleasant – you'll get a watered-down history of the city from the cabbie, plus you can get into 'Mediterranean mode' by haggling for the ride.

FORT ST ELMO This remarkable star-shaped building is strategically situated at the tip of Valletta, guarding the entrances to the two harbours. Every February, the area around Fort St Elmo comes alive with the Valletta Carnival, which celebrates the coming of summer. The fort itself used to house various workshops in which carnival floats were built. These were recently closed down, but might yet re-open. Nearby, in a disused church, is the workshop of one of Malta's carnival veterans, Pawlu Curmi, known as il-Pampalun, who creates amazing floats – also worth a visit. You'll notice that all around the St Elmo area there are a number of large stone caps. These are lids to granary silos, used by the knights for wheat storage, and today as resting areas for the weary visitor.

THREE CITIES On the other side of the Grand Harbour from Valletta are the historic fortified towns of Vittoriosa, Cospicua and Senglea, referred to as the three cities. They are older than Valletta and were home to the first Knights. You can get there by a ten-minute boat crossing, on a traditional Maltese dghajsa. It's good to see these boats in operation – there was a time when it seemed that they were slowly vanishing, and although today it's more of a tourist option than a means of transport for locals, it's still great that they're in use. Pay a visit to Valletta Market and make your way home by boat. A nice half-day activity.

WALKS AND ARCHITECTURE

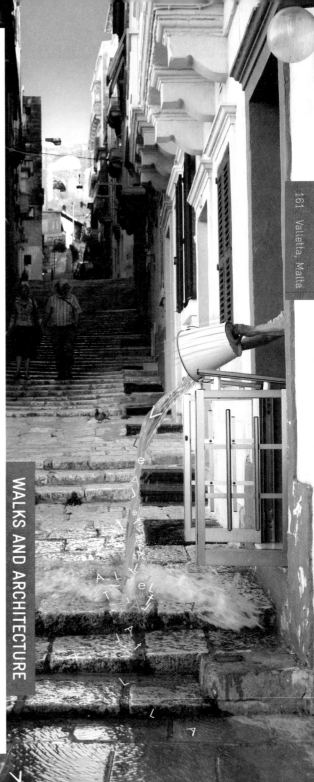

EDWIN VOLLEBERGH'S
DEN BOSCH
'S-HERTOGENBOSCH
BOIS LE DUC

The cumbersome name s'Hertogenbosch is a contraction of 'des Hertogen bosch' – literally 'the Duke's forest', but let's face it – it's kind of a mouthful, so us Dutch folk just call it 'Den Bosch' (and the French folk call it Bois le Duc). It's located 80km south of Amsterdam and is the capital of the province of North Brabant. In medieval times it was a very important city (the second biggest after Utrecht), and was a hub of industry and culture (most famously the birthplace and home of the great Hieronymus Bosch). It's a fortified town, and escaped the Second World War relatively unscathed, so most of its walls are intact, with its main ramparts still being used to keep out the water. Many other historical elements are also still standing, and there seems to be constant renovation of the numerous old buildings, fortifications, churches etc.

It's a relatively small city, with a population of around 150,000, and today is known mostly for its historical centre and for the shopping. Outside of this though, it also has a lively cultural scene and is a provincial centre for industry, education and administration. It also borders on a nature reserve that stretches all the way to Vught and a canal network called the Binnendieze, as well as containing many green spaces inside the city.

I always say to visitors 'It's not Amsterdam. But it is also true that Amsterdam is not Den Bosch.' What I mean is that it's not exactly a metropolis, but it has a lot to offer that a big city can't. The people are friendly and straightforward, and there's a great laid-back vibe that you can enjoy from the beautiful terraces of the countless restaurants and bars. Our studio (and apartment) is based in a romantically historical area behind the train station, with an amazing bakery next door. The kind of area that would be completely unaffordable elsewhere. Also, there's plenty of stuff to stimulate the mind – theatres such as the Konigstheater, Theatre Artemis and the cultural complex, Verkadefabriek, keep a vibrant dramatic arts scene alive, and a selection of small but interesting galleries keep people like me on my toes.

You can get around the centre very easily by foot, and there is plenty of transport out to the suburbs (although, really there's no reason to go there). A lot of the centre is pedestrianised, so if you come here by car you'll have to leave it at a car park somewhere near the periphery. It's a pretty safe town with a vibrant nightlife, so don't worry about getting home at night.

There are a handful of places to stay in the city, but nothing spectacularly interesting. We could do with a fresh new hotel – it could do good business. Any takers?

HOTEL CENTRAL This is a well known hotel right in the centre near the marketplace. It has 124 rooms, a beautiful Gothic vaulted cellar and a fairly mediocre terrace. Burgemeester Loeffplein 98, www.hotel-central.nl

JO VAN DEN BOSCH This place is a little bit old-fashioned, but nice and friendly and well located – a ten minute walk from the railway station. Boschdijkstraat 39A, www.jovandenbosch.nl

HOTEL TERMINUS Above a pub next to the central station, this is a good budget option. The rooms are simple and clean, with shared toilet and shower facilities. Most of them are on the second floor, so you don't get too much noise from the pub downstairs. Boschveldweg 15

CUBA CASA There are a few interesting B&Bs in the centre of town. This one is cosy and romantic with a view of the canal. Buitenhaven 4, www.hoteliers.nl/den-bosch

BRETON In the streets around Korte Putstraat, you'll find yourself practically stumbling over restaurants. One of my favourites is Breton, run by one of the best chefs in town, Mark Boumans. It's northern French cuisine, and they only serve starters (or rather, small plates), so you can order a couple. Delicious. Korte Putstraat 26, www.restaurantbreton.nl

D.I.T. Our studio designed this place, so we're a little bit biased, but it's a really nice cafe/restaurant, with good food and a pleasant atmosphere. Jacques, who runs it, keeps the menu changing all the time, with Turkish pizza, various salads and king prawns as staples. It's not a very child-friendly place though, so keep the kids at home. Snellestraat 23, www.eetbar-dit.nl

PUNTNL Situated next to the museum shop of SM (Stedelijk Museum), PuntNL is a hip cafeteria that's good at any time of the day. It serves Dutch cuisine at reasonable prices. My tip is the anchovy bread with Frisian Nagel cheese or the barbequed asparagus with veal bacon. Magistratenlaan 100, www.restaurantpuntnl.nl

DE BIJENKORF This restaurant is in a big warehouse, right on the market square. We come here after a night at the theatre. Markt 95, www.debijenkorf.nl

WILLY'S BONTE PALET There's nothing to say about this place except it's the smallest and cosiest bar in town. Great for an intimate drink. Hinthamerstraat 99

W2 POPCENTRE The W2 is a fantastic foundation promoting live pop music. They showcase a brilliant selection of alternative and emerging artists, both homegrown and international. It's based in the former Willem II cigar factory and has a great bar. Boschdijkstraat 100, www.w2.nl

CAFE HET VEULEN A traditional cafe/bar with an excellent selection of beers and a good cheese plate. Plus you get free peanuts – what more could you ask for? Korenbrugstraat 9A

PLEIN 79 This is a classic club/bar located in the cellar of a medieval building in the very centre. It's not amazingly trendy, but it's even cooler for that. They host great live gigs, and it's a favourite amongst locals. Markt 79, www.plein79.nl

Den Bosch is, and has always been, first and foremost a market town, and every day there is a market in the central square. The best day to go is Friday, when the produce is freshest, and you can get lots of nice organic meat and veggies. Apart from that, its history as a regional shopping destination has been preserved, and there are plenty of opportunities to spend money. Make sure to check out the area around Verwersstraat – where the best of the antiques and fashion shops can be found.

SUIT SUPPLY The friendly guys here will measure you up for a new custom-made suit, and the sewing machines in the shop are proof they mean business. Look sharp! Verwersstraat 7

COBRA This is a high-end shop stocking collections from names like Dries van Noten, Ann Demeulenmeester, Marc Jacobs etc. for both men and women. Naturally a fat wallet is a pre-requisite. Klein Lombardje 2 (behind the Gold Harnas), www.cobramode.nl

SHOPPING

OXO WOONWINKEL An interiors shop to really make you happy. They sell wallpaper, cushions, crockery and interior accessories by designers like Piet Hein Eek amongst others. They also make curtains and cushions to order. It draws customers in from all over the Netherlands. Highly recommended for the confident style mixer. Vughterstraat 72, www.oxowoonwinkel.nl

BLUE This shop sells used and new designer clothes by labels such as King Louie, Logo-shirt and Super-Seven. It also has it's own label called BlueByBettonvil, which uses a combination of new and recycled elements. Postelstraat 14

59 DESIGN Do you know your Braakman from your Castiglioni brothers? This shop has a spectacular array of vintage and contemporary furniture design – perhaps you're after an Aeron Chair by Bill Stumpf and Don Chadwick or a classic Pastoe dining set. 59 Design is one of those shops you just can't pass without popping in. Molenstraat 27B, www.59design.nl

DE KLEINE WINST This shop is actually the house where the famous Hieronymus Bosch grew up (although it's been burned down and rebuilt a few times since then). Bosch's surname was actually Van Aeken, but because this was his home town, he signed his work with 'Bosch'. In any case, today it's a souvenir shop selling rubbish made in China and surprisingly nice Delft tiles, which we bought when we were renovating our fireplaces. Markt 29

HIERONIMUS·BOSCH
PAINTER 2 1450 - 1516 ('s-HERTOGENBOSCH

ARTI CAPPELLI For the old masters, you'll naturally gravitate towards the Noordbrabants Museum, but I prefer to visit one of the galleries around Verwersstraat. Arti Cappelli is a particularly good one, presenting contemporary painting, sculpture and photography. Verwersstraat 20

MAJKE HÜSSTEGE A few doors down from Arti Cappelli is this much larger space, also exhibiting a diverse collection of contemporary artists from around the world, curated by Majke Hüsstege herself. Verwersstraat 28, www.majkehusstege.nl

ARTIS Another huge space is this converted 19th Century cigarette factory in the area around the station. It's an artist-run gallery founded in 1985, that serves as an exhibition space and an art laboratory that opens up space for discussion and inclusivity in the arts. Boschveldweg 471, www.artisdenbosch.nl

VERKADEFABRIEK This old factory has been brilliantly transformed into a cultural complex with an art-house cinema and a couple of theatre spaces showing everything from performance art to contemporary dance. It also has a nice restaurant serving light French food and an excellent bar. The interior renovations have been delicately carried out by Piet Hein Eek, with the original tiles left intact, and big banks of wooden tables. It's a friendly, funky place to spend the evening. Boschdijkstraat 45, www.verkadefabriek.nl

STEDELIJK MUSEUM (SM) A museum of contemporary art and design with an impressive collection, particularly in ceramic art and jewellery, and a varied programme of exhibitions. It is 'temporarily housed' in a factory renovated by French designer Matali Crasset. Let's hope they stay there because it's a fantastic space. Magistratenlaan 100, www.sm-s.nl

WHISPERING BOAT TOUR Den Bosch is at the Delta of three rivers; the Aa, the Dommel and the Dieze (that's why it's triangular, because in essence it's wedged between the Aa and the Dommel). The canal system of the Dieze river runs all the way through the city. Due to lack of space, over the course of history, some inhabitants built their homes over the canal. You can walk along the bits that are exposed, but a more interesting way of seeing the Binnendieze (inner Dieze) is by boat. Book a traditional open boat (called a whispering boat) in advance with a boat skipper. They will take you the whole length of the canal – with parts of your journey completely underground – and you will see the hidden corners of the Old Town, with a (hopefully) informative commentary. This trip is popular not just amongst tourists, but locals too. The tunnels have been restored to perfection (thank you European subsidies!), and it's almost inconceivable now that in the 1970s this was basically a festering open sewer that was going to be paved over. Boat booking: Molenstraat 15a

SINT JAN'S CATHEDRAL This cathedral, built in the 13th Century, is one of the most breathtaking cathedrals in the country. It's vast – 115m long and 73m high, and built in a Gothic style distinctive to this region of The Netherlands. Study the exterior, decorated with beautiful arches and statues – well, study the part you can see – it seems like this cathedral is being endlessly renovated – as soon as they finish one side, they start the next. So far the restoration budget is over €32 million. Inside are some murals possibly attributable to Hieronymus Bosch (although this isn't official). Torenstraat 16

PALEISKWARTIER Outside the old city walls, on the west side of the station, is a rapidly developing 'downtown area'. It's still under development, with about half the plans already built, and some very interesting architecture taking shape. Amongst other constructions, the 'Armada' consists of ten high-rise buildings designed by UK architect Anthony McGuirk with spherical facades that will be reminiscent of the sails of a fleet of ships. Also noteworthy is the Palace of Justice that gave the area its name. This was designed by Belgian architect Charles van den Hove, with internal contributions by artists such as Marlene Dumas, Rob Birza, Jan Dibbets and Luc Tuymans.

WALKS AND ARCHITECTURE

BOULEVARD THEATRE FESTIVAL AUGUST
This is the city's main summer event.
Lots of productions by theatre companies
big and small are put on in venues all
over town and in the surrounding fields
and villages. After the Boulevard Festival
finishes, the City Fair starts – small but
charming! www.festivalboulevard.nl

DESIGN ACADEMY SHOW JUNE Housed
in the old Remington factory, Maasland
architects have created a fantastic space
for the Design Academy. It's always worth
visiting the final show, where ceramics,
paintings and sculpture are sold for next
to nothing. Academy of Art and Design
Sint Joost, Onderwijsboulevard 256

AFS'H ART AND ANTIQUES FAIR APRIL
The oldest art and antiques fair of The
Netherlands has been going for over 40
years, and has expanded into a very big
event with 90-odd exhibitors from The
Netherlands, Belgium and Germany,
attracting many thousands of visitors.
www.afsh.nl

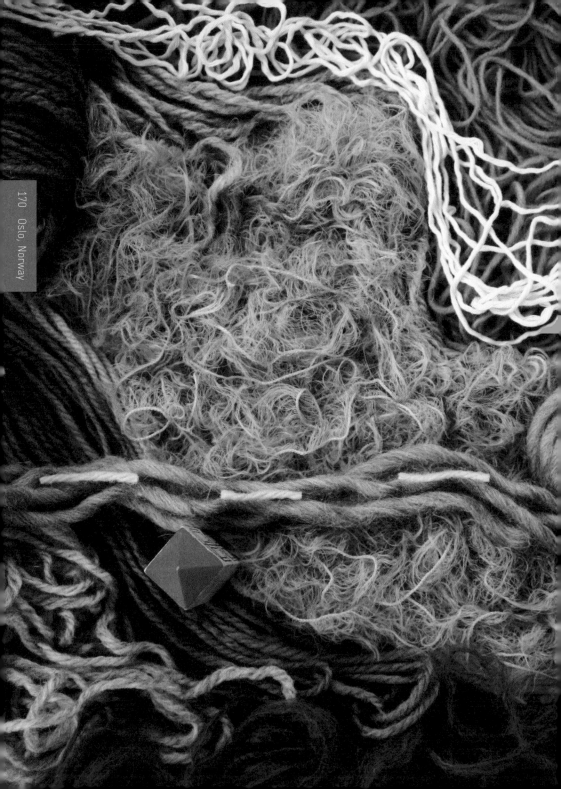

ANNA FRAGAUSDAL'S  Oslo

Although Oslo is geographically one of the largest capitals in the world, covering an area of 453km², it only has a population of 550,000. That averages out at just under 1km² per person, so as you might guess, this is a city that holds nature close to its heart. Its inhabitants love the great outdoors no matter what the weather, and are very proud of what Oslo has to offer. In winter you can hop on a tram and go straight to the ski slopes, and in summer you can jump on a ferry with the same standard ticket and go to one of the small islands off its coast for a picnic or a swim.

Despite its size, the city centre is fairly small and walkable (although the public transport system is also very efficient). The Akerselva River, which starts at Lake Maridalsvannet, divides the city into two – east and west. The neighbourhoods of Sagene, Grünerløkka and Grønland, in the inner east part of the city, are the up-and-coming, arty areas. They have exploded over the past 20 years, with cafes, bars, clubs and designer shops popping up everywhere. Design, advertising and film production companies have all set up shop along the east part of the river over the past decade, and big educational art and design institutions have followed suit. The inner west side of the city (the neighbourhoods of St Hans Haugen and Frogner) is far less happening. It's more posh and traditional, although it also has some very nice expensive designer boutiques and up-market restaurants and cafes.

Although the city has existed for over 1,000 years, its architecture is fairly modern, with most people living in apartment blocks built over the past 150 years. There is, however an 11th Century church that managed to survive the great fire of 1624, and this church and the surrounding area (known as Medieval Park) is the centre for the annual indie music festival, Øyafestivalen. Just across the road from the church is the new opera house, designed by Norwegian architects Snøhetta, and completed in 2008. It is a remarkable structure that seems to rise from the sea, with a white marble exterior and a wooden interior. It has really boosted the city's architectural self-esteem, and is a landmark building well worth seeing. If you look up at the hills from the opera house, you can see the newly renovated Ekeberg Restaurant, built in 1927. This is one of the finest examples of the Functionalist period of Norwegian architecture.

PLACES TO STAY

LOVISENBERG GUESTHOUSE

Most accommodation in Oslo is located downtown, which is not really where it's at. This newly refurbished guesthouse gives you a nice alternative, situated within walking distance of the eastern parts of town. There are plenty of cafes, shops and parks around. It's very reasonably priced and the rooms are really nice with old renovated furniture and lamps. The owners are Christians, and there's a chapel if you're so inclined. Don't worry if not, there are no early curfews or anything like that, although it probably isn't the place to have a huge party. Lovisenberggaten 15A, 0456 Oslo, www.gjestehuset. lovisenberg.no

MS INNVIK

The ship MS Innvik is a perfect budget option, brilliantly located just next to the new opera house – probably the most sought-after view in Oslo. There is a theatre on board, as well as an arty B&B. Although the rooms are a bit cramped, this is pretty good value for your money. And I would definitely recommend having a cold beer on the deck on a hot summer's day. Sweet! Langakaia, Bjørvika, 0150 Oslo, www.msinnvik.no

GRAND HOTEL

The Grand Hotel used to be an artists' hangout at the turn of last century. It's located on the main street, Karl Johan, a few blocks away from the Royal Castle. Most of the hotel is pretty posh in an old-fashioned way, but one floor, the 'ladies floor', has been modernised by Norwegian interior designers, using female Norwegian celebrities as the inspiration. I like the concept, but I would just as happily recommend the old part of the hotel. Karl Johans Gata 31, 0159 Oslo, www.grand.no

STUDENTERHYTTA

I really love the fact that Oslo can offer a few places far off the beaten track. Studenterhytta is in the middle of nowhere – but a really beautiful nowhere. In the summer you can go for a swim at the nearby lake, and maybe meet a moose on the way back, and in winter you can do some cross-country skiing. It's very cheap, and the staff are friendly, offering really great food ranging from warm elderberry juice to a three-course gourmet dinner. To get there you'll have to catch bus 41 to Sørkedalen Skole or Maridalen and walk 5km. Kjellerberget, Sørkedalen, 0758 Oslo, www. studenterhytta.no

GRIMS GRENKA

This is Oslo's first boutique hotel, designed by Norwegian design agency Uniform. It manages a to pull off a great combination of Scandinavian design and Eastern sensuality. Kongens Gata 5, 0153 Oslo, www.grimsgrenka.no

MADU A pricey but cool Asian fusion restaurant hidden away inside the Grims Grenka Hotel. You enter it by walking through the hotel lobby, and suddenly the wall just opens up and you enter a space with walls of glass and waterfalls separating the tables. Kongens Gate 5, 0153 Oslo, www.grimsgrenka.no

GREFSENKOLLEN At the top of Grefsenåsen mountain, this restaurant offers my favourite view of Oslo – you can see just about everything. The food is damn nice too – ranging from a traditional Norwegian waffle to a full-on gourmet meal. It's inside the majestic cog joint building, which was built by the Ringnes brewery in 1927, and has been a popular destination for decades. It has been recently renovated, and in the summer it offers outdoor seating so you can make the most of the view. Book ahead. Grefsenkollveien 100, 0490 Oslo, www.grefsenkollen.no

OLYMPEN (LOMPA) This used to be a kitsch local bar showcasing weird Eastern European bands, but was renovated in 2008, and is now a trendy bar/cafe/restaurant that serves traditional Norwegian food. It's a real piece of Oslo history with a huge painting by Hans Henrik Sartz Backer, illustrating scenes from the city. Check out the burlesque bar on the first floor. Grønlandsleiret 15, 0190 Oslo, www.olympen.no

KAMPEN BISTRO This is a cosy restaurant that only locals know about. It's nestled among the small wooden houses in Kampen, and it's got a great atmosphere – in winter it's intimate and warm, and in summer the roof garden is a great escape from the daily grind. Their menu changes every day, or you can just hang out and have a beer. You might even get lucky and catch a surprise gig. Bøgata 21, 0655 Oslo, www.kampenbistro.no

PALACE GRILL Ok, I've never really been here, but I sure want to go. It's expensive, but I've never heard a single complaint about this place. Palace Grill is extremely intimate, with just a few tables and an ever-changing ten-course menu. The waiter tends to get personal and don't be surprised it you end up having some late drinks with the staff. Unfortunately it is not possible to book a table, so get there early – and I mean really early. If you've got time, pop by the next-door bar Skaugum, especially excellent in summer. Solligata 2, 0254 Oslo, www.palacegrill.no

OSLO MEKANISKE VERKSTED This massive old welding shop has been successfully transformed into a theatre and a bar with a nice chilled-out vibe. It has kept a rustic feel with really high ceilings, raw brick walls and second-hand furniture. It's cosy in winter with a huge fireplace and relaxed in summer with a big outdoor area. A hidden treasure well worth a visit! Tøyenbekken 34, 0188 Oslo, www.oslomekaniskeverksted.no

BAR BOCA You can't be shy at Bar Boca. It's a tiny, intimate cocktail bar, done in funky 50s rockabilly style, with the coolest bartenders in Oslo. I love coming here – it feels like you're at a private party with a nice host serving you the best drinks ever. It gets very crowded, so if there's no room, you might get luckier a few metres down the street at another cool rockabilly place called Aku Aku. If you're travelling with your sweetheart make sure to order their volcano cocktail. Thorvald Meyers Gata 30, 0555 Oslo

BAR ROBINET You'll probably never bump into a tourist at this bar. It's as intimate as Bar Roca and also serves amazing cocktails. It is lit in red and has art by Norwegian cult artist Pushwagner. It tends to get cramped, but it's cosy. Cash only. Mariboes Gata 7A, 0183 Oslo

BLÅ My favourite thing about Blå is the interior – it's an old factory gone clubbing, and it's pretty rough. Blå was originally a jazz club, but has opened up to different music genres the last few years. This is a perfect spot to go dancing at the weekends, with great DJs and a nice crowd. The outdoor area just by the river is one of the best places for a beer in the summer. Brenneriveien 9C, 0182 Oslo, www.blaaoslo.no

TEDDYS SOFTBAR This bar actually has a preservation order from the government! It was established in 1958, and was the first of its kind, serving milkshakes, hotdogs, and other non-Norwegian food. Today it only sells beer and burgers, and comes with a hardcore rockabilly crowd, jukebox and booths. Brugata 3B, 0186 Oslo

BARS

175 Oslo, Norway

NORWAY SAYS This internationally renowned Norwegian design agency specialises in furniture, interiors and installation. They have a small shop inside their offices. Thorvald Meyers Gata 15, 0555 Oslo, www.norwaysays.com

PUR NORSK This is a small shop specialising in Norwegian design. It's pretty pricey, but they have really nice things – especially homeware. You can also check out their webshop. Theresesgata 14, 0452 Oslo, www.purnorsk.no

TORPEDO BOOKSHOP This is a small independent designer bookshop and publishing company. It also hosts exhibitions and events. Pop by for an intimate visit. Hausmannsgata 42, 0182 Oslo, www.torpedobok.no

HUNTING LODGE This is a shop and gallery space in one. They sell streetwear, art, books and toys. They have great exhibitions, taking advantage of the whole space. Shopping and installation in one – pretty neat. Torggata 36, 0183 Oslo, www.huntinglodge.no

FREUDIAN KICKS A cool shop in downtown Oslo offering small Norwegian designer brands as well as the big names like Acne. They put on fashion and art events and host exhibitions. A must if you're into fashion. Prinsensgata 10B, 0152 Oslo, www.freudiankicks.no

NORWAY DESIGNS PAPIRGALLERIET I love coming here. All the different paper never ceases to inspire me. I always end up spending too much money – be warned! Stortingsgaten 28, 0161 Oslo, www.norwaydesigns.no

THE MARKET AT BLÅ A designer/craft market, held at the Blå club every Sunday. It's fairly small, and I'm not crazy about all the stands, but there is some cool stuff. Brenneriveien 9C, 0182 Oslo

HUSFLIDEN Come here to experience Norwegian craftsmanship. The products are traditional, high-quality and expensive. It's worth a visit just to look at the folk costumes. Rosenkrantz' Gata 19-21, 0159 Oslo, www.dennorskehusfliden.no

KEM Large art supply shop – but be aware that Norway is not a cheap place for art supplies! Brenneriveien 9B, 0182 Oslo, www.kem.no

STANDARD A small gallery promoting Norwegian artists to an international audience. One of my personal favourites, Kim Hiorthøy, is one of their artists. Hegdehaugsveien 3, 0352 Oslo, www.standardoslo.no

TEGNERFORBUNDET (THE DRAWING ASSOCIATION) I really like this gallery, because it feels pretty down to earth and sometimes you can catch a real hidden treasure of an exhibition. Rådhusgaten 17, 0158 Oslo, www.tegnerforbundet.no

EMANUEL VIGELANDS MUSEUM This is actually a mausoleum housing the remains of the brother of sculptor Gustav Vigeland. It's dimly lit, but as your eyes adjust you'll see that every inch of the 800m² space is covered with fresco paintings depicting the various stages in a man's life – many of them quite erotic. Grimelundsveien 8, 0775 Oslo, www.emanuelvigeland. museum.no

KUNSTVERKET A small, private contemporary art gallery, which hosts a broad variety of exhibitions, happenings and installations. Well worth a visit. Tromsøgata 5B, 0565 Oslo, www.kunstverket.no

DOGA DogA (The Norwegian Centre for Design and Architecture) was established in 2004 as a meeting point for design and architecture. I love this exhibition space, which is often used for industry events, like fashion shows and Pecha Kucha nights. Check out the small but nice shop. Hausmannsgata 16, 0182 Oslo, www.doga.no

THE DESIGNER CHRISTMAS MARKET DECEMBER Every year this completely packed market is held at DogA. If you're in town, make sure to stop by; there are some really nice things to be found here. Hausmannsgata 16, 0182 Oslo, www.doga.no

DESIGNERS SATURDAY SEPTEMBER Designers Saturday is a showcase for interior design that happens every other year. The latest and greatest national and international design products are exhibited at 30 showrooms around town. www.designerssaturday.no

AKERSELVA LIGHT FESTIVAL SEPTEMBER One night around the autumnal equinox, you can experience the walk down by the river Akerselva after dark. The whole distance is lit and there are lots of activities and events along the way. It is extremely popular and gets really packed. Starts at Maridalsvannet.

ØYAFESTIVALEN AUGUST Annual indie music festival, which has a really strong design profile throughout. Cool bands, nice crowd, no camping and organic food. At the Old Church Ruins in Gamlebyen, www.oyafestivalen.no

MUSIKKFEST OSLO JUNE For one day in early June, Oslo is transformed into a massive festival featuring everything from world music to house to rockabilly. It lasts 12 hours and is spread across 30 stages around the city. www.musikkfest.no

THE RIVER WALK The Akerselva River divides the city into the eastern and western parts, and it's well worth taking a walk down this dividing line – but be warned, parts of this walk might be too snowy and icy in the winter. Start from the top, near the drinking water reserve Maridalsvannet. This bit is very green, with lots of nice swimming opportunities in the summer. Be careful of the crazy people on bikes – they go really fast! After a while you'll reach Sagene, Grünerløkka and Grønland – the funky parts of the city, and you'll end up near the new opera house. It will probably take you a couple of hours, but it will give you the highlights of Oslo in one – nature, city-life and an architectural highlight at the end.

THE EKEBERG RESTAURANT This is probably the most famous architectural landmark in Oslo, if you ask the man on the street. It was designed by Lars Backer in 1927 and left to rot for years before it was renovated in 2008. Today it's a gourmet restaurant with an amazing view over Oslo. I would recommend taking a walk in the surrounding area in the afternoon, and finish it off at the outdoor cafe area with a cold beer in the sun. Kongsveien 15, 0193 Oslo, www.ekebergrestauranten.com

WALKS AND ARCHITECTURE

THE BOTANICAL GARDEN This is a really old Botanic Garden, established in 1814. It's a beautiful, peaceful retreat. Have a stroll around and check out the zoological museum or the nice, quiet cafe. The Munch Museum is just across the road. Located at Tøyen

VILLA STENERSEN The renowned Norwegian architect, Arne Korsmo, designed Villa Stenersen in 1938. It was originally built as a private home for a wealthy broker and art collector and is one of the most famous Modernist buildings in Norway. The house, which has a big art collection, is open for guided tours on the first Sunday of the month, or if you're in a group you can book another time. Tuengen Allé 10C, 0374 Oslo, www.villastenersen.net

VIGELANDSPARKEN Gustav Vigeland's beautiful monumental sculptures in the middle of the huge park Frognerparken never cease to amaze me. This is a must see! Get up early to avoid the touristy masses. The park at dawn is precious. Located at Majorstua

BYGDØY Bygdøy is a peninsula packed with expensive houses, museums and beaches. The Folkemuseet (Folk Museum) is worth a visit. I especially like their permanent exhibition 'Living in the City' which features a restored apartment building from 1865. You can walk around the different apartments and see how the style has changed over the past 150 years. If you're here in summer, make sure to go for a swim. I would recommend Paradisbukta rather than the packed main beach Huk.

KORKETREKKEREN/THE SCREWDRIVER The old bobsleigh slope from the Winter Olympics in 1952 is an extremely popular winter activity. Grab a sleigh and go down the slope – fast! Between Frognerseteren Restaurant and Skistua, www. akeforeningen.no

THE CITY BICYCLES Cycling is a great way to see any city. Buy an 80 NOK bicycle pass at a newsagents and pick up a bike from 90 different locations around the city. You'll have to return it within three hours, and it's not available in winter. www.oslobysykkel.no

Yarn from Husfliden

Jan Kallwejt's Warsaw

There are lots of things I love and hate about Warsaw. It has wide, tree-lined streets and many beautiful parks dotted around the city. On the other hand there is virtually no town planning and the architecture is a real mixed bag of beautiful, interesting and downright hideous. On a global level, I basically love the city in summer and hate it in winter, when temperatures plummet below zero. May to September is definitely the time to come here.

You probably already have some sense of Warsaw's tumultuous history over the past century. It was all but razed to the ground during the Second World War, and rebuilt with Russian 'help' in the style of Socialist Realism (Socrealizm in Polish). The buildings are mostly what you would expect of this style, with a handful of very interesting ones, although even these are much maligned by the locals, due to the bad memories they evoke. After the fall of communism, there was a chaotic attempt at modernisation. Again, there has been a lot of criticism of the complete lack of planning that went into the building works – but here too, I still like some of the skyscrapers that resulted, some of which were designed by top international architects.

Running through the city is the Vistula River. For many years, the city had its back to the river, as it were, with the interesting areas located away from its axis, and its banks left neglected, but this is gradually changing. On the right side of the Vistula is the Praga district. It suffered less during the war, but was left to fall into ruin. It's now becoming more and more hip as artists move there and new cafes, galleries and shops pop up every year.

On the left side of the Vistula, there is the city centre, Śródmieście, which contains within it the Old Town. This is worth visiting – even though it is packed with a constant stream of tourists. Surrounding the city centre there are four districts. From north to south they are: Zoliborz; a relaxing neighbourhood full of green spaces; the industrial district of Wola, where most of the new architcture may be found, as well as some interesting renovation projects; Ochota, a district with a tranquil, pretty old section, featuring a remarkable 19th Century water filteration facility (more impressive than it sounds!); and finally Mokotow - the area where I grew up and lived for many years - a calm, beautiful district that I still have a lot of affection for.

As you might imagine, I have never stayed in a hotel in my hometown, so please take these recommendations with a pinch of salt!

INTERCONTINENTAL HOTEL The luxury option in a new 40-storey skyscraper with great views over the city. It's very centrally located. Emilii Plater 49, 00 Warsaw, www.warszawa.intercontinental.com

JOLIE BED AND BREAKFAST A tiny, elegant B&B in the peaceful Zoliborz district. Henryka Wieniawskiego 6, 01 Warsaw, www.jolie.pl

HOTEL HETMAN This is in the Praga district, about 20 minutes from the city centre. It's a good place to be if you want to experience the funky bars and restaurants of the area. It's not exactly stylish, but good value for money. Księdza Ignacego Kłopotowskiego 36, 03 Warsaw, www.hotelhetman.pl

BOUTIQUE B&B A nice B&B that has a few standard rooms and a few apartments that might be good for families. Smolna 14, 00 Warsaw, www.bedandbreakfast.pl

ZIELNIK A small restaurant situated next to Dreszera Park in my beloved Mokotow district. It's a bit pricey, but the food is delicious – a modern take on traditional Polish cuisine. It has a great atmosphere, and in the spring they run a barbeque garden in the park across the road. Odynca 15, 02 Warsaw

MILK BAR BAMBINO Milk bars were very popular in Poland during the communist era, serving cheap foods based on milk products. In the 1990s, most of them were closed down or went bankrupt. One of the handful left standing is Bambino. The interior is totally untouched, and they serve great food at unbelievably low prices. Krucza 21, 00 Warsaw

CAFE KARMA This is a great cafe/bar in a beautiful square, which is very popular amongst the actors and artists of Warsaw. I love their non-alcoholic cocktails. They also offer a tasty vegetarian light menu as well as nice coffee and tea. Plac Zbawiciela 3/5, 00 Warsaw

QCHNIA ARTYSTYCZNA Avant-garde restaurant with an interesting menu located in Ujazdowski Castle. It has a big terrace with a beautiful view, and is a great place to go after visiting the Centre of Contemporary Art, which is also located in the castle. I have a soft spot for this place, because I used to work there as a waiter when I was a student. Zamek Ujazdowski, Jazdow 2, 00 Warsaw

PLACES TO EAT

CAFE KULTURALNA A cafe/bar/club located in the Palac Kultury building next to Dramatyczny Theatre. It's got funky, retro décor, good DJs, film screenings, and live music (jazz and funk but other stuff too), attracting a friendly crowd. Plac Defilad 1, 00 Warsaw

11 LISTOPADA 22 The three clubs Zwiaz Mnie, Hydrozagadka and Saturator are all located in the same courtyard and are all very cool places with their own vibes. Saturator is a three-floor, wacky venue, Sklad Butelek (the bottle warehouse) is in an industrial basement and is decorated with old furniture and candle-lit corners – very chilled, with lots of live events, and Zwiaz Mnie specialises in old-school and funk. 11 Listopada 22, 03 Warsaw

CHLODNA 25 A cafe/bar that is the unofficial home of counter-culture. It hosts talks, poetry slams, exhibitions and concerts, with parties going on in the evening. It brings the art community in in droves, and has a great atmosphere. Chlodna 25, 00 Warsaw, www.chlodna25.blog.pl

REGENERACJA A popular bar in Mokotow that's usually bustling with people – and sometimes dogs too. A great place for drinks and snacks, with a dance floor downstairs, where you can often stumble upon a cool party that goes on until 4am. Pulawska 61, 02 Warsaw

MUSEUM OF ETHNOGRAPHY I'm a big fan of Polish naïve art – especially painters from Silesia – a post-industrial area of Poland full of old mines and a tradition in textiles. The Museum of Ethnography may sound boring – and for the most part it is – but it has a great collection of folk art painting and wooden sculptures. Kredytowa 1, 00 Warsaw, www.pme.waw.pl

WILANOW POSTER MUSEUM Most tourists visit the palace at Wilanow, but when I go, it's usually for an event at the Poster Museum. There are regular temporary exhibitions, and you should check their website to find out in advance what's on. The most interesting time to visit is during the International Poster Biennale. St Kostki Potockiego 10/16, 02 Warsaw, www.postermuseum.pl

RASTER Based in a private apartment, the Raster Gallery is famous for curating exhibitions of interesting, young Polish artists, including the popular painter Wilhelm Sasnal, who was promoted here at the beginning of his international career. Check opening hours before you go. Hoza 42/8, 00 Warsaw, www.raster.art.pl

CENTRE FOR CONTEMPORARY ART Situated in Ujazdowski Castle, the exhibitions here are constantly changing, and it also hosts workshops, concerts and performances. ul Jazdów 2, 00 Warsaw, www.csw.art.pl

FABRYKA TRZCINY This is one of the oldest industrial sites in the Praga district. In its early days it housed a marmalade production facility, later becoming the headquarters of the Polish rubber industry. Its 2000m² space has recently been converted into an artistic centre with a theatre, club, two bars, a restaurant and a gallery. It hosts some great events and jazz concerts. Otwocka 14, 03 Warsaw, www.fabrykatrzciny.pl

WARSZAWSKA NIKE The only place in Warsaw where I can buy shoes. It's a small, exclusive Nike shop with an assortment of limited editions, run by Warsaw streetwear pioneer, 'Serek'. There are a few other interesting clothing shops that have appeared recently on the same street. Mokotowska 24, 00 Warsaw, www.warszawskanike.pl

GALLERIES AND CULTURE

BARS

SHOPPING

CZULY BARBARZYNCA The name of this bookshop/cafe translates as 'The Gentle Barbarian'. It's very light with a modern, tranquil vibe, and it hosts lots of author events, readings and discussions in the evenings. It is situated near the university library, which is also worth a visit. Dobra 31, 00 Warsaw, www.czulybarbarzynca.pl

MAGAZYN PRAGA Eclectic design boutique selling design objects, carpets and furniture. It's located in the old Konoser vodka factory in Praga, which also houses the Bochenska Gallery and the Wytwornia Theatre, as well as a restaurant. In the summer there's an outdoor cinema round the back. Zabkowska 27/31, 03 Warsaw, www.magazynpraga.pl

MYSIKROLIK A tiny tailor's shop, craft-store and gallery, which hosts small art exhibitions and events. Okolnik 11A, 00 Warsaw, www.mysikrolik.com

WARSZAWA

POWAZKI The oldest and most beautiful cemetery in Warsaw. On the evening of All Saints Day, thousands of candles are lit on the graves. It's a truly magical experience.

PALAC KULTURY I NAUKI The Palace of Culture and Science is one building you don't want to miss – although it's not something that Warsavians are particularly proud of. A huge 42-storey monument in the style of Socialist Realism, with a dose of Art Deco and Polish Historicism thrown in for good measure, it was built in the 1950s as a gift from the Soviet Union to the people of Poland. Most tourists only go as far as the lift takes them (to the panoramic terrace on the 30th floor), but the rest of the building is really worth exploring. It's home to countless institutions and offices, as well as public spaces such as a big swimming pool, gymnastic arenas, winter gardens, theatres, a cinema and museums. You can take a guided tour, or just visit some of the public spaces. There are many deep basements and dungeons, and some closed areas with no public access. A fascinating place definitely worth visiting. Plac Defilad 1, 00 Warsaw, www.pkin.pl

PRAGA WALK On a warm afternoon, I would suggest a walk in Praga. Start at Warsaw Zoo on Florianska Street. Walk past St Florian and St Michael Cathedrals, then turn right onto Jagielonska Street, and after several meters left onto Okrzei Street. After you pass Targowa, turn into Zabkoska Street. This street is a good example of how Praga has changed in recent years – some buildings are virtually derelict, others have been restored, and some modern architecture has sprung up in between. Walking along Zabkowska, you'll finally reach the old Warsaw Vodka Factory. It doesn't produce alcohol any more, but has been converted into a cultural centre with galleries, a theatre and a concept store (see Shopping). If you're not too exhausted, keep going along Zabkowska until it ends, turn into Kaweczynska and then left into Otwocka (you should be aware that you're now in an area that's considered dangerous). End your route at Otwocka 14, 'Fabryka Trzciny' (see Galleries) for some culture and maybe a drink. www.warszawskapraga.pl

WARSAW FILM FESTIVAL OCTOBER A ten-day international film festival, hosting lots of interesting events. www.wff.pl

WARSAW SUMMER JAZZ DAYS JUNE-JULY A long festival that pretty much runs through the summer, featuring free and ticketed concerts by jazz musicians from around the world. It's at venues around the city, with lots of open-air concerts in Zamkowy Square.

NOC MUZEÓW (LONG NIGHT OF MUSEUMS) MAY Noc Muzeów is the one night of the year that museums and galleries are open well into the night. Thousands of people turn up, and cafes are also open late for tea or an ice cream. It can be lots of fun.

Neste espaço só se escreve a direcção.

Liza' Ramalho and Artur Rebelo's Porto

The geography of Porto is what makes our city special. It sits on a mountain between the Atlantic Ocean and the Douro River, and these bodies of water define the look and feel of the city, making for views that surprise and impress around every corner.

Porto is the second largest city in Portugal, but in itself it only has a population of 240,000. However, the surrounding small cities of Gaia, Maia, Matosinhos and Gondomar have all merged together, and this conglomorate (known as Big Porto) has in excess of one million inhabitants. Gaia (full name Vila Nova de Gaia) lies directly opposite Porto on the Douro. It is connected to the city with six bridges – the most famous of which is the Dom Luis bridge, designed by the engineer Teofilo Seyrig. If you look across at it, one of the things you'll notice is the logotypes of the Port wine company. This world famous fortified wine is made here. Make sure to order some white port to accompany your tripe (the local speciality).

The Ribiera is the old part of Porto on the left shore of the Douro. It is a typical Old Town with narrow twisting streets bustling with people and cafes. There's some great typography around here, with fantastic tiling covering buildings and pavements. There are even original street signs designed by Thom, which are unfortunately currently being replaced. We like walking around the streets surrounding the Praça General Humberto Delgado, to get some inspiration.

Rising above the city is a Baroque tower designed by Nicolau Nasoni, called the Clérigos Tower, which is considered the city icon. In 1917, in one of the first publicity stunts in the country, two acrobats climbed to the top of the tower, had a cup of tea and some cookies, and showered pamphlets on the city below, promoting the Cookies Invicta Company. Today you can climb the 225 steps of the tower and enjoy the view of the Old City below.

In Western Porto, not far from the Contemporary Art Museum designed by Álvaro Siza Vieira, there is a friendly park that links the city to the Atlantic Ocean. This is where we go to relax – walking from our studio across the park to the ocean, and then back along the river to the Old City.

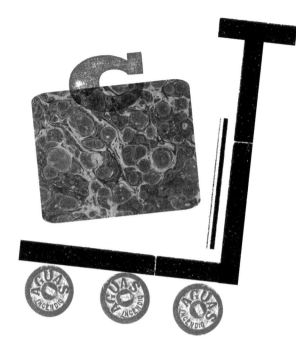

POUSADA DA JUVENTUDE This youth hostel is not the most interesting or elegant building, but it is the cheapest option and it offers an excellent view over Douro River. Rua Paulo da Gama 55, 4169-006 Porto, www.pousadasjuventude.pt

CASTELO DE SANTA CATARINA An enchanting castle built at the turn of the century that is totally over the top, with ornate furniture and loads of kitsch stuff. It's in uptown Porto and is surrounded by lovely gardens and scenery. Reasonably priced. Rua Santa Catarina 1347, 4000-457 Porto www.castelosantacatarina.com.pt

HOTEL BOAVISTA A basic mid-range hotel, which is well located, and offers some great views of the beach and of San João Baptista Fortress. Esplanada do Castelo 58, 4150-196 Porto, www.hotelboavista.com

GRANDE HOTEL DO PORTO Built in 1880, this is an old style Grand Hotel in the heart of Porto's downtown. It's not cheap, but it's an elegant option. Rua de Santa Catarina 197, 4000-450 Porto, www.grandehotelporto.com

GOSHO We love sushi, and this is the best sushi in town. It was designed by ANC Arquitectos, and it has some beautiful touches evoking Japanese architecture. It's situated in a five-star hotel, so it's not the cheapest place to go. Avenida da Boavista 1277, 4100-130 Porto

ROTA DO CHÁ A good place for a light meal and a cup of tea when you are visiting the galleries on Miguel Bombarda Street. Rua Miguel Bombarda 457, 4050-379 Porto

SESSENTA SETENTA This is one of our favourite restaurants. It's in the beautiful old Convento de Monchique and it's all built out of stone. The food is imaginative, fresh and delicious, and while you eat you can enjoy a spectacular view over the Douro. It's expensive but worth every penny. Rua Sobre o Douro 1A, 4050-592 Porto

CASA NANDA This is a typical restaurant with wood panelled walls, and a very local vibe. The portions are big and everything is cooked on a wood-burning stove. Rua da Alegria 394, 4000-035 Porto

COMETA A really intimate and cosy place, owned by a friend of ours, who's done it up with beautiful retro fittings. It attracts a funky clientele and serves great food! Rua Tomás Gonzaga 87, 4050-607 Porto

SALTA O MURO This is the best fish restaurant in town – and that's saying something. We love coming here. It's in a street full of nice restaurants, next to the fish market in Matosinhos – plus it's very cheap! Rua Heróis França 386, 4450-155 Matosinhos

CASA Pinto

PASSOS MANUEL A very nice, trendy bar in an old movie theatre, where you'll often find us after work. It has DJ settings and live events, and attracts the design/architecture crowd. Rua Passos Manuel 137, 4000-385 Porto, www.passosmanuel.net

MAUS HÁBITOS This bar (whose name translates as 'bad habits') is situated on the fourth floor of a spectacular Modernist car garage. It serves as a cultural centre too, with an art space and regular concerts and events. It's got a fantastic chilled-out atmosphere and a lovely terrace. Especially good for vegetarians. Check website for opening times. Rua Passos Manuel 178, 4000-382 Porto, www.maushabitos.com

GALERIA DE PARIS Rua Galeria de Paris is a busy street with several interesting bars, and a good area to spend a night bar hopping. This eponymous bar has a cosmopolitan, chic vibe going on, but not in an intimidating way. Like many other bars on this street, it's open till the wee hours of the morning. Rua Galeria de Paris 56, 4050 Porto

CASA DO LIVRO This is one of our favourites – an old bookstore beautifully and elegantly transformed into a bar with good music, good atmosphere and good drinks. Rua Galeria de Paris 85, 4050 Porto

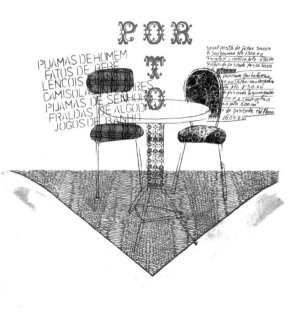

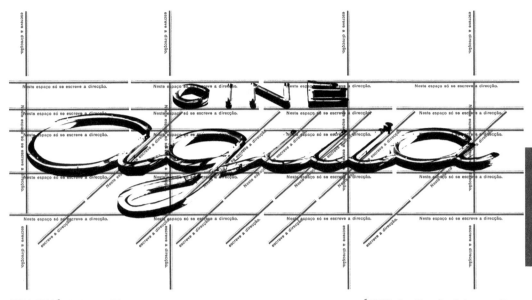

CASA DE LÓ A shop selling delicious traditional Portuguese cakes. Travessa de Cedofeita 20A, 4050-183 Porto

ARTES EM PARTES This is an ultra-cool four-storey shopping centre where you can buy vintage records (Musak) and ephemera (Matéria Prima) as well as designer clothing. It also has a gallery space and a nice cafe at the back. Rua Miguel Bombarda 457, 4050-381 Porto

A PÉROLA DO BOLHÃO Once a tea shop, this is now a wonderful grocery shop with a beautiful Art Nouveau façade located near the Bolhão Markett. Rua Formosa 277/81, 4000-252 Porto

CC BOMBARDA This is a small shopping mall, where you can find one-offs by Portuguese designers, and other really nice design objects. Rua Miguel Bombarda 285, 4050-382 Porto, www.ccbombarda. blogspot.com

PAPELARIA MODELO This shop was established in 1921, and still has the original signage. Good for drawing materials. Largo dos Lóios 68, 4050-338 Porto, www. papelariamodelo.pt

MARIA VAI COM AS OUTRAS A well-designed bookshop/cafe stocking art and design books and magazines as well as nice tea and wine. It also sometimes hosts live music events. Rua do Almada 443, 4050-037 Porto, www.Maria-vai-com-as-outras. blogspot.com

ÍNDEX A gallery/bookshop worth checking out for its films and exhibitions as much as for its stock. Rua D Manuel II 320, 4050-343 Porto

BOLHÃO MARKET This is the old food market where all the regional foodstuffs can be found. It's very authentic with old ladies selling chillies and maize bread, and pigeons and salt cod (a local favourite dish) everywhere you look. A must see. You can enter it from any of the following streets: Rua de Fernandes Tomás, Rua Formosa, Alexandre Braga, Sá da Bandeira.

SHOPPING

RUA MIGUEL BOMBARDA This is a sedate residential street that is home to around a dozen contemporary art galleries. It attracts all art lovers, and it gets really animated at the openings, which happen on the first Saturday of every month.

FÁBRICA DO SOM An alternative music venue with lots of funky concerts and an annual experimental electronic music festival. It's an intimate venue and gets some great acts. Av de Rodrigues de Freitas 23-27, 4300-456 Porto, www.fabricadosom.com

IN-SONORIDADE An arts academy that hosts rock and jazz music concerts. 4th Floor, Rua do Breyner 65, 4050-126 Porto

GALERIA DAMA AFLITA A new, very funky gallery that specialises in drawing and illustration exhibitions among other nice events. Rua da Picaria 84, 4050-478 Porto, www.damaaflita.com

MUSEU SERRALVES The contemporary art museum designed by Álvaro da Siza Vieira was built on the large grounds surrounding the impressive Art Deco Serralves house, and the gardens surrounding it are still very beautiful. Exhibition openings usually take place on a Friday night, and the art world is always out in force. Rua D João de Castro 210, 4150-417 Porto, www. serralves.pt

GUINDAIS FUNICULAR Pick up the funicular in Ribiera, near the Dom Luís I Bridge, enjoy the three-minute ride up to Batalha Square, admire the beautiful view and then go for a coffee and a spot of shopping. Rua Augusto Rosa, 4000-098 Porto, www.metrodoporto.pt

CASA DA MÚSICA This is the new venue designed by Rem Koolhaas, dedicated to the creation, performance and study of music. It's an amazing building of steel, aluminium and glass with suspended walkways and a vast entrance hall. Av da Boavista 604-610, 4149-071 Porto, www.casadamusica.com

PALÁCIO DE CRISTAL GARDENS A landscaped park near the Rua Miguel Bombarda gallery district. The original glass crystal palace (modelled on London's building of the same name) has been replaced by a domed iron and glass building that holds concerts and sporting events. If you go to the bottom of the gardens you'll see one of the best views of the river. Rua Dom Manuel II, 4050-345 Porto

THE ÁLVARO SIZA VIEIRA SEASIDE TOUR

Álvaro Siza is probably Portugal's most important architect. His buildings are experimental, defiant and playful. He was born and raised in Matosinhos, and there are many of his buildings around Porto. One of the most popular is the swimming pool in Leça da Palmeira. Using rough concrete, Siza created pools that offer uninterrupted views of the sea and merge artlessly with the natural rock formations. It's a great family-friendly place to go. Just down the road from there you'll find the Casa do Chá da Boa Nova (Boa Nova Tea House), one of Siza's first built projects (1956). It seems to emerge from the cliff at the shore of Matosinhos. Avenida da Liberdade, Leca da Palmeira.

SERRALVES EM FESTA JUNE A 48-hour festival in the grounds of the Serralves Museum with music, exhibitions, shows and a big turnout. Rua D João de Castro 210, www.serralvesemfesta.com

PECHA KUCHA NIGHT A regular night – find out places and dates online. www.pecha-kucha.org/cities/porto

SAO JOÃO FESTIVAL 23RD JUNE Saint John is the city's patron saint, and this is a huge street party with fireworks, barbecues in the streets, and lit-up balloons floating in the sky. Afterwards, the streets fill with people pounding each other on the head with plastic hammers and wild garlic stalks. The party continues on the beaches until the morning. Awesome!

FANTASPORTO FEBRUARY A really fantastic film festival that started as a haven for sci-fi and fantasy films and has grown to embrace all genres. It's one of the biggest in Europe. www.fantasporto.com

NIGHTLIFE
LOCAL FLAVOUR
CULTURE
EATING

- bamboo & kristal clubs
- dristor kebab
- obor market
- carol park
- posibilă gallery

UNIVERSITATE & LIPSCANI AREA

- all hotels here
- caru cu bere
- expirat & other side
- club control
- rozalb de mura
- cochet shop
- atelier 35 gallery

VICTORIEI PLAZA AREA

- barka saffron
- picollo mondo
- studio martin
- karousel gallery
- naser restaurant
- bureşti & matache area

ROMANĂ & AMZEI AREA

- galeron cafe
- 115.ro gallery
- cărtureşti bookshop
- green hours cafe
- athenaeum

- botanical garden

- valea cascadelor flea market

- fantastic club

- mnac

Lucian Marin's Bucharest

Bucharest, like many Eastern Bloc capitals, still bears a clear imprint from its communist period. First of all, it is one of the biggest cities in Eastern Europe, with a population of close to four million. Its size is due in part to the massive urbanisation campaign by Ceauşescu (who ruled from 1965–1989), coupled with his ban on abortion and contraception, leading to substantial natural growth. In atmosphere too, the residues of communism are apparent: from dusty dark museums, to local markets, derelict apartment buildings and abandoned construction sites. These are some of my favourite things about Bucharest, and what makes the city unique. I like going to these areas and taking pictures of abandoned cars, auto repair shops and little cobbler shops tucked between the endless rows of Soviet apartment blocks in my area.

Bucharest is situated on the banks of the Dâmboviţa River, which flows into the Argeş River, a tributary of the Danube. Most of this river is now underground, and as the city is quite flat, it can be hard to get your bearings. If you're only coming for a short visit, you're probably best off sticking to the Lipscani and Amzei areas. This is where you'll find all the essentials – bars, clubs, museums, restaurants and shops. They're also some of the oldest areas in the city, so they should give you a taste of Bucharest's multi-layered identity. Many of the places I go to are then focussed around three main points: Victoriei Plaza, Romana Plaza and Universitate Plaza. Much of the nightlife is in these areas, although you'll also find some of the biggest and blingest clubs a bit further away, such as Studio Martin, Kristal or Bamboo. Bucharest has been undergoing a lot of modernisation in recent years, and has experienced a real economic boom since joining the EU in 2007. This is evident in a lot of these more up-market venues.

To get around the city, your safest bet is by taxi. They're pretty cheap at €1 per 2km. However, if you want to experience the socialist underbelly of the city, take the metro. The central terminals and the trains have been modernised, but there are plenty of original stations outside of these. Romania's public transport system is one of the largest in Europe, and it can be tricky to navigate. Avoid taking the bus unless you speak some Romanian. There are no bus maps and it can be very confusing.

CAPSA HOTEL A five-star hotel in grand, old-school European style. The building has been beautifully restored and it's located right in the heart of historic Bucharest. There is a famous cake shop in the hotel, which is open to all. 36 Calea Victoriei, www.capsa.ro

REMBRANDT HOTEL A small, classy hotel that has been recently (and tastefully) renovated. It's in the Lipscani neighbourhood, near Universitate Plaza. 11 Smardan Street, www.rembrandt.ro

BANAT HOTEL This feels like travelling back in time to the pre-revolutionary days of Bucharest. The building is old, beautiful and centrally located, and the interior has a totally socialist look and feel. It's basic, but reasonably priced. 5 Piata Rosetti

FUNKY CHICKEN HOSTEL The website hypes it up as a cool anarchic hostel. That's probably not entirely accurate, but nonetheless it is an extremely cheap option (€9.50 a night), and a very central location, ten minutes from Universitate Plaza and Cismigiu Gardens. 63 General Berthelot Street, www.funkychickenhostel.com

PLACES TO STAY

CARU CU BERE This is one of the oldest beer houses in Bucharest, serving traditional Romanian dishes in traditional Romanian surrounds. It often features live Romanian music and dancing too. It's a good pick if you're looking for local flavour in the Old City, but book ahead – it can get packed. 5 Stavropoleos Street, www.carucubere.ro

BARKA SAFFRON An artsy and intimate Asian restaurant (but quite pricey!). The Indian owner is very friendly, and has a tendency to circulate around the tables chatting and joking. I come here for birthday dinners and other occasions. 1 Sanatescu Street, www.barkasaffron.ro

PICCOLO MONDO Don't be fooled by the Italian name, this restaurant, which is part of a hotel of the same name, serves fantastic Lebanese food. It's not that fancy, but it's very popular, thanks to the quality of the dishes. 9 Clucerului Road (behind 1 Mai Square), www.piccolomondo.ro

NASER This is my favourite restaurant in the city – I come here twice a week. It's located near the Domenii Market, and serves great Arab food (kebabs, ayran, baclavas and kataiffs, labane etc.) in simple surrounds. The owner plays cards and backgammon with his mates all day long, smoking a hookah (which you are also welcome to try after your meal). Make sure to taste the cookies! 86 Dumitru Zosima Street

SAORMA DRISTOR A street food restaurant, selling the Romanian version of kebabs. It's a very popular place to go after a party on a Saturday night, and it's crowded all night long. Get a taxi there and back. The driver will know where to take you. 1 Camil Ressu, www.dristorkebab.ro

GALERON This cafe/bar/restaurant is in a traditional Romanian villa, with various rooms inside, each done in a different theme. There's a nice terrace, and an alcove that offers great views of Nicolae Golescu and Episcopiei Streets. The food is fresh, and it's centrally located in Amzei Plaza. It's the best place to go for a drink or a business meeting. 18A Nicolae Golescu Street, www.grandcafegalleron.ro

ORIENT CAFE One of my favourite bars, with a great cocktail list. I go there after work on Fridays. 16 Calea Victoriei, www.orient-cafe.ro

STUDIO MARTIN Situated in a famous cinema, this is one of Bucharest's most established clubs. It's open on Friday and Saturday nights, and books the best DJs in town, playing house, electro and minimal music. Check their website for details. 41 Iancu de Hunedoara, www.studiomartin.ro

KRISTAL This is a clubber's club, frequently listed in the top 50 worldwide. They get some top European DJs and it has a glam interior to match. One of the best in town. 2 J S Bach, www.clubkristal.ro

BARS

CLUB BAMBOO Only the richest and most beautiful Romanians frequent this posh club, and you have to be dressed to the nines to get in. Very bling – entrance and drinks are expensive. 39 Rămuri Tei, www.bamboosportingclub.ro

GREEN HOURS This is a courtyard cafe/bar with a laid-back atmosphere attracting a young-ish crowd. In the evening it turns into a jazz club, and occasionally hosts live music, theatre and vintage clothing and book fairs. Take a walk in the surrounding area – it's situated in a prime spot between Amzei and Universitate Plaza. 120 Calea Victoriei, www.green-hours.ro

EXPIRAT AND OTHER SIDE Two clubs in one small building in the old centre. One entrance (on Lipscani) leads you to a mainstream club, while the entrance on Brezoianu takes you to The Other Side – a more edgy, funky venue. Some of my friends play there regularly, and this is where the Hot Chip guys came for their afterparty. 5 Lipscani / 4 Ion Brezoianu, www.expirat.org

FANTASTIC CLUB It's easy to miss this dark building on a dark street – look for the candles in the entrance, and check their Facebook site – sometimes you need a password to get in. Inside it's equally dimly lit, with hidden rooms. It's crowded – but usually a nice crowd, and the music is great. They have their own form of currency in the form of buttons (from clothes) and cloakroom tickets are used as playing cards. 147-153 Calea Rahovei (in Biblioteca Palat Bragadiru)

CONTROL This is a big, new alternative/indie club. It's well laid out, with a space for live music. Check out their events online. 19 Academiei Street, www.control-club.ro

I like looking at all the antique shops in the Buzesti and Lipscani areas. You can find genuine souvenirs from post-war Bucharest – old prints, newspapers from the 1950s, number plates and household objects.

CARTURESTI Bookshop, art gallery and cafe set over two floors. It mostly sells books in Romanian, but has English language and art book sections, as well as stocking old movies, music and gifts. 13 Arthur Verona, www.carturesti.ro

ROZALB DE MURA The shop of this avant-garde, up-market Romanian fashion designer, who designs for Roisin Murphy. 9-11 Selari Street, www.rozalbdemura.ro

SHOPPING

KOMBINAT A concept store selling cool clothing alongside a gallery space, tea house and fanzine library – all contained in a well designed interior. 22 Tudor Arghesi Street, www.kombinat.ro

COCHET This is a very hip store in an old club that sells everything from vintage clothing to limited edition prints, Björk DVDs and international and local brand names such as Ana Alexe. In fact, everything in the shop is for sale, down to the furniture. It has a cafe, and might be a venue for live events in the future. It's pricey, but not ridiculously so. 3A-3B Ion Otetelesanu, www.cochetcochet.ro

PHILATELIC CLUB This is where you'll find me on a Sunday morning, hunting out beautifully designed stamps. It's a serious time-travel experience. Calea Dorobanti (near the Perla Restaurant)

MY GRANDMA'S BACKYARD A friendly and cool fair for handmade and vintage clothes and accessories. Check the blog for the dates. www.ciudat.blogspot.com

FLEA MARKETS There are two flea markets worth visiting – one at Valea Cascadelor (on Thursday, Saturday and Sunday) and one at Vitan (only on Sundays). Find the cool stuff at the back behind the car dealers and the cheap plastic junk – bikes stolen in Berlin, old televisions and cameras, Russian figurines, Bakelite phones and many many other weird and wonderful things.

MATACHE FRUIT AND VEGETABLE MARKET AND BUCUR OBOR This is where I go for produce far fresher than that in the supermarket. You can also get homemade cheese, honey, jams and horseradish. Bucur Obor is the bloody and visceral meat market in the grand hall, which is in a permanent state of commercial chaos. Get there early and watch your pocket. Piata Matache, Buzesti Street, near Victoriei Plaza

MNAC The relatively new museum for contemporary art is located in a wing of the monstrous Casa Poporului (Palace of Parliament). It has some interesting experimental exhibitions and events, great parties in the summer and a nice rooftop cafe. It also manages the Kalinderu MediaLab, which caters specifically to multimedia and experimental art. 2-4 Izvor Street (entrance from Calea 13 Septembrie), www.mnac.ro

GALERIA POSIBILA A private gallery that I've only visited once to see an exhibition of works by Dan Perjovschi, one of the best living Romanian artists (in my opinion). 6 Popa Petre, www.posibila.ro

KAROUSEL A gallery that exhibits the best of contemporary Romanian photography. 5A George Calinescu, www.karousel.ro

ATELIER35 A nice space for young artists in the old centre. They host exhibitions, installations and performances, as well as various workshops throughout the year. 13 Selari, www.atelier35.eu

OLD-SCHOOL MUSEUMS I like dusty places that haven't changed for decades like the Railroad Museum, Technical Museum, Firefighters' Museum, Military Museum, or the Village Museum, which is open-air, with life-size exhibits of traditional buildings. Village Museum: 28 Kiseleff Road, www.muzeul-satului.ro

GALLERIES AND CULTURE

ROKOLECTIV FESTIVAL APRIL This festival of electronic music and related art takes place over the course of a weekend and attracts some reasonably big names (DAT Politics, Underground Resistance and Jean-Jacques Perrey have featured in the past). The last day of the festival takes place in the MNAC Gallery. www.rokolectiv.ro

ENESCU FESTIVAL SEPTEMBER A three-week festival of classical music featuring around 3,000 musicians from all around the globe. The artistic director, Ioan Holender, makes sure that despite the modest budget, there's always an impressive line-up. www.festivalenescu.ro

EVENTS

CASA POPORULUI – PALACE OF PARLIAMENT
Don't miss this. In one word, it's vast. Ceauşescu's most tremendous vanity project is still the third largest building in the world, with 1,100 rooms extending over 12 storeys high, and eight storeys deep. It's built in Neo-classical style, and is kitted out with crystal mirrors, chandeliers galore and one million cubic metres of Transylvanian marble. One fifth of the city was destroyed to build it. There are tours every half hour.

BELLU CEMETERY This is the most famous cemetery in the city, in use for 200 years. A place for peaceful reflection.

BOTANIC GARDEN This was once a pleasure park for the royal family and it is very beautiful, covering 17.5 hectares. Go there early on weekdays and you'll have it all to yourself. Highly recommended in spring or autumn. www.gradina-botanica.ro

CAROL PARK A public park (called Liberty Park in communist times) designed by French landscape artist Édouard Redont at the turn of the century. It's very large and has many features including the Tomb of the Unknown Soldier and a Modernist mausoleum for various communist leaders designed by architects Horia Maicu and Nicolae Cucu in the 60s.

WALKS AND ARCHITECTURE

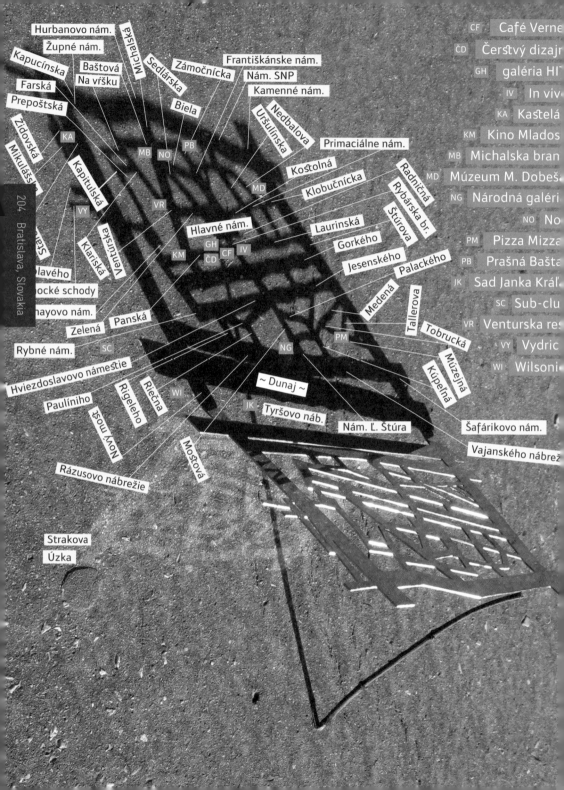

Hurbanovo nám.
Župné nám.
Michalská
Kapucínska
Baštová
Sedlárska
Zámočnícka
Na vŕšku
Farská
Biela
Prepoštská
Židovská
Mikulášs
Nedbalova
Františkánske nám.
Nám. SNP
Kamenné nám.
Uršulínska
Primaciálne nám.
Kapitulská
Košťolná
Klobučnícka
Radničná
Rybárska br.
Štúrova
Hlavné nám.
Laurinská
Gorkého
Jesenského
Palackého
Medená
Tallerova
Tobrucká
Múzejná
Kúpeľná
Venturska
Kláriská
lavého
ocké schody
nayovo nám.
Zelená
Panská
Rybné nám.
Hviezdoslavovo námeśtie
Paulíniho
Riečna
Rigeleho
Nový most
Mostová
Rázusovo nábrežie
~ Dunaj ~
Tyršovo náb.
Nám. Ľ. Štúra
Šafárikovo nám.
Vajanského nábrež
Strakova
Úzka

KA
MB
NO
PB
MD
VR
VY
KM
GH
ČD
CF
IV
SC
NG
PM
WI
JK

CF   Café Verne
ČD   Čerstvý dizajn
GH   galéria HIT
IV   In viv
KA   Kaštelá
KM   Kino Mlados
MB   Michalska bran
MD   Múzeum M. Dobeš
NG   Národná galéri
NO   No
PM   Pizza Mizza
PB   Prašná Bašta
JK   Sad Janka Kráľ
SC   Sub-clu
VR   Venturska res
VY   Vydric
WI   Wilsoni

marcel benčik's bratislava

Bratislava is the only European capital that borders two countries – Austria and Hungary. It is only 60km away from Vienna, and could almost be considered a suburb of that city. Nonetheless, it has its own identity (quite a mixed one given the history of repeated conquest), and its own individual vibe.

The part you're most likely to want to visit is the Old Town. It's much more compact than some European Old Towns – you can walk from one side to the other in less than ten minutes. It's very pretty, with winding narrow streets, a lot of Baroque and medieval architecture, and a pedestrianised area that was renovated in the 1990s. Surrounding the Old Town are big concrete blocks called 'panelaks'. I spend my time either in the Old Town or in Dullovo Namaste, where my studio is based – about ten minutes' walk from the centre, not far from the bus station.

In terms of green space, Bratislava has its fair share. The Danube River runs through the middle of it (the town bridges both banks – check out the communist icon Novy Most – New Bridge – the longest cable-stayed bridge in the world, in case you were wondering). Also the Carpathian mountain range starts here, with the Malé Karpaty (Little Carpathians). These are densely forested, and you can visit the Forest Park, which is 27km^2, and has a nice cafe and pub that attracts students from the nearby university.

Bratislava embraced capitalism warmly and with vigour. Over the past 20 years, the authorities have done just about anything to attract foreign investment and the economy has boomed. There has been a lot of construction, and the city really offers a mix of old-world charm and youthful modern vitality. I grew up in a city in northern Slovakia called Žilina, and went abroad to study. At the academy one day, I suddenly had a revelation that I really like Bratislava and actually miss it – it is dynamic and full of opportunity, but still feels like home.

MAMA'S BOUTIQUE HOTEL A new four-star hotel in a quiet area near the centre. It has a sushi restaurant that I'm told offers great value for money, and a rooftop terrace with great views, a jacuzzi and deck chairs. Chorvatska 2, www.hotelmamas.sk

HOTEL MICHALSKA BRANA Located in the pedestrianised part of the Old Town, this is a nicely decorated and reasonably priced guesthouse that's cosy and friendly with a good breakfast and a patio. Bastova 4, www.hotelmichalskabrana.com

VENTURSKA RESIDENCE New serviced holiday apartments in the heart of the Old Town. They're very spacious and modern and not too expensive. Venturska 3, www.venturskaresidence.com

BOTEL MARINA An old riverboat located on the river a few steps from the city centre. The rooms are, as you might expect, very small, but it's a nice, quirky budget option. Nabrezie arm gen L Svobodu

Azovská **BBB** Babuškova Bagarova Bachova Bajkalská Ba Banskobystrická Banšelova Bardejovská Bárdošova Barónka ažantia Beblavého Bebravská Beckovská Belehradská Beli Beniakova Beňovského Bernolákova Beskydská Betliarska ova Blagoevova Blatnická Blumentálska Bočná Bodrocká ova Borovicová Borská Bosákova Boskovičova Bošániho ratislavská Bratská Brečtanová Brestová Brezová Brezov roskyňová Brusnicová Břeclavská Bučinová Budatínska Bú Bulharská Bulíkova Bullova Buzalkova Bystrická Bzovícka esta na Kamzík Cesta na Klanec Cesta na Senec Cigeľská Cíg **ČČČ** Čachtická Čajakova Čajkovského Čaklovská Čalovská evského Černicová Červená Červený kríž Červeňáková Čer ohorská Čiernovodská Čierny chodník Čiližská Čipkárska Č Damborského Dankovského Dargovská Datelinová Daxnerov eviata Devínska cesta Dlhá Dlhé diely Dneperská Dobrovi olnozemská cesta Domašská Domkárska Domové role Donne ementisa Dražická Drevená Drieňová Drobného Drotárska cesta Dudova Dudvážska Dulovo nám. Ďumbierska Dunajs Einsteinova Eisnerova Elektrárenská Estónska Exnárova **F** edáková Fedinova Ferdiša Kostku Ferienčíkova Fialkové údo rancúzskych partizánov Františkánska Františkánske nám. Fur Galandova Galbavého Gallayova Gallova Galvaniho Gašp ercenova Gerulatská Gessayova Gettingova Gordova Gogo ová Gruzínska Gunduličova Guothova gusevova **HHH** Haan uliakova Hanácka Handlovská Hanulova Hany Meličkovej H a Havrania Haydnova Hečkova Herlianska Heydukova Heyr inická Hlučínska Hnilecká Hodálova Hodonínska Hodžovo r Horná Hornádska Horská Hospodárska Hrabový chodník H rdličkova Hrebendova Hríbová Hriňovská Hrohákova Hrobár a Humenské nám. Hummelova Hurbanovo nám. Husova Hú ydinárska Hýrošova **ChChCh** Chalupkova Charkovská Chemic riisková Iljušinová Ilkovičova Ilová Inovecká Ipeľská Irkut olinského Jabloňova Jačmenná Jadranská Jadrová Jahodov onáša Jána Poničana Jána Raka Jána Smreka Jána Stanislava a Janotova Jánska Janšákova Jantárová Jantárová cesta Ja strabia Jašíkova Javornská javorová Jazdecká Jedenásta J enského Jiráskova Jiskrova Jókaiho Jozefa Hagaru Jozefská Jurovského Jurská Justičná **KKK** K Horárskej studni K Železne Kamenárska Kamenné nám. Kamilková Kapicova Kapitulská arpatské nám. Kašmírska Kaštieľska Kaukazská Kazanská emensova Klenová Klimkovičova Klincová Klobučnícka Kllo ohútova Koľajná Kolárska Kolískova Kollárova Kollárovo ná árska Koncová Koniarkova Konopná Konventná Kopanice osatcová Kôstková Kostlivého Kostolná Košická Kovácsova a Kpt. Jána Rašu Krahuľia Krajinská Krajinská cesta Krajn rasovského Kratiny Krátka Krčméryho Kremeľská Kremenc ova Kubániho Kubínska Kudlákova Kulkovská Kúkoľová Ku urucova Kutlíkova Kutuzovova Kuzmányho Kvačalova Kveti adislava Sáru Ladzianskeho Ladová Lachova Laliová Lamač erského Latorická Laučekova Laurinská Lazaretská Ledir esnícka Lečkova Letecká Letná Levárska Levická Levočska ova Lipová Lipského Liptovská Lisovňa Listová Líščie nivy cka Lotyšská Lovinského Ľubietovská Ľubinská Ľublanská Luhačovická Lužická Lýcejná Lykovscová Lysáková **MMM** ová Magnezitová Magurská Macharova Máchova Majakovsk sko Malinová Malodunajská Malokarpatské nám. Malý trh Markova Maróthyho Marákovej Martinčekova Martinengova ána Hella Mečíková Medená Medveďovej Medzierka Medzil ichalská Mikovíniho Mikulášska Milana Marečka Milana Pišú lynská dolina Mlynské luhy Mlynské nivy Modranská Modrý oravská Morušová Moskovská Mostná Mostová Mošovskéhc nova Mudroňova Muchovo nám. Muránska Murgašova Muš a doline Na grbe Na hrádzi Na Hrebienku Na hradkach Na K

CAFE VERNE This is my favourite place – hidden away in the basement of Bratislava Academy of Fine Arts. I come here for breakfast, lunch and sometimes drinks in the evening. They do a fine continental breakfast and scrambled eggs. You can hang out on the ancient velvet sofas, surrounded by antique radios, Jules Verne inspired decorations, and young students and bohemian intellectuals. Hviezdoslavovo namestie 18

THE VIENNESE GROCERY This is another of my favourites. It's a Viennese grocery store that has space to sit. It's a pretty ugly joint, but I can honestly say it serves the best strudel I've ever eaten. Plus it's dirt cheap. Páričkova 6

PRAŠNÁ BAŠTA This is a very popular place, so avoid it at peak times. They've served the same reassuringly nice meals for as long as I can remember and have a peaceful garden area in the summer. Zámočnícka 11, www.prasnabasta.sk

PIZZA MICA (PIZZA MIZZA) Another popular staple of Bratislava's lunch hour. A good Italian with a lovely summer terrace – and the biggest pizza in town – 50cm diameter! Tobrucka 5, www.pizzamizza.sk

TAVERNA Right by my studio, ten minutes out of the city centre there's a really good Greek restaurant – at least I think it's Greek – everything inside is blue and white, with cheesy traditional music playing in the background. If you can handle the slight tackiness, you'll be rewarded – the food is just great. Fresh ingredients, carefully prepared, and reasonably priced. It never gets overcrowded, so you can always find a seat, and in the summer they set up tables on the sidewalk, so you're spared the interior décor. Košická 39, www.greckataverna.sk

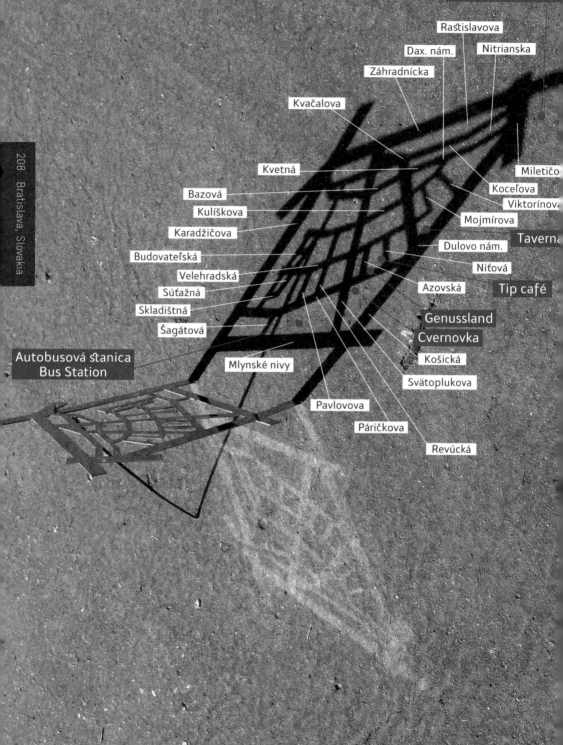

Raštislavova

Dax. nám.

Nitrianska

Záhradnícka

Kvačalova

Kvetná

Miletičo

Koceľova

Bazová

Viktorínov

Kulíškova

Mojmírova

Karadžičova

Dulovo nám.

Budovateľská

Niťová

Velehradská

Azovská

Súťažná

Tip café

Skladištná

Genussland

Šagátová

Cvernovka

Taverna

Autobusová stanica
Bus Station

Mlynské nivy

Košická

Svätoplukova

Pavlovova

Páričkova

Revúcká

Most of the bars in Bratislava are in walking distance from one another. They're all pretty similar, and I like bar-hopping from place to place. The thing I like about all these venues is that they're straightforward – you go there to get loaded and have fun – but all of them are friendly, and usually attract a crowd of cool people who are not afraid of talking to strangers.

TIP CAFE A weird place near my studio with a crowd of grumpy old men and gamblers – but friendly waiters, and the best coffee in town. Páričkova 31

VYDRICA On the side of the Castle Hill in a nice neighbourhood you'll find this very laid-back, local pub. Open till very late. Beblaveho 6

KASTELÁN CAFE A restaurant/bar in the centre. In the summer there's a small terrace, and on Friday nights there are often theme nights, with good music and a nice vibe. Židovská 19

PIVNIČKA A small basement bar with live jazz/blues/reggae concerts every Thursday. It's very dirty, but cheap and somehow great. Palackého 2

SUB CLUB This is a great club in a nuclear fallout bunker right next to all the above bars. They have a lot of house and techno here, but also ragga, rock and drum and bass. I like the 'Sub-urb' nights, which bring in excellent DJs. The space is cavernous with winding corridors. Nabrezie arm. gen. L. Svobodu, www.subclub.sk

CVERNOVKA My studio is in the old rivets factory, which ceased production in 2004. It's now the base of lots of designers and artists, and quite often holds private parties with DJs or live acts. It might be a bit tricky to get into – you'll have to call and ask about it, or know someone who's based in the building. It's worth it – the parties are lots of fun. Páričkova 18

Bratislava isn't really a shopping town – come here for eating and drinking and do your shopping in London or Berlin. I barely ever go shopping – twice a year on average.

CERSTVY DIZAJN (FRESH DESIGN) Located in the school building, you can find cool objects, jewellery and fashion by young Slovak designers. There's always at least one extremely good piece hidden somewhere inside. Hviezdoslavovo namestie 18, Bratislava

IN VIVO Near to Cerstvy Dizajn, this is a more run-of-the mill design shop, stocking standard fare – nothing special really. Panska 13, www.crazy-design-invivo.sk

NOX For those who are into vintage clothing, there are a few shops dotted around the city. This is probably the best of the lot – with a more interesting selection. Michalská 14

CENTRAL MARKET MILETICOVA (CENTRALNE TRHOVISKO) This is where the locals shop, and it has a really unique atmosphere. The fruit and vegetables are great, and they also sell homeware and other goods. The best time to go is on Saturday but it's open every day. It's got good lunch options too, with plenty of small kiosks selling food and drink. Miletičova Street

FLEA MARKET On the first Saturday of every month, there's a neighbourhood flea market at Horsky Park (get there by trolleybus 207). Letna 1

GALLERIES AND CULTURE

GALERIA HIT I'm not a big gallery-goer. The galleries in Bratislava are much like elsewhere – quiet and predictable. This is the one exception and I come here again and again. It's a tiny place in the AFAD (Academy of Fine Arts and Design) building. To get there you have to go through to the backyard and look for the metal door with the green sign. It shows work by young Slovak talent, and is run by very cool people, who make sure the atmosphere is homely and warm. The opening nights are very good. Check opening hours before you go – it's often closed. Hviezdoslavovo namestie 18, www.vsvu.sk/galeria_medium

13M³ An interesting multi-disciplinary space focussing on new media to bridge the arts, sciences and technology. Their exhibitions are often humorous and inspirational, with an urban vibe. Transit Studios, Student 12, www.13m3.sk

SLOVAK NATIONAL GALLERY The National Gallery occasionally puts on very good exhibitions (they had a great one of Slovak art from the 1980s). It's in an old-looking building, which is actually a reconstruction that was built in the 1950s, and has an interesting extension on the back from the 70s. They have a good collection of 20th Century Slovak art. Esterházy Palace, Námestie L Štúra 4, www.sng.sk

KINO MLADOST An old-school, traditional cinema, established in 1913 and located in the heart of downtown, screening a selection of art-house/indie movies. Hviezdoslavovo namestie 17

kova Nerudova Neváidzova Nezábudková Nezvalova Nitov é záhrady Novinárska Novobanská Novodvorská Novohorská Obchodná Obilná Oblačná Oblúková Očovská Odbojárov kárska Olivová Olšová Ondavská Ondrejovova Ondrejská iešková Ormisova Osadná Oskorušová Osloboditeľská Ôsm vocná Ovručská Ovsištské nám. Ožvoldíkova **PPP** Pajštúnska Panónska cesta Panská Papraďova Parcelná Páričkova Pa a Pavlovova Pavlovská Pažického Pažítkova Pečnianska P Petzvalova Pezinská Piata Pieskovcová Piesočná Peišťar átennícka Plavecká Plickova Pluhová Plynárenská Plzens snou hôrkou Pod lipami Pod Lipovým Pod násypom Pod Rov Zečákom Podbrezovská Podháj Podhorská Podhorského P hradná Podtatranského Poddunajská Podzáhradná Pohranic ká Poludníková Poniklecová Popolná Popovova Popradsk a Požiarnická Pračanská Prašná Prestaničné nám. Porep ánskom mlyne Pri hradnej studni Pri hrádzi Pri kolíske Pri kr i Starom mýte Pri strelnici Pri Struhe Pri Suchom mýte Pri š ibylinská Pridánky Priečna Priehradná Priekopnícka Priek ká Prípojná Prístavná Prokofievova Prokopa Veľkého Pro uškinova Pútnická Prenejská Pod Kobylou Pod Krásnou hôrko žami Pod Válkom Pod vinicami Pod záhradami Pod Zečákom dlesná cesta Podolučinského Podniková Podpriehradná Po olianky Poľná Poľnohospodárska Poloreckého Poľská Poluč čná Považanova Považská Povoznícka Povraznícka Požiarn Pri Bielom kríži Pri dvore Pri Dynamitke Pri Habánskom mly ej prachárni Pri Starom háji Pri strarom letisku Pri Starom m och Pri zvonici Priama cesta Pribinova Pribišova Pribylinsk ká Príjazdná Príkopova Primaciálne nám. Primoravská Pr vosienková Pšeničná Púchovská Púpavová Pustá Puškino iová Radlinského Radničná Radničné nám. Radvanská Raj á Ráztočná Rázusovo náb. Ražná Rebarborová Remeselníc edová Riazanská Ribayova Ríbezľová Riečna Rigeleho tovská Rošického Rovná Rovniankova Rovníkova Royova F idnícka Rumančekova Rumunská Rusovská cesta Rustaveli 1. Rybničná Rytierska **SSS** Sabinovská Sadmelijská Sadová dmokrásková Segnáre Segnerova Sekulská Sekurisova Ser zova Silvánska Sinokvetná Skalická ceste Skalná Skerličo lkovičova Sladová Slatinská Slávičie údolie Slepá Sliačska Slovinská Slovnaftská Slowackého Smetanova Smikova olíkova Sokolská Solivarská Sološnická Somolického Sos :nevského Srnčia Stachanovská Stálicová Stanekova Stan á vinárska Staré grunty Staré ihrisko Staré záhrady Starhrad avbárska Staviteľská Stepná cesta Stodolova Stolárska S ná cesta Strmé sady Strojnícka Stromová Stropkovská St zdná Suchá Suché mýto Suchohradská Súkennícka Súľovs a Svoradova Svrčia Syslia **ŠŠŠ** Šafárikovo nám. Šafranov :ínska Ševčenkova Šiesta Šikmá Šinkovská Šintavská Šíp ortová Šrobárovo nám. Šťastná Štedrá Štefana Králika Šte ská Štúrova Štvrtá Štymdlova Šulekova Šumavská Šuň icova Táborská Tajovského Talichova Tallerova Tatranská locvičná Tematínska Teplická Terchovská Teslova Tešedíkc Tokajícka Tolstého Tománkova Tomanova Tomášikova To išovská Trenčianska Treskoňova Tretia Trhová Trnavská ce a Tuhovská Tulipánová Tupého Tupolevova Turbínová Tur Údernícka Údolná Ulliská Uhorková Uhrova Uhrovecká ca Planét Ulica svornosti Úprkova Úradnícka Uránová Urb :rého V záhradách Vajanského náb. Vajnorská Valachovej savská Vavilovova Vavrínová Vazovova Važecká Vážska V pvá Vetvárska Vetvová Vidlicová Viedenská cesta Vietnam Vlárska Vlastenecké nám. Vlčie Hrdlo Vlčkova Vodný vrch :ňanská Vrbenského Vŕbová Vresová Vretenová Vrchná okohorská Vyšehradská Vyšná Výtvarná Vývojová **WWW** nicou Za tehelňou Záborského Zadunajská cesta Záhoracka

SAD JANKA KRÁĽA I don't do enough walking. When I do manage to shift myself, I cross the river and stroll through Sad Janka Kráľa – one of the biggest green spaces in town. It can be a bit depressing in winter, but in summer it's a great place to be – very chilled-out. You can get there by crossing the big concrete Novy Most Bridge, with its crazy revolving UFO restaurant at the top of one of its pillars (which serves bad food but has great views).

SLAVIN AND HORSKY PARK This is a cemetery at the top of the hill behind the castle, with amazing views over the city. It has a monument in memory of Soviet casualties in the liberation of Bratislava in the Second World War. On summer nights it's quite romantic – you can sit under the monument looking at the lights below. North of Slavin is the very spacious Horsky Park (Forest Park) which has a little cafe and a pub, and is a civilised place for a walk.

DEVIN CASTLE This is one of Slovakia's historical icons, and is basically the remains of an old fortification with commanding views of the Danube and the Morava rivers. It's located 25km away from the Old Town, surrounded by green hills. You can get there by bus.

WILSONIC MARCH A festival of electronic music, situated in the park in the heart of the city. It's a small festival with a wonderful atmosphere, and all the designers and artists in Bratislava congregate there. www.wilsonic.sk

PECHA KUCHA NIGHTS A regular event that I often go to. It's a great place to meet people working in culture and the arts and is very popular. www.pechakucha.sk

INTERNATIONAL FILM FESTIVAL BRATISLAVA DECEMBER A festival featuring films from around the world – particularly films by new directors and independent movies. It takes place at the Aupark Shopping Centre across the Danube from the Old Town. www.iffbratislava.sk

beautiful sky

PLEČNIK'S STADIUM

3.5A to Wien

1 hour to Alps

Park

Railway Station

Tivoli Pond

FRANCESCO ROBBA

Slovenska AVENUE

CESTA

Mr. Josef Plečnik

Edvard Ravn

Main Square

LJUBLJANICA RIVER

2¾ hour to Venice

OLD TOWN

lift

GRAD

FRENCH REVOLUTION SQUARE

Castle Hill

HAPPY En

ZOISOVA C.

City Do

Good morning

KARLOVŠKA CESTA

LJUBLJANICA

1 HOUR TO THE SEASIDE

SWAMP

TRNOVSKA CESTA

R. JENKO'S
Ljubljana

I have lived in Ljubljana most of my life and it's a city I really love. There is a great balance between nature and the bustle of the city. It's not a huge city, but there's no shortage of things to do. There is a flea market on weekends, workshops for children, galleries and independent theatres that hold open-air performances. There are over 40 festivals going on in summer and a Christmas fair in the winter. Castle Hill rises above the city and offers a great view.

One of the most amazing attractions of Ljubljana is its central food market (travellers claim that it's the best in the world). I especially like going there in summer, when it becomes a feast of colours and smells. The market – and most of the city centre – was designed by greatest Slovenian architect Jože Plecnik, who studied under the Austrian architect Otto Wagner. He left an enormous mark on the city with his civic structures – including the Triple Bridges (Tromostovje), Žale cemetery, and office buildings such as Triglav Insurance Company Palace, which has an incredible trapezoidal staircase adorned with marble columns.

There's a lot of development going on in Ljubljana as it begins to reconfigure itself as a modern European metropolis. It's got a very strong local character but is also only 250km from Venice and 380km from Vienna, lying at the crossroads of Mediterranean, Slavic and German cultures. It has a lot of really interesting architecture, and this is going to be a focal point for development. There are a few really beautiful Art Nouveau buildings, and these, as well as those designed by the city's signature architects – Plecnik, Fabiani, Šubic and Ravnikar (check them out!) – will be preserved, whilst new spaces are simultaneously developed by contemporary Slovenian and international architects. The vibrant Old Town is gradually reshaping and becoming an even more popular hangout place, and on the opposite side of the Ljubljanica River, which runs through the city, the new Centre of Contemporary Arts is becoming the hub of a buzzing art district.

If green spaces are more your cup of tea, the Alps are only an hour away to the west (for skiing), and the magic Venetian gem of Piran is an hour to the south. The city also has two big parks (Tivoli and Žale). To put it simply, it's got something for everyone.

CELICA HOSTEL Once a military prison, this building was renovated by more than 80 Slovenian and international artists, and converted into a youth hostel in 2003. Despite its popularity (Rough Guide put it in the top 25 places to stay in the world, and the Lonely Planet described it as hippest hostel #1), it is still worth staying at. Metelkova ulica, www.souhostel.com

FLUXUS HOSTEL This small, friendly hostel is very well located in an old apartment building next to Nama department store in the middle of the city centre. It only has 16 beds and one double, so worth booking in advance. Tomšiceva 4, www.fluxus-hostel.com

ANTIQ HOTEL Styled with Biedermeier chairs and wallpapers and old Ljubljana newspapers, this place borders on kitsch, but is nonetheless very cosy and welcoming. Rooms range from budget to superior, and it is excellently located in the old part of the city centre. Gornji trg 3, www.antiqhotel.si

PLACES TO STAY

XXI This place is run by an architect friend of mine, whose love is food and music. A concert piano is free for anyone to use, and so impromptu concerts are common events. Ingredients for wonderful dishes are passionately sourced directly from local farmers and fishermen. Rimska Cesta 21

RIVER HOUSE Excellent ambiance on the river banks, friendly staff, funky music and great food. Very nice cocktails too. Gallusovo Nabrežje 31, www.riverhouse.si

RESTAVRACIJA JB This is a glamorous restaurant specialising in modern European cuisine. It is in a Plecnik building rich with Art Nouveau elements. Miklošiceva 17, www.jb-slo.com

AS RESTAURANT AND LOUNGE Hidden in a passage within the pedestrian area of the city centre, this place never sleeps. I've had many an evening in the party venue in the basement, and it's a guaranteed good time. This is a slow-food fish restaurant, and it's full of surprises, if you have time to enjoy them. Knafljev prehod, Copova ulica 5A, www.gostilnaas.si

NOBEL BUREK A small kiosk close to the main railway station churning out steaming hot burek (cheese or meat in puff pastry) for those who like to do their fine dining in the street. Excellent value, excellent fast food. Miklošiceva 30

PLACES TO EAT

BIKOFE BiKoFe – literally meaning 'Would you like a coffee?' in local slang – is a small urban art scene oriented bar. There's always a nice mix of designers, artists, musicians and students, most of whom know each other – and the waiters. There are monthly art exhibitions, and some evenings DJs play underground music. Židovska steza 2

SAX PU I really like popping by this little place. It's great for jazz lovers and is especially nice in summer, when you can have a beer in the garden. Decorated with murals and graffiti. Eipprova ulica 7

ŽMAUC The name of this bar is short for 'Od Žmauca sosed pa ud brata prjatu' which translates as 'Žmauc's neighbour and brother's friend'. I think that says it all. Admire the painted facade and meet interesting and/or weird regulars there. It's been 'the place' for more than a decade. Has Wi-Fi. Rimska 21

CAFEE OPEN Gay-friendly and generally friendly place. Foreign newspapers are available and they organise occasional concerts and literary evenings. Snacks and coffees are really good. Has Wi-Fi. Hrenova ulica 19, www.open.si

CAJNICA CHA This is the best place if you want a decent tea of any sort (and I mean ANY sort) although I sometimes find it a bit too crowded. Great snack lunch too. Stari trg 3, www.cha.si

BAR SLAŠCICARNA VIKI This is a very laid-back coffee house that looks like it's come from another era. Nothing has changed here for decades, but their cakes are delicious. It's a God-forgotten-place, but somehow always busy with customers. Ziherlova 2

Beauty is balance.

ALTERNATIVE CULTURE

METELKOVA MESTO This newly-revamped centre for alternative culture is a member of Trans Europe Halles, and it stretches all the way from the corner of Metelkova Street to Masarykova Street near the main railway station. It is a creative hub for urban culture and graffiti artists, and offers studio space for artists and musicians. A diverse crowd hangs out there, ranging from high school kids, to students, local artists, musicians and fans of various subcultures (punk, metal, reggae, you name it). It houses several clubs: Menza Pri Koritu, Gala Hala, Club Gromki, Chanell Zero, Jalla Jalla, Teahouse at Marici's, a gay club called Tiffany, and a lesbian club called Monokel. During the day there is an independent political social library and info shop, but the place really gets going around midnight, and keeps rocking till the morning. Metelkova City, www.metelkova.org

KLUB K4 This legendary underground club was the first of its kind in Ljubljana, opening in 1989 and introducing punk, rock, funk and disco to the then socialist city. Many famous musicians started out here, and it was the city's first gay-friendly club. The interior has been recently redone and its rough industrial look is really well designed. At K4 you'll find VJs spinning their visuals and new, alternative styles of mainstream underground music. Pink Saturdays are regular gay nights. Kersnikova 4, www.klubk4.org

SUB SUB This alternative nightclub has a vibrant live programme. It features some fine visual artists as well as internationally renowned music acts and DJs. Hala Tivoli, www.subsub.si

Basically, the city centre is packed with small designers' shops (some of which are part of the designers' studios): Cliché, Almira Sadar, Vodeb, Devetka, Draž, Butanoga handmade shoes, Marjeta Grošelj's bags and Akultura are all worth looking at and all within walking distance of one another.

ROGAŠKA STORE An exceptionally well-designed glassware shop with fantastic presentation, music and lighting as well as excellently trained staff. Mestni trg 22, www.rogaska-crystal.com

CUKRCEK A chocolate and sweet shop (its name translates as 'Sweetie'). Friendly staff and handmade chocolates make it a great destination at the end of an afternoon walk. Mestni trg 11, www.cukrcek.si

ARS GALLERY Sells interesting paintings and jewellery by independent designers and artists, and also art supplies. Jurcicev trg 2

SMET UMET This is the shop of a cultural-ecological society, which designs products from used and recycled materials. Malgajeva 7, www.smetumet.com

POZITIVE Independent design shop. A must visit. Zrinjskega ul 5, www.pozitive.si

SREDA Recently opened designers' shop with innovative Slovene designs. You can buy everything that you see in the store, from a key chain to the table. Passage Ajdovšcina, www.sreda.si

ARTIST MARKET On certain days in the summer, an artists' market is added onto the flea market that takes place every Sunday morning in the old part of the town. Cevljarski most, Gornji trg

BEŽIGRAJSKA GALLERY This is part of the City Gallery and they house a big collection of visual and concrete poetry. Good idea to make an appointment. Vodovodna 3, www.mestna-galerija.si

NATIONAL AND UNIVERSITY LIBRARY Rokopisni Oddelek (rare books and manuscripts) has a splendid collection and a vast array of Slovenian posters. The building itself is very interesting. Make an appointment. Turjaška 1, www.nuk.uni-lj.si

ARCHITECTURAL MUSEUM This museum caters not only for architecture, but also for graphic and industrial design. Archives cover most of Slovene graphic design history. Interesting exhibitions and lecture series. Fužinski grad, Pot na Fužine 2

GALERIJA GLESIA A glass gallery founded by contemporary artist Tanja Pak, which holds contemporary glass exhibitions. Precna 6, www.glesia.si

GALLERY T5 This newly-renovated tobacco factory is now a concept gallery for contemporary design and architecture. Pecha Kucha nights are regularly held here. Tobacna ul 5, www.t-5.si

KUD FRANCE PREŠEREN This is an institution in itself. It holds cultural events, exhibitions, experimental theatre, street performances and workshops for diverse age groups. Their summer Trnfest Festival is a definite must. Karunova ul 14, www.kud-fp.si

ŠKUC GALLERY One of the pillars of non-governmental culture in Slovenia for over 30 years now, it has become a prominent international art centre for exhibitions, events, publishing and documentation. Still fresh as ever. Stari trg 21, www.galerija.skuc-drustvo.si

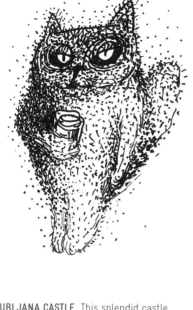

BIENNALE NEODVISNE ILUSTRACIJE
Biennial of independent illustration.
www.bienaleneodvisneilustracije.com

MESEC OBLIKOVANJA Organised
by Foundation Big it has grown into
a big design event. Loads of events
in diverse locations throughout the
city usually in the month of October.
www.mesecoblikovanja.com

**BIENNIAL OF VISUAL COMMUNICATION
ARTS** Organised by the Brumen
Foundation, this is the most important
national competition of visual
communication. Usually takes place
in autumn. www.brumen.org

TIPO BRDA SOCIETY A society which
organises type design workshops and
exhibitions. www.tipobrda.com

LJUBLJANA CASTLE This splendid castle
offers a great view of the whole basin.
The castle complex is very interesting and
includes several renovated buildings which
hold regular exhibitions.

CLASSIC ARCHITECTURE To get an overview
of the local architecture, start your walk at
the Plecnik's brilliantly designed market at
Plecnikova tržnica, then head towards the
Triple Bridge (Tromostovje), turn towards
City House (Mestna Hiša) and explore the
little cobblestone streets: Mestni trg, Stari
trg, Gornji trg. The architecture ranges
from Baroque to Art Nouveau.

TOURIST BOATS To see the city from a
different angle, pick up one of the tourist
boats that leave from Tromostovje.

ŽALE CEMETERY AND TIVOLI PARK Two
really special green spaces that can
provide a tranquil break from the city.

KINODVOR MESTNI KINO This is a proper
European cinema institution. Recently
renovated, it's the place for cineastes
and connoisseurs. Kolodvorska 13,
www.kinodvor.org

ASTRID STAVRO'S
BARCELONA

The best way to get into Barcelona is by plane. The view of the sea, the beaches, and the city from above is stunning (tip: make sure you sit on the right side of the plane to get the best views). Flying into the city also helps you understand its geography - with the sea on one side and the Tibidabo mountain crowning the city on the other. If you keep this in mind, it's quite easy to find your way around; the mountain is uptown, the sea is downtown.

Barcelona is reasonably large, and is divided into various areas. The old medieval town known as 'Ciutat Vella' is located downtown. It is split into four quarters: Barceloneta, known for its sandy beaches and restaurants and cafes along the boardwalk, Casc Antic, which includes Borne and La Ribera, Barri Gòtic, the medieval quarter, and Raval, formerly known as 'Barrio Chino'. Ciutat Vella is where most tourist attractions - besides Gaudí - are, which makes it the most packed area of Barcelona regardless of the time of the year. It is also the most beautiful part of the city, full of great restaurants, boutiques, museums, Gothic arches and Roman ruins.

The Eixample quarter is the Modernist quarter. It begins where the medieval city walls end. Designed in the middle of the 19th Century by Ildefons Cerdà, the Eixample is an enormous grid of rectangular blocks in a continuing repeating layout. The city's most famous examples of Catalan Modernism can be found here - La Pedrera, Casa Batlló, and la Sagrada Familia. Gràcia is the other main district, a former independent town that joined the city in the 20th Century. Gràcia still maintains a 'pueblo' character with its small houses and life lived in public squares. It is the most distinctively Catalan neighbourhood to be found in easy walking distance of the centre. Less well-known but equally fascinating is the Poblenou suburb, which is Barcelona's equivalent of London's Shoreditch - an industrial district filled with warehouses and factories, some of which are now trendy lofts, and others which are derelict. It's home to many artists and designers.

Two languages are spoken in Barcelona: Catalan and Spanish. For political reasons, most signs are indicated only in Catalan. The language issue is a sensitive one – while adding richness and culture to the city, it is also part of a larger debate concerning Catalonia's relationship to Spain and its desire for autonomy.

HOTEL OMM This top-end hotel is the creation of architect Juli Capella and interior designers Sandra Tarruella and Isabel López, and is located in Barcelona's fashionable Passeig de Gràcia area. It is spacious, warm and totally unique. It also shares the block with renowned architect Antonio Gaudi's buildings La Pedrera and Casa Mila. Rosselló 265, 08008 Barcelona, www.hotelomm.es

BANYS ORIENTALS The success of this pioneer boutique hotel is partly due to its location (El Born), and its motto should be: 'great value for money'. It's set in a 19th Century mansion with spacious, well-designed rooms that would not be out of place in a hotel four times as expensive. The hotel shares a premises with the classic Barcelonese restaurant Senyor Parellada. Argenteria 37, 08003 Barcelona, www.hotelbanysorientals.com

PARK HOTEL This laid-back hotel is a unique example of mid-20th Century Rationalist architecture. The foyer has a sleek, mosaic-tile bar. Barcelona's best-kept secret is a room with a big terrace on the top floor. Marqués de l'Argentera 11, 08003 Barcelona, www.parkhotelbarcelona.com

CASA CAMPER This hip hotel (run by the guys who own the shoe company of the same name) is a rather odd hybrid of indulgence and asceticism that feels like Julian Schnabel meets Mother Teresa. But somehow it works. Carrer Elisabets 11, 08001 Barcelona, www.camper.com

CAL PEP Iconic and boisterous Cal Pep is a permanent feeding frenzy and has been this way since forever. It has Barcelona's best and freshest selection of tapas, and is popular with visitors and locals alike. The door opens at 8pm but make sure you get there at 7.45. The best spot: the left end side of the 'barra'. Plaça de les Olles 8, 08003 Barcelona, www.calpep.com

ELS PESCADORS This is THE (with capital letters) fish restaurant in Barcelona. It is conveniently located slightly off the main drag in the working-class suburb of Poblenou. In summer, the restaurant has a lovely terrace looking out over a forgotten little traffic-free, tree-lined square. Plaça Prim 1, 08005 Barcelona, www.elspescadors.com

LA TORNA The temptation will be to eat next door, in the hip and flashy Mercado Santa Catarina by the Tragaluz Group. But this little circular 'barra' on the edge of the market is where the local connoisseurs go to enjoy fresh fish and meat straight from the market. Don't forget to look at the Mercado's colourful ceiling on your way out, designed by Italian architect Benedetta Tagliabue. Inside the Mercado de Santa Caterina, Av de Francesc Cambó, 08003 Barcelona

EL XIRINGUITO DE ESCRIBÀ Definitely the best place for eating a good paella and marisco right on the beach. Keep some space for the amazing desserts. Litoral Mar 42, Playa Bogatell, 08005 Barcelona, www.escriba.es

RESTAURANTE AGULLERS This is our studio's favourite restaurant. Some of us eat there every day of the week. As a matter of fact, Ana is possibly the most regular customer Agullers ever had…. Delicious homemade food at affordable prices. Agullers 8, 08003 Barcelona

EL VASO DE ORO This noisy and crowded cruise ship-style tapas bar is literally a long and narrow corridor. To find a seat along the 'barra' you need to actually leave the place and walk back in through one of its numerous doors. Balboa 6, 08003 Barcelona

ALASTRUEY This place hasn't changed an inch in the past 50 years. It serves traditional cuisine using fresh produce from the market. Mercaders 24, 08003 Barcelona, www.restaurantalastruey.com

ENVALIRA Profoundly traditional restaurant with moderate prices and delicious food. Try the rice dishes and the superb cannelloni. Plaza del Sol 13, 08012 Barcelona

EL PARAGUAYO Extraordinary fat, juicy steaks and hot yucca near the beach. Parc 1, 08002 Barcelona

EL TOSSAL If you find this restaurant in a guide – which is very unlikely – you'll read that they cook what is available in the market. But this is inaccurate. The only waitress is the wife of the owner, a hunter. What you eat is what the husband caught the prior weekend in the forests of northern Spain. Try the excellent homemade stews and the speciality of the house, wild boar civet. The decor looks like something from David Mamet's movie *State and Main*. Tordera 12, 08012 Barcelona, www.eltossalbcn.com

CARBALLEIRA I love the old-fashioned decor in this Galician restaurant with its enormous old fish tank in the entrance. It serves great seafood and one of its longest-serving waiters was once a model in one of Camper's magazines – you'll recognise him for his Fernando Trueba-ish looks. Reina Cristina 3, 08003 Barcelona

IL GIARDINETTO RESTAURANT Designed by architects Correa & Milà, it won the FAD interior design award back in 1974, but it is no less cutting-edge today. The two levels are dominated by columns with painted branch motifs and the walls are decorated with foliage cutouts. It's an old-school restaurant serving delicious Italian food, and is an all-time favourite of the uptown arts crowd. La Granada del Penedès 22, 08006 Barcelona

BARS

BAR MARSELLA This is the oldest bar in Barcelona, opened in 1820, and was a favourite haunt of Ernest Hemingway. Today it is a packed, boisterous place that attracts a young crowd. The ceiling is stained caramel from decades of cigarette smoke, the ornate chandeliers flicker feebly and the floors are beautiful mosaics. Carrer de Sant Pau 65, 08001 Barcelona

GINGER A 70s stylish, split-level cocktail, wine and tapas bar on a beautiful Barri Gótic square. It's on the same street as our studio so you could say its our local pub – I guess it's lucky that the cocktail list and the tapas are both excellent. Lledó 2, 08002 Barcelona

LA CONCHA Located in a picturesquely dingy street just off Las Ramblas, this popular Raval bar has a Moroccan gay kitsch vibe. Its name is a clever play on words meaning both a shell and a slang term for female genitalia, and it is an authentic slice of bohemia, with yellow-red lighting, a low ceiling and a sexually ambiguous crowd. Guàrdia 14, 08001 Barcelona

PIPA CLUB This pipe club is in a labyrinthine apartment on the second floor of an old house in Plaza Real. Buzz at the door to be let in. Beautifully decorated old vitrines containing an impressive pipe collection and old tobacco tin boxes decorate the walls. The place has a good atmosphere and is certainly very different from your average bar. Plaza Real 3, 08002 Barcelona, www.bpipaclub.com

BOADAS Located in the middle of Las Ramblas, this 1940s cocktail bar with no tables retains its original charm. Tallers 1, 08002 Barcelona

IDEAL An English style, old-fashioned 'cockteleria' that has the biggest selection of whiskies in Europe. They also make the best, and I mean the best gin and tonics. Aribau 89, 08036 Barcelona

GIMLET A great place for cocktails. It is a crowded, little, and lovely little bar. Try the eponymous gimlet. Rec 24, 08021 Barcelona

LORING ART Bookshop specialising in contemporary art. Gravina 8, 08001 Barcelona, www.loring-art.com

LA CENTRAL Barcelona's best bookstore, and one of the studio's main clients, La Central, stocks everything from McSweeney's to small edition literary gems. There are a few branches around the city. The Raval branch is in the former chapel of the Casa de la Misericordia. The architecture is stunning and the lunch menu is delicious. Calle Elisabets 8, 08001 Barcelona, www.lacentral.com

VINÇÓN Fernando Amat, Vinçón's founder and director, still holds walk-in sessions for people with fresh ideas and interesting products every Tuesday afternoon. This reflects the philosophy of his fantastic design emporium, which is filled with the best Spain has to offer. Housed in the former home of artist Ramón Casas, the window displays alone are worth seeing. Passeig de Gràcia 96, 08008 Barcelona, www.vincon.com

LA BOLSERA Art supplies, party and carnival gear, wrapping and packing materials, and a place to hang out when looking for inspiration. Calle de Xuclà 15, 08001 Barcelona, www.labolsera.com

RAIMA Raima is the most famous stationers in Barcelona. Located in a beautiful old building in the Gothic Quarter, the store is well stocked, but has very rude and obnoxiously slow staff. Calle Comtal 27, 08002 Barcelona, www.raima.com.es

SERVEI ESTACIÓ Bricolage paradise over six floors, each floor specialising in something else. It is by far the most inspiring and messy shop in Barcelona. Aragó 270-272, 08007 Barcelona, www.serveiestacio.com

GRANJA MASCARBÓ Don't expect to find anything to taste or buy in this old granja (milk bar). You will only find Montse, an old woman who will update you on the local gossip of this beautiful street in the Barri Gótic. The sign on the entrance is a museum piece itself. Lledó 78, 08001 Barcelona

SAN ANTONIO MARKET On Sundays between 8am and 3pm, just outside the food market, you'll find this specialist old books and coins market. Ronda Sant Pau/Carrer Comte d'Urgell, 8015 Barcelona

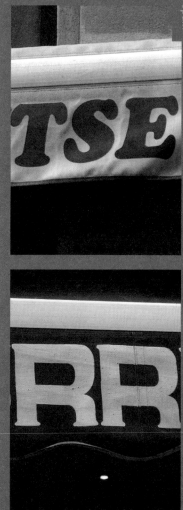

SONAR JUNE A three day 'festival of advanced music and multimedia art', which offers round-the-clock concerts and interesting exhibitions. www.sonar.es

SANT JORDI 23RD APRIL St Jordi is the Catalan equivalent of Valentines Day. Traditionally men give women roses and women give men books. It is one of the most popular and interesting celebrations in Catalonia.

LA MERCÈ 23-27TH SEPTEMBER This is the festival of festivals. There are hundreds of activities from street concerts to acrobatics, dancing, performance art, parades and correfocs (fire runs).

CHILL LAUS A series of laid-back, informal conferences with interesting, cutting edge designers and art related people. www.chilllaus.net

GALLERIES AND CULTURE

CENTRE DE CULTURA CONTEMPORÀNIA DE BARCELONA (CCCB) A great place to discover interesting exhibitions, concerts, courses, lectures, debates and festivals. Montalegre 5, 08001 Barcelona, www.cccb.org

DISSENY HUB BARCELONA The Design Hub Barcelona building is currently being built by architect Oriol Bohigas. In the meantime it's housed in the former textiles museum, and is holding a series of interesting small exhibitions as a warm-up for the opening. Palau de Pedralbes, Av Diagonal 686, 08034 Barcelona, www.dhub-bcn.cat

JOAN MIRÓ MUSEUM A museum dedicated to Joan Miró that hosts interesting temporary exhibitions. The building alone, built by Catalan architect José Luis Sort, who also designed the Maeght Gallery in St.Paul-de-Vence, is worth the trek. Inside the Parc de Montjüic, 08038 Barcelona, www.fundaciomiro-bcn.org

CINEMA VERDI Screens a wide range of mainly independent international films in original versions with subtitles. Verdi 32, 08012 Barcelona, www.cines-verdi.com

There is plenty of interesting architecture in Barcelona beyond the Modernista buildings that it's famous for. These are a few of my favourites.

MIES VAN DER ROHE PAVILION
Designed as the German Pavilion for the 1929 Barcelona Internacional Exhibiton, this key piece of 20th Century architecture was disassembled, and then reassembled in 1983 on its original site in Montjüic by Oriol Bohigas and a team architects. Av Marquès de Comillas s/n, 08038 Barcelona, www.miesbcn.com

MARITIME MUSEUM
I'm not that interested in the contents of the museum, but the building itself is an amazing civil Gothic building and a Mies van der Rohe favourite. Av de les Drassanes s/n, 08001 Barcelona, www.mmb.cat

MUNTANER 342
A building designed by Catalan architect Josep Lluis Sert, who also designed the Joan Miro Museum. Carrer de Muntaner 342, 08022 Barcelona

MONTJUIC CEMETERY
This spectacular cemetery is the final resting place of Joan Miró, musician Isaac Albéniz and the painter Santiago Rusiñol amongst many others. Overlooking the sea, it is Barcelona's biggest cemetery, and is a great place to get lost. Mare de Déu de Port 54-58, 08038 Barcelona

PALO ALTO
Palo Alto looks like a beautiful, decadent Tuscan villa that has been miraculously transported to the middle of the industrial district of Poblenou. It houses several design and architecture studios including that of illustrator Javier Mariscal, as well as a nice canteen. Pellaires 30-38, 08019 Barcelona, www.paloaltobcn.org

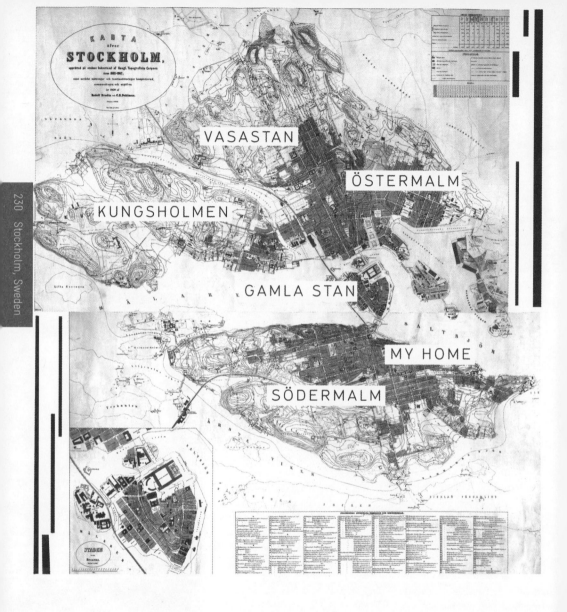

VASASTAN

ÖSTERMALM

KUNGSHOLMEN

GAMLA STAN

MY HOME

SÖDERMALM

STOCKHOLM MINUS SUBURBS

NILLE SVENSSON'S STOCKHOLM

Depending on your flight route, when you land at Stockholm Airport, you pass over nothing but woodland punctuated by the occasional farmhouse. In winter especially, the landscape can seem so solemn and empty. Whenever I have spent any length of time abroad, I always think what a contrast this is to the urban sprawl you usually fly over when landing in a capital city. A friend of mine always talks about how provincial Stockholm is, and how despite the recent awakening of cosmopolitan sophistication in the city, 'we are all just one generation away from being farmers'.

Stockholm is situated at the narrow passage that connects the big inland sea of Mälaren and the saltier waters of the Östersjön, or the Baltic Sea as it is internationally called. It was initally founded as a fortification for keeping control of this passage, and the 'Innerstaden' (Inner City) is still based around those islands on which it was established. This area is divided into five neighbourhoods: Gamla Stan, Norrmalm, Östermalm, Kungsholmen, Södermalm and Vasastan. Each of these has its own distinct character, which can be crudely sketched out as follows: Gamla Stan is the oldest district, Norrmalm is the downtown area, Östermalm the upper class neigbourhood, Södermalm the poor-turned-arty area, Kungsholmen the non-descript-area-which-everybody-thinks-will-turn-arty-but-it-just-doesn't-seem-to-happen and Vasastan the young urban professional area.

Having said that, the socio-economics of Sweden don't really allow for a lot of fundamental differences in residential areas (although, unfortunately this is rapidly changing). What differences there are, are far more noticeable when comparing the Inner City and the suburbs. The general trend now is that "gentrified" Stockholm is growing southwards, especially along the red subway line, by assimilating areas that were hitherto considered suburbs.

Oh, yes, there are three more islands in the Inner City worth mentioning – Skeppsholmen, which is where the Museum of Modern Art is, Djurgården, which is a big park/recreation area, and Långholmen, which is Södermalm's Djurgården.

Finally, if after reading this guide, you decide that Stockholm does not seem to be your kind of place, please watch the forgotten, but entrancing Paul Newman film – *The Prize*. It might just make you change your mind.

I have always thought that asking someone about hotels in the city they live in is begging for an ill-informed answer. Let me tell you straight away that I have never stayed at any of these places and honestly have no clear idea of what to expect.

AF CHAPMAN An old sailing ship converted to a hostel. If you're a born Stockholmer you would probably think this choice is a bit unimaginative since it is such a well-known landmark, but objectively it is hard to beat the location and price. Probably a good thing to book well in advance. Skeppsholmen, 11149 Stockholm, www.stfturist.se

LYDMAR Low-key, fancy, central as hell. If you are allergic to art photography – steer clear! Sturegatan 10, 11435 Stockholm, www.lydmar.com

COLUMBUS A kind of up-market hostel/hotel located on Södermalm. My girlfriend's parents always stay here when they are in Stockholm, partly because we live next door, and it seems to be a nice place. Tjärhovsgatan 11, 11621 Stockholm, www.columbus.se

FINNHAMN This is a good option for an overnight/weekend trip. It's a huge old summerhouse converted into a hostel (ok, so I like hostels), on a beautiful and accessible island on the skerries east of the city. It has a nice restaurant, which is always surprisingly busy compared to the calm tranquillity of the area. You can also rent your own cabin on the island, and I once arranged a very successful bachelor party here with the aid of the people who run it. 13025 Ingmarsö, www.finnhamn.se

THE DAYS OF THE BOUTIQUE HOTELS
ARE FINALLY OVER

PLACES TO STAY

CLARION Let's face it, the days of the boutique hotels are over. Nowadays when I go somewhere I want a hotel with lots of rooms and a stimulating hubbub in the foyer – a constant stream of people, conversations in exotic languages, taxis coming and going, fights between rockstars and model girlfriends etc. If you book me into one more room with a dark wood panel behind the bed and a faucet that comes directly out of the wall, I'm staying home. The Clarion Hotels, one in the southern part and one in the Inner City offers a nice way to kick the boutique hotel habit, being a sort of in-between kind of place. The southern Clarion calls itself an 'art hotel', which I guess is the new 'design hotel'. Ringvägen 98, 10460 Stockholm, www.clarionstockholm.com

Of course there are more places than this. Damn this guide writing thing is so hard. It's hard to find good seafood or good Asian food in Stockholm, but apart from that there is a lot to choose from. Booking in advance is highly recommended, especially weekends. If you are low on cash (as we freelance designers always are) check prices before you go to save yourself an unwanted surprise. If you go to a restaurant, cafe or bar and you see a little dragon-logo, it tells you that the place has won a local culinary award called 'gulddraken'. Guess who designed that logo?

EN FLICKA PÅ GAFFELN Very nice local eatery in the northern part of the city, serving traditional continental cuisine. Frejgatan 79, 11326 Stockholm, www.enflickapagaffeln.se

CLOUD NINE A new, carefully designed restaurant near the northern Clarion Hotel that has a special dessert room. One of the owners is an avid surfer who has run other restaurants in Stockholm and his crowd of customers are bound to follow him here. Linnégatan 89E, 10055 Stockholm, www.cloudnine.se

MATKULTUR Stockholm is small and nothing is really off the beaten track and hidden for very long, but normally you would probably not venture this far east on Södermalm. This restaurant, and the bar next door have a nice atmosphere and the bar includes what is probably the smallest art gallery in town. The menu changes regularly and the quality of the food varies but the ambition is high, with a kind of 'world-food' profile. Erstagatan 21, 11636 Stockholm, www.matkultur.nu

LANDET Ok, I lied. This restaurant is off the beaten track, but as it happens to be on the designer-student beaten track, located right next to the art and design university Konstfack, it is relevant to include in this guide. It's a popular place with a nice restaurant on the ground floor and a too-cool-for-art-school micro-venue upstairs. LM Ericssons väg 27, 12637 Hägersten, www.landet.nu

BERNS ASIATISKA Maybe the best modern Chinese food in town. It's in a big 19th Century building in the heart of the city that also houses a hotel, theatre, bar and club. To my taste this place is hopelessly uncosy, but nice if you like über-designed open spaces. Berzelii Park, 10325 Stockholm, www.berns.se

ROXY One of the few places I regularly frequent. Nice food with a sort of modern Spanish twist and a great bar. They have also taken over the basement next door and sometimes host events and club nights there. Nytorget 6, 11640 Stockholm, www.roxysofo.se

TEATERGRILLEN Top-notch, top-dollar, with food by top chef Tore Wretman, and a very nice interior that hasn't changed since 1968. Nybrogaten 3, 11434 Stockholm, www.teatergrillen.se

ALLMÄNNA GALLERIET This restaurant/gallery is located a few floors up in an industrial building, behind an anonymous entrance. Ever since smoking was banned, there can be a weird smell in the bar late at night. This has something to do with the plumbing. Kronobergsgatan 2, 11233 Stockholm, www.ag925.se

LE ROUGE Fairly recently opened, this place has a fantastic ambience and attracts a lot of media-type people. Me like a lot. They say the food is great too, but on the pricey side. It's in the Old Town so check out the old houses on your way here. Österlånggatan 17, 11131 Stockholm, www.lerouge.se

INDIGO Someone once called this 'the only bar in Stockholm'. It's got a European vibe and the DJs are really good, playing music your grandparents warned your parents about. 200m further down, on the other side of the street, the restaurant Ljunggrents has a really cool roof terrace. In the summer you can eat there and then go to Indigo. Götgatan 19, 11646 Stockholm

TRANAN The problem with all city guides is that the information can get dated. But as far as hangouts go, I think it is safe to say that this bar and also Riche (below) will continue to attract the same type of cool crowd for at least a generation to come. Karlbergsvägen 14, 11327 Stockholm, www.tranan.se

RICHE A popular watering hole for the arty and beautiful (who would sacrifice arty if they had to give up one of them). Sometimes they have exhibitions that make you go 'hmm', but it's all part of the charm. To say 'I ended up at Riche' is a way of saying that you had a good night out (if you're 35+, otherwise it is a way of saying that something went wrong). Birger Jarlsgatan 4, Stockholm, 11434, www.riche.se

GONDOLEN This bar is suspended beneath the Katarinahissen walkway, 30m above the water. The view and cocktails are very nice, but it's not the kind of place you want to hang around in all night. Best for early drinks or for lunch on weekdays. Stadsgården 6, 10465 Stockholm, www.eriks.se

THERE IS A NICE VIEW
FROM GONDOLEN

WE ENDED UP AT RICHE

KONSTIG A slightly run-of-the mill design bookshop that has some good stock. The lady who runs it has a bit of an attitude, which makes it cooler than some. There's a sneaker shop next door if you're into that kind of thing. Asogatan 124, 11624 Stockholm, www.konstig.se

PAPER CUT A bit like Konstig, but more focused on DVDs and magazines. It's located on a street that is becoming more and more interesting shopping-wise, so browse around…. Krukmakargatan 3, 11851 Stockholm, www.papercutshop.se

MICKES SKIVOR Second-hand vinyl/CD place with an excellent assortment. Maybe not the best in Stockholm but definitely one of the better. Good starting point for a stroll through the area west of this street where there are lots of cafes and generally a nice ambience. Långholmsgatan 20, 11733 Stockholm, www.mickes-cdvinyl.se

RAINBOW MUSIC If you take your second-hand vinyl as seriously as I do, forget the Inner City hipster-traps and go outside the city to this vinyl lair. I can spend hours here. Höstvägen 7, Solna, www.rainbowmusic.nu

10 GRUPPEN Probably as close to Marimekko as Swedish design will ever get without lawsuits happening. Some of the stuff is really nice.Götgatan 25, 11646 Stockholm, www.tiogruppen.com

PUB This classical department store has undergone a recent makeover. It's divided into independent shops and concepts, with an emphasis on Scandinavian fashion. Two that I particularly like are +46 and Aplace. Hötorget, 11157 Stockholm, www.pub.se

KONSTNÄRERNAS CENTRALKÖP Hard to find, but one of the best places to buy art supplies. It's actually run by an artists' collective and you can become a member. For more graphic design-related stuff try Matton downtown. Fiskargatan 1, 11620 Stockholm, www.konstnarernas.se

BLACK MARKET Serious fashion shop with both local and international stuff (including one of my favourites, Peter Jensen). Located in the gallery area in Vasastan. Eriksgatan 79, 11332 Stockholm, www.blackmarketsthlm.se

SERIESLUSSEN COMIC STRIP Magazines are one of my main sources of inspiration – encapsulating a moment in contemporary culture in a way that books, movies and more 'serious' forms can't. This shop stocks vintage magazines from around the world. If your language skills extend to Swedish with a Finnish accent, you can have fascinating conversations with the owner. The best comics store is located right around the corner. Bellmansgatan 26, 11847 Stockholm

ALEWALDS SPORT I love it when on winter days you see Japanese tourists walking around in huge down parkas, which they bought upon arrival in an attempt to survive the cold. If you need warm clothes or hiking gear, this is the shop to go to. Kungsgatan 32, 11135 Stockholm, www.alewalds.se

SIVLETTO A huge basement/garage type of shop, hairdresser and cafe. They specialise in 1950s rockabilly/tiki/hotrod stuff with an enthusiasm that is genuinely inspiring. Malmgårdsvägen 16-18, 11638 Stockholm, www.sivletto.com

PUB DEPARTMENT STORE AT HÖTORGET

CRYSTAL PALACE Very interesting gallery operating in the art/crafts field. Karlbergsvägen 44, 11362 Stockholm, www.crystalpalace.se

HUDIKSVALLSGATAN A building containing a cluster of galleries. They usually synchronise opening nights (Thursdays), and combined with nearby Crystal Palace you can get a lot of art in one evening. Hudiksvallsgatan 6-8, 11330 Stockholm

INGER MOLIN This was one of the first galleries to treat crafts in the same way as art. It always has good shows. Kommendorsgatan 24, 11448 Stockholm, www.galleriingermolin.se

MAGASIN 3 Privately owned art exhibition hall just outside the Inner City. It usually exhibits cutting-edge international art and installations. 1st Floor, Stockholm Konsthall, Frihamnen, 11556 Stockholm, www.magasin3.com

VISNINGSLÄGENHETER Both the City Museum and Nationalmuseet have preserved flats or houses around the city. They are in their original states and provide insight into the daily life of Stockholmers in previous centuries and recent decades. Check the websites for details. www.stadsmuseum.stockholm.se, www.nationalmuseum.se

DANSMUSEET This is a gem. A small museum with an impressive collection of dance-related material from all over the world. The scale model of Legér's costume and scenography work alone is worth the entrance fee. Gustav Adolfs Torg 22–24, 11152 Stockholm, www.dansmuseet.nu

TENSTA KONSTHALL A hip art space located in a faraway suburb that always has good shows. Taxingegränd 10, 16304 Spånga, www.tenstakonsthall.se

PASS THE GRAND HOTEL TO GET TO
THE MUSEUM OF MODERN ART

STADSHUSET The City Hall provides a very nice example of what you can do if you have a trillion bricks lying around. Look closely at how the facades of the tower are slightly curved in order to create the right tension of the form – like a Greek column. I might be wrong, but I've heard the architect Ragnar Östberg forced the builders to tear down the walls and start all over because he was not satisfied with the way the curvature turned out. Ragnar Östbergs Plan 1, 11220 Stockholm

MARKELIUSHUSET If you go to Stadshuset you can continue along the water up to Markeliushuset. It was built as a cooperative, Functionalist dream, housing a restaurant, food store and child care centre all run by the inhabitants of the building. Today there is a very nice lunchtime restaurant and a bakery on the ground level called Petitfrance. The tiny transport elevators that sent goods straight from the kitchen to the apartments are still operating. John Ericssonsgatan 6, 11222 Stockholm

GLOBEN The Stockholm Globe Arena (which is primarily used for ice hockey tournaments) is big, spherical and pretty ugly. But quite cool in a kind of post-modern kitsch way. Arenavägen 60, 12177 Stockholm, www.globearenas.se

SKÄRGÅRDEN If you are in Stockholm in the summer, and you don't take the chance to visit the skerries, there's just something wrong with you. There is a lot of information about the destinations elsewhere but I would reccomend you try Finnhamn, Sandhamn or Rödlöga.

TUNNELBANAN A lot of the subway stations are artistically decorated and some of them are completely commissioned to artists. I think a map can be obtained at the place you buy travelcards. Karlavägen Station is where I got off every morning during the four years I went to art school. There is a huge photo montage on the wall which had and still has a profound effect on me.

NOTICE THE CURVATURE OF
THE STADSHUSET TOWER

I think jogging is one of the best forms of sightseeing. This is a nice route that I often take along the Årstaviken – the waters south of Södermalm – perfect if you're staying at the southern Clarion. Start by running down to the bridge over Hammarbyslussen. Cross it and take an immediate right after the bridge. Continue along the water, behind the boat shop, and then past the two bridges and into the new residential area. If you stick by the water, you'll have to turn right, and then left. Run up the stairs to the big bridge that goes over to the northern side (Södermalm). Take a left after the bridge, run down to the waterfront, turn left and just stay on the path all the way back to the hotel. It's about 8km in total. If you make it in under 44 minutes you are faster than me. The beautiful but strangely red-coloured bridge you pass under is designed by Norman Foster.

MERET AEBERSOLD'S ZURICH

There are lots of things that I love about Zurich – it's compact, accessible, close to nature and has a wealth of culture on offer. I have lived around Europe, and I'm currently working in London, but Zurich is always the place I go back to when I want to relax and enjoy the simple life. It's a very easy place to live.

Zurich has many different faces: it is divided into 12 districts, called Kreise, each containing one or two neighbourhoods with their own distinct feel. When I live there or go back to visit, I often find myself in Kreise 3, 4 and 5. These are the old working class/red light districts, and they are still where a lot of the nightlife happens. They have lots of bars and restaurants, as well as cool galleries and independent shops. Zurich is known as the wealthiest city in Europe, and was voted in a number of surveys as having the best quality of life. If you want to experience this posher side of Zurich, you should stick around the city centre in Kreise 1 and 2, and around the end of Lake Zurich in Kreis 6.

The city is objectively very beautiful. It's surrounded by woodland, and is situated at the point where the river Limmat meets Lake Zurich. The river and the lake lend a defining character to Zurich, really enriching the quality of life. There are lots of lidos and parks around the water, and at nighttime these lidos often turn into bars, where you can enjoy the warm summer nights with drinks and food. It is also easy to access the surrounding mountains and countryside, as well as the towns of Basel and Bern, which are less than an hour away by train.

Getting around within the city is also very easy. The public transport system is good (with trams, buses and trains), and as it's fairly compact, you can walk around most of it. However, I would recommend renting a bicycle at the main train station, so that you can really explore the city and its surrounds.

HOTEL ROTHAUS This hotel, which used to be a brothel, is centrally located right on the Langstraße in the middle of vibrant Kreis 4. It has a nice little bar on the ground floor, where I like to have drinks with friends, and is relatively affordable. Sihlhallenstraße 1, 8004 Zurich, www.hotelrothaus.ch

HOTEL GREULICH I know this design hotel quite well because we did a project with my industrial design course there. The rooms are built around a courtyard, next to a birch garden, and are very minimal and light. The restaurant is top notch, serving Mediterranean and experimental cuisine. Herman-Greulich-Straße 56, 8004 Zurich, www.greulich.ch

GASTHAUS ZUM GUTEN GLÜCK This recently-opened guesthouse provides the much needed budget option that Zurich was lacking. The rooms are simply and lovingly designed. There's a nice bar/cafe there as well. Stationsstraße 7, 8003 Zurich, www.zumgutenglueck.ch

PLACES TO STAY

ROSSO This Italian restaurant is one of my absolute favourites. It's situated in an old warehouse and still has a waxed concrete floor and other original features. I always order a pizza and their legendary chocolate bomb for desert. Book ahead if your party is bigger than two. There is a nice second-hand furniture shop in the basement of the same building. Geroldstraße 31, 8005 Zurich, www.restaurant-rosso.ch

ITALIA Another great Italian – this one is very traditional – an uncomplicated Osteria for the everyday, with everyday prices to match. The antipasto misto and the sepia pasta are highly recommended. Book ahead at weekends. Zeughausstraße 61, 8004 Zurich, www.ristorante-italia.ch

LILY'S STOMACH SUPPLY For decently priced Asian cuisine ranging from Thai to Indian, this is the place to go. It's like a mixture of Busaba and Wagamamas. Langstraße 197, 8005 Zurich, www.lilys.ch

VOLKSHAUS A nice, intimate space in which to enjoy traditional (and very rich) Swiss cooking. I also love coming here for drinks or coffee at the spacious, folksy bar at the front. Stauffacherstraße 60, 8004 Zurich, www.restaurantvolkshaus.ch

MAISON BLUNT A Moroccan restaurant near the Langstraße that's been converted from an old garage. The combination of traditional Moroccan décor with the original look of the garage is very carefully and beautifully done. They have a great variety of mezze plates. Gasometerstraße 5, 8005 Zurich, www.maison-blunt.ch

PLACES TO EAT

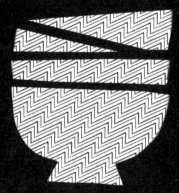

BARS

If you travel to Zurich between May and September (depending on how warm it is), there are a few fantastic bars near the lake and river, where you can sit outside, drinking in the booze and the atmosphere. I love them all equally.

PRIMITIVO A nice, simple outdoor restaurant on the river Limmat. You can get your food and drink to take-away or sit on top of the roof and enjoy the the view and the table service. It's also a good spot for a swim. Oberer Letten, Wasserwerkstraße, 8037 Zurich

EISENBAHNWAGEN 200m away from the Primitivo is the Eisenbahnwagen. As the name suggests, this bar is built out of an old railway carriage. It is a bit less crowded and touristy than the Primitivo, and I often go there for a catch-up with friends and a beer after work. Oberer Letten, Wasserwerkstraße, 8037 Zurich

BADI UNTERER LETTEN This old lido, built 3m over the Limmat, stays open at night in July (check the website for specific dates), screening films onto the wall and serving drinks. A unique experience not to be missed. Wasserwerkstraße 131, 8037 Zurich, www.filmfluss.ch

SEEBAD ENGE This lido at Lake Zurich is built out onto the water. In the winter it's a sauna and in summer it's a swimming pool during the day (with a women's only section), and a floating bar at night. Whenever you go, the view of the Alps will impress. Mythenquai 9, 8002 Zurich (in Rentenanstalt Park), www.seebadenge.ch

If you're not lucky enough to go to Zurich in the summer, all the previous listings will be of little use to you, so try one of the following 'normal' bars instead:

TOTAL BAR This bar was bought as part of the house where the owners live, and the bar pays off their mortgage. It's got an uncomplicated, egalitarian atmosphere and style. Tellstraße 19, 8004 Zurich, www.totalbar.ch

CASABLANCA CAFE-BAR This cosy venue is a trendy spot for a coffee during the day and a drink at night. I like to sit in the window and watch people passing by. Langstraße 62, 8004 Zurich, www.cafe-casablanca.ch

LONG STREET This bar used to be a strip club, and the décor hasn't changed much – lots of red velvet and a lap bar. It's the perfect bar to get into a party mood – it's always crowded with a nice mix of trendy people, and there's a small dancefloor upstairs that opens at midnight. Langstraße 92, 8004 Zurich, www.longstreetbar.ch

STERNWARTE URANIA At the top of a 48m high observatory tower, this bar offers great views over the city, and is where I take people visiting Zurich for the first time (check their opening hours). Uraniastraße 9, 8001 Zurich, www.urania.astronomie.ch

Z AM PARK A lovely cafe on the Fritschiwiese Park. The interior was designed by Studio Aekae, who recycled the damaged parquet flooring to build the bar and furniture. The chairs are reworked by selected designers and auctioned off a few times a year. Zurlindenstraße 275, 8003 Zurich, www.zampark.ch

ZUKUNFT This club in the Langstraße area hosts a great selection of parties and gigs. I've seen DJs like Sonar Kollektiv, Richard Dorfmeister and bands like The Whitest Boy Alive all play here. Their monthly printed programme is usually designed by interesting artists. Dienerstraße 25, 8004 Zurich, www.zukunft.cl

HIVE The urban west end of Zurich turns into one big party from Thursday to Sunday, and Hive is right in the middle of it. It was recently redesigned by my friends Christian Kaegi and Fabrice Aberhard (Aekae Designers), with two spacious dancefloors. They have a great lineup of live gigs from the alternative electronic music scene. Geroldstraße 5, 8005 Zurich, www.hiveclub.ch

HELSINKI KLUB Although Helsinki is not far from Hive, it's a completely different type of venue. It's a small club in a little old garage, run by Tom Rist, brother of the artist Pipilotti Rist. It has a cool underground vibe, and showcases live jazz, blues and hip-hop acts. It is also known for its jukebox, which is programmed every couple months by specially selected musicians, artists and friends. I often go there after dinner at Rosso next door to enjoy the chilled-out atmosphere and take a chance on a new band. Geroldstraße 35, 8005 Zurich, www.helsinkiklub.ch

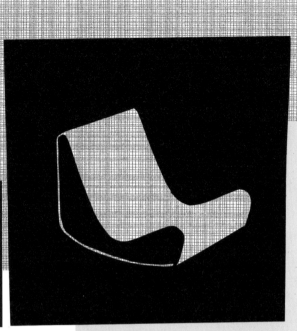

MAKING THINGS Based in Kreis 4, Making Things is a small shop and studio run by three local fashion designers. They sell their own creations of printed clothes and jewellery, as well as a selection of international and Swiss labels. You can find some lovely things there. Gruengasse 20, 8004 Zurich, www.makingthings.ch

ELASTIQUE This shop, just opposite Making Things, makes me feel like I'm in a James Bond movie. It stocks high-end vintage furniture from the 1950s, 60s and 70s and is almost like a design museum. Gruengasse 19, 8004 Zurich, www.elastique.ch

ONYVA A new store in the Old Town selling affordable clothes and accessories from international labels. I love the innovative use of charity shop furniture in the interior. Zaehringerplatz 15, 8001 Zurich, www.onyva.ch

FIDELIO A high-end shop stocking designer brands like Costume National, Viktor & Rolf and Raf Simons, with a nearby branch (Fidelio 2) catering for a younger market. Munzplatz 1 (Fidelio 1) and Nuschelerstraße 30 (Fidelio 2), 8001 Zurich, www.fidelio-kleider.ch

KANZLEI FLOHMARKT You can find everything at this flea market from shoes to 70s lamps. It's open every Saturday from early in the morning till afternoon. It's in a schoolyard, which also houses the Xenix bar and cinema, which screens open-air films in the summer. Helvetia Platz, 8004 Zurich, www.flohmarktkanzlei.ch, www.xenix.ch

LUX PLUS A trendy second-hand shop with a nice selection of clothes and accessories. Ankerstraße 24, 8004 Zurich, www.luxplus.ch

ERBUDAK I love this atmospheric little boutique. The owner, Dilara Erbudak, has infused it with a really glamorous vibe, stocking brands like Les Prairies de Paris, John Smedley and Jerome Dreyfuss. Engelstraße 62, 8004 Zurich, www.erbudak.com

16 TONS This is where I come to supplement my sneaker collection. They sell vintage clothes and dresses, second-hand music (reggae and dancehall) and sneakers from all decades, and everything at very fair prices. If you like reggae and dancehall, this is the place to go! Anwandstraße 25, 8004 Zurich, www.16tons.ch

ORELL FÜSSLI KRAUTHAMMER My absolute favourite design bookstore in the middle of the old part of Zurich. I could spend days rummaging through their art books! Marktgasse 12, 8001 Zurich

MUSEUM FÜR GESTALTUNG I know this museum well, as it's right next door to the Zurich University of the Arts. It has an excellent programme of theme-based temporary exhibitions. It also has two satellite spaces: the Plakatraum, which has a great poster collection, and the Museum Bellerive – a big villa that hosts temporary exhibitions throughout the year. Ausstellungsstraße 60, 8005 Zurich, www.museum-gestaltung.ch

MIGROS MUSEUM FÜR GEGENWARTSKUNST This is a centre for contemporary art in all its forms. It's funded by Migros, the big Swiss co-operative supermarket chain. Limmatstraße 270, 8005 Zurich, www.migrosmuseum.ch

GALERIE FREYMOND-GUTH A small, underground gallery for contemporary arts that was founded by artists and spun out of the non-profit project space Les Complices in 2006. Brauerstraße 51, 8004 Zurich, www.freymondguth.com

GRAPHISCHE SAMMLUNG This is Switzerland's second largest art collection. It's mostly old masters, however, the more recent collections focus on international contemporary art and emerging Swiss artists. It's a great place to come for inspiration. Rämistraße 101, 8092 Zurich, www.graphischesammlung.ch

FOTOMUSEUM WINTERTHUR This gallery, based out in Winterthur (about 30 minutes from the centre), puts on fantastic photography exhibitions on subjects ranging from historical photography to applied photography in industry, architecture and fashion. Gruzenstraße 44–45, 8400 Winterthur, www.fotomuseum.ch

HAUSKONSTRUKTIV This is a museum of Constructivist art, following the development from Modernism till today. I love it for its relevance to design, but it's worth going just for the building. Selnaustraße 25, 8001 Zurich, www.hauskonstruktiv.ch

DE PURY AND LUXEMBOURG An international gallery for contemporary art. Limmatsraße 264, 8005 Zurich, www.depuryluxembourg.com

RIFF RAFF This is my favourite cinema in Zurich. It's beautifully designed, and shows lots of independent movies. It also has a great bar and bistro. Neugasse 57, 8005 Zurich, www.riffraff.ch

ROTE FABRIK Situated in a beautiful warehouse, this is a left-leaning centre for theatre, music, politics and art. In the summer they put long tables outside, where you can eat and drink. I like the down-to-earth atmosphere. Seestraße 395, 8038 Zurich, www.rotefabrik.ch

GALLERIES AND CULTURE

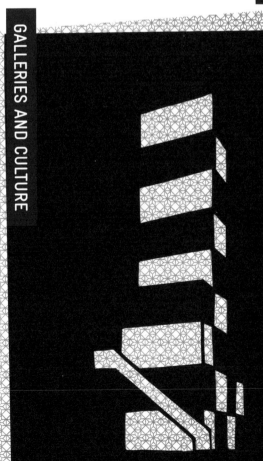

THERME VALS A two and a half hour trip from the city, this is a thermal spa set into the mountain slope. Built by the Swiss architect Peter Zumthor, it's one of the most beautiful buildings in the country and is a totally relaxing, totally Swiss experience. www.therme-vals.ch

BAHNHOF STADELHOFEN Designed by Santiago Calatrava in 1990, this train station is an amazing multi-level structure that provides different perspectives of the platforms, the underground arcade and the hillside behind it.

HEIDI WEBER HAUS This is the last building designed by Le Corbusier, on the banks of Lake Zurich. It's made of concrete and stone, and houses various sculptures, paintings, furniture and writings by the great architect. Höschgasse 8, 8008 Zurich, www.centrelecorbusier.com

LINDENHOF PARK An elevated park in the centre of Zurich. It's built around the relics of an old Roman fort and customs house. It's a beautiful spot to rest and enjoy a magnificent view of the Old Town, the river Limmat and the surrounding hills. The nearest tram stop is 'Rennweg'.

EVENTS

ZÜRCHER THEATER SPEKTAKEL AUGUST
A lakeside theatre festival that I have been
going to since I was a kid. Lots of great plays,
street theatre and open-air restaurants and
bars. www.theaterspektakel.ch

BLICKFANG NOVEMBER Part of an
international network of design trade
shows, with 200 designers selling furniture,
fashion, jewellery and everything else.
A good place to buy Christmas pressies
and get inspired by other people's work.
Kongresshaus Zurich, Gotthardstraße 5,
8002 Zurich, www.blickfang.com

İSTANBUL BOĞIZA/THE BOSPHORUS

Muzedechanga •

Dank! •

Ortaköy •

Touchdown •

9 Ece Aksoy •

Büyük Londra Oteli •

Mısır Apt •

Kahve Altı

Cezayir

Sofyalı Sokak •

Çukurcuma

Istanbul Modern

Galata Tower •

Spice Bazaar •

Grand Bazaar •

• Çemberlitaş Hamman

Bianca Wendt's
ISTANBUL

When my boyfriend was offered a job in Istanbul, it didn't even seem worth considering. I had just finished my MA, and was quite settled in London. We decided to just go for the weekend – after all, spring was on the way and someone else was paying. Much to my surprise, I fell in love with the city from the start, and shortly after packed my bags.

Istanbul is situated on either side of the Bosphorus – the narrow strait that separates the Black Sea from the Marmara Sea, and it bridges Asia and Europe both physically and culturally. It really has everything: mosques, palaces, smoky bars, ancient tea houses, hedonistic clubbing, swimming in the sea, antiques, shopping, and modern art.

The official population is 13 million but unofficially it's closer to 20 million. As you might imagine, it's a sprawling city with various neighbourhoods, each with its own distinct character. Beyoğlu is probably the most relevant area. This is the old Christian quarter, in which grand 19th Century buildings stand side by side with modern galleries and shops. İskiklal Caddesi runs through the middle – a pedestrianised walkway with cafes, bars, galleries and shops. Within Beyoğlu are several neighbourhoods with an artistic bent: Cihangir offers its trendy inhabitants European-style cafes and bars, as well as amazing views of the city. Cukurcuma, the antiques district, is very up-and-coming, as is the historic area of Galata. If you're after nightlife, Tünel is the place to go.

Outside of Beyoğlu, the places to visit are: The old port area and Tophane, where you can smoke a nargile and play backgammon on the water. Nişantaşı is the poshest suburb – filled with expensive shops and quite a lot of Eurotrash. Sultanahmet is a historical area where you'll find hamams and harassment in equal measure, and the Black Sea coast has beaches, fish restaurants and music festivals. Finally, the districts of Fener and Balat have a rich history within their Byzantine walls, and are currently being renovated with EU funding.

I am always aware of my 'foreignness' in Istanbul, but feel welcome at the same time. People are friendly and happy to help, even if it does involve strangers actually getting into the taxi with you to show the driver the way. History is everywhere, but the city is constantly changing. Beautiful, timeless, always on the move. Even after decades of unsympathetic city planning, Istanbul manages to retain its charm.

BÜYÜK LONDRA Built in 1892, this used to be the most prestigious place to stay in the days of the Orient Express. Today, its appeal lies in its faded grandeur. The rooms are a bit shabby but affordable. But the best part is the lobby bar, with live-in parrots, surly barmen, DIY drinks, a record player and vinyl collection. You'll always meet a character or two there. Not long ago, I randomly spent an evening in the company of a group of Swedish writers, including crime writer Håkan Nesser, and a flamboyant British Council worker who later tried to steal my coat. Meşrutiyet Caddesi 117, Taksim, www.londrahotel.net

WITT ISTANBUL In Cihangir, the bohemian part of the city, this hotel has rooms that are more like apartments, designed by Wallpaper* award-winners Autoban. They are large, with marble kitchens and bathrooms, modern furniture and some have views of the Bosphorus. Defterdar Yokuşu 26, Cingahir, www.wittistanbul.com/eng

HOTEL LES OTTOMANS For something completely decadent, this waterfront hotel was originally built in the 1790s for a Pasha. Restored and lavishly decorated in traditional Ottoman style, with the benefit of all the mod cons. Oh, and don't let the website put you off…. Muallim Naci Caddesi 68, Kuruçeşme, www.lesottomans.com

VILLA ZURICH Design-wise there's nothing special about this hotel, but it's in a great location in the arty area of Cihangir, and is cheap, clean and inoffensive. There's a busy cafe/bar downstairs that spills onto the street in summer, and one of Istanbul's best fish restaurants (Doğa Balık) on the roof. Akarsu Yokupu Caddesi 44–46, Cingahir, www.hotelvillazurich.com

DOKUZ ECE AKSOY Tiny and cosy, serving wonderful home-cooked food with evocative names like 'it snowed on tomatoes'. Oteller Sokak 9, Tepebası, Istanbul, www.dokuzeceaksoy.com

KARDEŞLER KEBAB This used to be my local and I make sure to visit it every time I come back to Istanbul. It's slap bang in the middle of Cihangir, and as basic as you can get. Sit outside, listen to the call to prayer from the adjacent mosque and watch the world go by. You can eat really well (try the lentil soup and the lahmacun) for about €1. I think it's open 24 hours; well, I've never seen it closed. Agahammam Caddesi 1, Cingahir

CEZAYIR Housed in a beautifully restored building from 1901 that was built by the Italian Workers' Society. There's a restaurant, lounge, bar and a big garden open in the summer. 'Cezayir' means Algerian in Turkish: Algerian Street, where the restaurant is located, became French Street and was given a clichéd 'French' makeover after an injection of funds from the French government. Cezayir stands out from the crowd of pastiche. Hayriye Caddesi 12, Galatasaray, www.cezayir-istanbul.com

Mesut ERSOY
34 THB 78

Kadir KAPLAN
34 TFD 62

MÜZEDECHANGA
This restaurant is some way outside the city. You can get there by car or taxi, and the journey itself is interesting; you'll pass through the wealthy waterside neighbourhoods of Bebek, Ortaköy and Arnavutköy, with an increasing sense of space as you go. The restaurant itself lies in the extensive grounds of what was the Sabancı family's residence, and is now an art gallery. Sakıp Sabancı Caddesi 22, Emirgan

KAHVE ALTI
My favourite place for breakfast, this used to be a vintage clothing shop with a small cafe attached, but in typical Turkish style, the food won out and the cafe has now taken over. Head out the back to the relaxing courtyard. I recommend the simit plate, a fresh orange juice and a glass of cay (tea). Perfect. It's also open for lunch and dinner. Anahtar Sokak 15, Cihangir

WWW.YEMEKSEPETI.COM
I wouldn't normally recommend staying at home staring at a computer screen, but if you have a deadline or a hangover or it's raining outside, this website can be a godsend. Any type of food imaginable (traditional Turkish, kebab, sushi, icecream, even McDonalds) is delivered to your door within half an hour of ordering. Most of it is in English, too.

SOFYALI SOKAK
This street in lively Tünel and its surroundings is the place to go for a night out. You can enjoy a mezze plate washed down with raki, rock and beer, play a game of backgammon or sip a demure cocktail.

TOUCHDOWN
In the swanky shopping district of Nişantaşı, with an interior inspired by American football and located in a shopping arcade, this place never seems to go out of style (personally I'm not sure why!) If you want to hob nob with media / advertising / publishing people, it's the place to go. Abdi Ipekçi Caddesi 61, Nişantaşı

NU TERAS
Can be a bit Euro-tastic, but worth braving for the sheer decadence of partying on an open rooftop of a 200-year-old building with Istanbul spread out below you. Come during the week rather than at the weekends and bring a fat wallet. It's actually a restaurant that turns into a nightclub as the sun goes down, so be warned: eat quick or there will be people dancing in your face (or your dinner)! Meşrutiyet Caddesi 149/7, Tepebaşı

Muhammet FAKIBABA
34 TAH 93

Ahmet Çiçek

ABDULLAH, THE GRAND BAZAAR Well, you have to go to the Grand Bazaar – even if it is increasingly filled with touristy tat, it's still an amazing spectacle. Abdulla is a shop inside the bazaar and is the place to come for traditional crafts, all natural sheets, towels, blankets and soaps. Halıcılar Caddesi 62, Kapalıçarsı, www.abdulla.com

MISIR ÇARSISI (SPICE BAZAAR) A lot less touristy and smaller than the Grand Bazaar, this market, also known as the Egyptian Bazaar, sells weird and wonderful spices, all laid out with a keen shopkeeper's eye for colour and arrangement. Cardamom, green cumin, red pepper, curry, sesame, ground coconut, yellow turmeric and saffron fill bags and boxes or are heaped in piles, while strings of dried okra, peppers and aubergine dangle overhead. You'll also find a large variety of oils, rose water, and the hand-woven kese, which are used in Turkish baths for scrubbing. Near the Galata Bridge

MIDNIGHT EXPRESS Housed in the beautiful Mısır Apartment on İskiklal Caddesi, this shop is a treasure trove of handpicked Turkish fashion, with a small selection of homeware and jewellery. Owned by husband and wife designers Banu Bora and Tayfun Mumcu, it was inspired by a recent visit to Istanbul by Suzy Menkes. 2nd Floor, Mısır Apt, İskiklal Caddesi 163/5, Galatasaray, www.midnightexpress.com.tr

ETERNAL CHILD The creation of Central Saint Martins alumni Gül Gürdamar, this is a young and fresh collection of easy knitwear in colourful shades with unusual details and textures. Sold in Beymen Shopping Centre, Abdi Ipekci Caddesi 23, Nisintasi, www.eternal-child.com

ECE SÜKAN VINTAGE Vintage isn't big in Turkey, but Ece Sükan, a well-known Turkish model and stylist, is looking to change perceptions with a handpicked a collection of women's fashion from the 1920s to the 1990s. Ahmet Fetgari Sokak 152, Teşvikiye, www.ecesukanvintage.com

34 TEB 67
Dilkan Gülcücük

ROBINSON CRUSOE Small and inviting, this is my favourite bookshop in Istanbul. With a great English-language selection of literature, guidebooks, history, art, design and film titles, as well as magazines, I never leave empty-handed. İskiklal Caddesi 389, Beyoğlu

ÇUKURCUMA The Çukurcuma district of Istanbul is where you can find serious antiques, old junk, and everything in between. This area is in the heart of arty Beyoğlu, which is slowly becoming gentrified and done up. I wouldn't recommend a particular shop in this area: try them all, you never know what you'll find.

DANK Housed in a 650m² underground carpark, this is not easy to find but worth the trip if you are looking for vintage furniture. The stock of slightly damaged 1960s and 70s furniture is always changing, and comes from importers and manufacturers' warehouses. I recently bought an Eames side chair with a slight scratch for about £35. Otlukbeli Caddesi, Yol sok, Mayadrom Uptown Etiler Alışveriş Merkezi P2 Garaj Katı, Etiler, www.dank-design.com

There are 18,000 taxis in Istanbul, and it is impossible to imagine the city without them. One of the first things I was warned about upon my arrival was to look out for unscrupulous taxi drivers, who would take you the 'scenic route', pretend not to know where they were going, or charge the night rate in the day time. It didn't take long to figure out that most of these taxi drivers were actually decent guys. Never short of an opinion, a cigarette or honk of the horn (but always short of a seatbelt), their daily lives are intertwined with those of their many passengers. No two taxis are the same: although all are yellow, there is a large amount of poetic licence as to what colour 'yellow' is. Also of note is the weird and wonderful array of typefaces used to denote the licence number on the taxi doors (in black or various shades of blue), the names of the driver's children sometimes found on the back, Turkish flags, secondary information such as the taxi rank name and logo, coloured trims – the list goes on. (Concept and art direction: Bianca Wendt, photography: Mine Kasapoğlu)

OKAN ASART 34 TEP77

GALLERIES AND CULTURE

ISTANBUL MODERN An old warehouse on the pier has been transformed into a showcase for modern Turkish and international art. The standards of the exhibitions can be patchy, but it's definitely worth a look. Visit the Istanbul Modern Cafe while you're there, full of mid-century furniture and right on the water. There's also a sculpture garden, video and photography gallery and a cinema showing classic films. Meclis-i Mebusan Caddesi 4, Liman Sahasy Antrepo, Tophane, www.istanbulmodern.org

GALERIST Located in the Mısır Apartment, Galerist is a stylish and innovative gallery dedicated to showing contemporary Turkish artists and designers, including Hussein Chalayan. Mısır Apt 311/4, İskiklal Caddesi 163, Beyoğlu, www.galerist.com.tr

URA! Turkish artist Mihda Koray founded this gallery, also in the Mısır Apartment, in 2007 when she realised that there was a youth culture/subculture niche missing in the Turkish art world. URA! has a roster of international and local talent and does not distinguish between visual artists, musicians and writers. It also publishes a zine. 1st Floor, Mısır Apt, İskiklal Caddesi 163, Beyoğlu, www.ura-project.org

PLATFORM GARANTI This gallery sees itself as a hub and a facilitator for art and research practices. It has an archive and research spaces upstairs, and exhibits contemporary art from Turkey and abroad. İskiklal Caddesi 115A, Beyoğlu, www.platformgaranti.blogspot.com

BAS This tiny space in Beyoğlu, run by artist Banu Cennetoğlu, produces and exhibits artists' books and printed matter. Some, such as the Bent series, are produced by Bas, while others are from a collection. Meşrutiyet Caddesi 92A, Tünel, Beyoğlu, www.b-a-s.info

34 TAZ 01

Tevfik ŞAPÇI

ISTANBUL GRAPHIC DESIGN WEEK MAY Workshops, exhibitions and talks run by designers from all over the world. www.grafist.org

ISTANBUL BIENNIAL SEPTEMBER-NOVEMBER A large-scale international art event with exhibitions, workshops, lecture series and all the other things you would expect. www.iksv.org

ÇEMBERLITAŞ HAMAMI This traditional Turkish bath is an architectural marvel in itself. A large domed marble space, with sunlight streaming through small star-shaped holes in the roof, it has been in use continually since it was built in 1584. Although catering largely to tourists, and priced accordingly, it's a great introduction to the hamam if you're feeling nervous. You'll come out revived and cleaner than you ever thought possible. Vezirhan Caddesi 8, Çemberlitaş, www.cemberlitashamami.com.tr

YEREBATAN SARNICI Located in the old part of Istanbul, this is the largest of the underground cisterns built to irrigate the gardens of Byzantine Constantinople. It's a magical underground forest of columns. When not filled with bad classical muzak, you can hear the calming drip, drip, drip of water. It's the perfect place to cool down on a hot day. Yerebatan Caddesi 13, Sultanahmet, www.yerebatan.com

ATATÜRK KULTUR MERKEZI This tribute to Atatürk, father of modern Turkey, was built in 1956-7 and is one of the city's few Modernist gems. Originally designed as an opera house, today it also shows theatre and ballet. Taksim Square, Kocatepe

34 TJY 06

EROL KAPLAN

broadway

BARBICAN

st martins

CUBE

WHITE

bistrotheque

PASSING

Eye

in the

MUSEUM 52

Soho

TATE

5

may

brick lane

southbank

24hr

magma

st bride's

hayward

DESIGN MUSEUM

MAN&EVE

borough

wapping

JOANA NIEMEYER'S
LONDON

Dr Johnson famously said 'when a man is tired of London, he is tired of life; for there is in London all that life can afford', and in my experience, having lived in London for the past 11 years, he got it absolutely right. Pretty much every interest of every type of person imaginable is catered for, and the challenge is really just to figure out who and where is catering to yours. It's one of the biggest capital cities in Europe, and to the outsider, it can seem dauntingly huge, with the connections between its various centres appearing oblique at best. Especially if you're using the tube as your primary means of transport, it can seem like a strange constellation of hubs – and in a way it is. The way I see it, London has maintained the essence of its origins as a series of villages that have merged, and one of the ways to make it feel manageable is to know what your village has to offer.

My village is the East End. People either love or hate the East End of London. It's a classic case of a rough area that was colonised by poor artists, and suddenly became super-trendy and filled with annoying people with wacky moustaches who left Stockholm because it's not edgy enough there. Despite this, you can't deny that it's still a truly vibrant area, and that it remains the beating heart of London's art and design scene. Most of my recommendations are focused here, with a few in the other design islands of London.

One of the things I love about London in general and the East End specifically is the diversity of people that live here. Britain has a reputation for great design, but if you look closely at the scene, you realise that the reason it's so good is because it's made up of top designers from every country in the world. In fact over the entire time I've lived here, I've only made four friends who are through and through British. And that's not down to some weird Anglophobia on my part – it's a genuine representation of the mix of people around me. So my village is made up of the best of the world in one place. What more can a city offer? Ever since I was a kid, I've been scared of missing out. In London I never have that feeling. I'm right in the centre of it all.

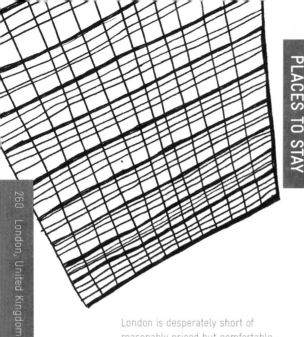

London is desperately short of reasonably priced but comfortable places to stay – especially in the East End – where all the accommodation seems to be either achingly cool, and therefore expensive, or a total slum.

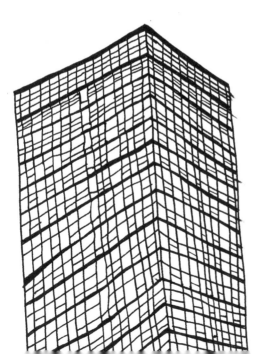

THE ZETTER A boutique hotel in the middle of Clerkenwell – which is where almost all the design studios are based. The area is a bit dead at the weekend, but the East and the West Ends are both easily accessible from here. I like the restaurant as well – it's a good place to meet clients. 86-88 Clerkenwell Road, London EC1M 5RJ, www.thezetter.com

HOXTON HOTEL I have never stayed here myself, but have heard great things about it. It's got funky, contemporary design and it's in the middle of Shoreditch/Hoxton – which might get a bit crazy on a Friday or Saturday night, but is definitely good if you like being in the heart of things. 81 Great Eastern Street, London EC2A 3HU, www.hoxtonhotels.com

THE ROOKERY This is a new hotel, also conveniently located on a quiet side street in Clerkenwell. It looks like an old-school English members club – all paneled wood walls and antique furniture – very James Bond. It has a sister hotel in Soho, that's apparently got even nicer design. Peter's Lane, Cowcross Street, London EC1M 6DS, www.hazlittshotel.com

ROUGH LUXE Across the road from King's Cross, this is a brand new hotel that has striking design – half luxury half ruin. The walls are stripped plaster and there is a strong focus on contrasting materials and styles. At this price you wouldn't expect to share a toilet, but maybe it's part of the experience…. 1 Birkenhead Street, London WC1H 8BA, www.roughluxe.co.uk

CAMDEN SQUARE B&B This is the best budget option I could find. It's in a sedate, residential area not far from the grungy mania of Camden Town, and is run by an architect and his wife. They rent out two rooms, a single and a double, at £50 per person. The house was designed by the owner, and is open and light with a slightly Japanese-y vibe. You can easily get into the East End on the overground train at Camden Road. 66 Camden Square, London NW1 9XD

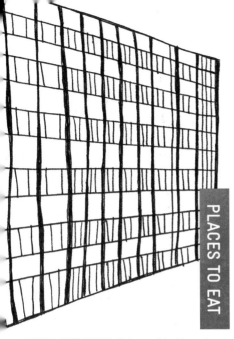

CANDID ARTS TRUST This must be the only place in Angel that hasn't been touched for the past 20 years. Tucked in an alley off City Road, the cafe is on the second floor, up a tatty old staircase. It's like walking into someone's living room – with couches and candles spread around. The food is cheap and decent. Good for lunch. 3 Torrens Street, London EC1V 1NQ, www.candidarts.com

SONG QUE This is the best of the many Vietnamese restaurants around Hoxton, serving delicious, cheap food. You might have to queue at the weekend, but it's worth it. Try the beef in battle leaf followed by the beef soup. 134 Kingsland Road, London E2 8DY

ST JOHN BREAD & WINE The original St John is in Clerkenwell, but I prefer this branch in Spitalfields Market. The food is fantastic – creative interpretations of traditional British food (bone marrow and parsnips or potted rabbit anyone?) and they do a whole roast pig for a big party. I once took a leftover pig's head home in a plastic bag, stopping at the Ten Bells pub for a quick pint first. Vegetarians might want to go somewhere else. 94-96 Commercial Street, London E1 6LZ, www.stjohnrestaurant.co.uk

THE PRINCESS This gastro-pub has a normal pub space downstairs and an elegant dining room upstairs, both serving delicious food. Great for a romantic dinner or a Sunday roast. Every designer in Hoxton comes here for their after-work pint. 76 Paul Street, London EC2A 4NE, www.theprincessofshoreditch.com

BUSABA The identity by North Design is probably as famous as the restaurant itself, but the food is good and reasonably priced. It has two branches in Soho, and if you get a seat at the window you can watch the craziness of Soho as it walks past. 8-13 Bird Street, London W1U 1BU, 106-110 Wardour Street, London W1F 0TR, www.busaba.com

LMNT One of the craziest decors ever. You can sit in a littletree house and listen to opera singers while having a great Sunday roast. Pay special attention to the drawings in the women's toilet. 316 Queensbridge Road, London E8 3NH, www.lmnt.co.uk

MANGAL One of the best Turkish restaurants on Kingsland Road. If you come here in the evening, you'll be guaranteed to spot the artists Gilbert and George, who come every day for dinner (they famously don't have a kitchen at home). 14 Stoke Newington Road, London N16 7XN, www.hasanmezemangal.co.uk

BISTROTHEQUE This hidden gem in industrial Hackney hosts almost every magazine launch in London, and is the place to be seen. It has great food, a great bar and hosts a regular gay cabaret. The area is fashionably dodgy. I came here once with my old boss and he was convinced someone would steal the wheels off his fancy car. 23-27 Wadeson Street, London E2 9DR, www.bistrotheque.com

BARS

ICA BAR I'm always relieved to remember this place when I'm in the West End. They have events ranging from gay bingo to creative speed dating, their food is good and their bookshop has one of the biggest magazine and independent DVD sections in town. The Mall, London SW1Y 5AH, www.ica.org.uk

FREUD This discreet basement bar serves the best cocktails ever. The bar closes when the ice runs out and one time this was at 10pm – so get there early! It's also a good place to come for lunch if you're shopping in Covent Garden. 198 Shaftesbury Avenue, London WC2H 8JL, www.freudliving.co.uk

PRINCE GEORGE This is my local pub and one of my favourites. It has quiz nights on Mondays, and at 11pm the landlady closes the curtains and 'locks' you in till she goes to bed. For a real taste of London order a pint of Flowers and a pickled egg. 40 Parkholme Road, London E8 3AG

NOTTING HILL ARTS CLUB A fun bar/club in West London, responsible for discovering producer Mark Ronson. They host various art and music nights and according to the director, David, Wednesdays are the best day to come. I once hosted a show here about badges called *Stuck on Me.* 21 Notting Hill Gate, London W11 3JQ, www.nottinghillartsclub.com

JAGUAR SHOES This was once a hot tip, but now everyone knows about it and Saturdays are ridiculously packed. It's at its nicest mid-week and still hosts interesting illustration exhibitions. 34-36 Kingsland Road, London E2 8DA, www.jaguarshoes.com

CAFE OTO This is a bar/music venue that hosts lots of experimental music acts as well as book launches for beautiful Swiss publications affiliated with the Helvetic Centre. 8-22 Ashwin Street, London E8 3DL, www.cafeoto.co.uk

NO-ONE/THE OLD SHOREDITCH STATION This is a shop, cafe, bar and exhibition space in one. It's a great place where you can spend whole afternoons using their Wi-Fi to turn it into your office. 1 Kingsland Road, London E2 8AA, www.no-one.co.uk

DALSTON JAZZ BAR This is the best place to finish the night. It's packed with beautiful people (too packed for my liking on Saturdays). Around 9pm all the tables and chairs get put away and everyone starts dancing. The DJs tend to be of the stubborn variety – not taking requests and then playing Mambo Number 5 three times in a row – but it's still a guaranteed fun night out. 4 Bradbury Street, London N16 8JN

TATE MODERN BAR I bring every friend that visits me here. It has the best view in London – making the city look big but manageable at the same time. If you're lucky, you can get a seat on a sofa and spend half the day there. Members can sit on the balcony. 53 Bankside, London SE1 9TG, www.tate.org.uk

SHOPPING

BEYOND THE VALLEY Set up by a student of Central Saint Martins this is a little shop, which has grown in reputation. Situated behind Carnaby Street, you can buy objects and clothes by emerging London designers – or alternatively sell your work there. It transformed Newburgh Street into a very interesting shopping destination with little wine bars and funky boutiques. I particularly like the jewellery by Noemi Klein. 2 Newburgh Street, London W1F 7RD, www.beyondthevalley.com

MAGMA BOOKS This is THE graphic design bookshop in London. It has branches in Farringdon and Covent Garden, and is the place I go to get inspiration or presents. They also produce *Graphic Magazine*. 117-119 Clerkenwell Road, London EC1R 5BY, 8 Earlham Street Covent Garden London WC2H 9RY, www.magmabooks.com

HURWUNDEKI This is one of my favourite shops for its contents and décor. It sells new and vintage clothing on two floors and the selection is immaculate. It's possibly overpriced, but you don't need to rummage to find the gems here. 98 Commercial Street, London E1 6LZ, www.hurwundeki.com

SHELF Cheshire Street is a pretty little turning off Brick Lane and has a couple of really nice design shops that are open Friday till Sunday. I love this one, which sells prints, tiles and ceramic letters. 40 Cheshire Street, London E2 6EH, www. helpyourshelf.co.uk

SPITALFIELDS AND BRICK LANE MARKETS On Sundays the area around Brick Lane and Spitalfields explodes. Brick Lane used to be the old traditional market, and Spitalfields was the trendy, arty alternative. Today they are filled with people selling everything from old rubbish to funky new design. It can get almost unbearably packed, so I tend to go to Up-Market – a relatively new offshoot of Spitalfields, which is less crowded and has a nice area selling German food, Afghan food and everything in between. Alternatively you could go to Spitalfields between Tuesday and Friday, when it has various events (an antiques market on Thursdays and a record market on Wednesdays) and is much more chilled. Commercial Street, London E1 6BJ, www.visitspitalfields.com

COLUMBIA ROAD FLOWER MARKET Every Sunday from very early in the morning, this pretty little street is transformed into an amazing flower market. It's really old-school – you can buy amazing flowers really cheaply – and weirdly complements the trendy shops and galleries that have begun to pop up on either side, such as the fantastic Ryan's World, which sells work by this lovely artist at very reasonable prices. There are plenty of nice cafes and pubs around. Columbia Road, London E1, www.columbia-flower-market.freewebspace.com

BROADWAY MARKET Within walking distance of Columbia Road and Brick Lane, this is a small farmers' market not far from where I live, open on Saturdays. It's an oasis of trendiness in a rough area, with London Fields park at the end of it. You can go for a swim in the open-air lido (open all year long) or grab a coffee to take away from one of the many cafes, and sit by the ping-pong table, watching every trendy person in London walk by. Try not to take them as seriously as they take themselves! Broadway Market, London E8, www.broadwaymarket.co.uk

MAN&EVE This gallery blurs the boundaries between art and design, taking a very graphic approach to their exhibitions. I collect their Private View invites, designed by Matilda Saxow who works for *Grafik Magazine*. Keep an eye out for the cats that roam freely around the space. 131 Kennington Park Road, London SE11 4JJ, www.manandeve.co.uk

DESIGN MUSEUM I worked here all through my studies and met some really interesting people. It's on the river with nice views from upstairs, and there can be some really excellent exhibitions. After the Tate Modern you might think 'why do I have to pay for a much smaller exhibition?' but as the museum is still waiting to be supported by government funding, it has to charge. I like going there on Fridays, when they stay open until 10pm. 28 Shad Thames, London SE1 2YD, www.designmuseum.org

WAPPING PROJECT This is off the beaten track, far out east towards Canary Wharf, and I only discovered it recently. It's in a converted power station, and its curator is the Jerwood Moving Image Award judge, Jules Wright. Most people just go there for the food, which is very good, but I think the art is even better. Wapping Wall, London E1W 3ST, www.thewappingproject.com

WHITE CUBE Right in leafy Hoxton Square, this is a must see – for its building, its significance in the art world, and occasionally also for its exhibitions. In the summer the square is taken over by a big installation. 48 Hoxton Square, London N1 6PB, www.whitecube.com

MUSEUM 52 Set up by the former assistant of Sam Taylor-Wood, this is somehow the child of the White Cube, and it represents one of my favourite artists, Philip Hausmeier. It's on Redchurch Street, which has a number of other galleries worth checking out. Go there on private view nights – usually the last Thursday of the month. 52 Redchurch Street, London E2 7DP, www.museum52.com

FORMCONTENT A new art project set up by three Goldsmiths art graduates that aims to encourage collaboration between artists and curators and create experimental exhibition formats. They have a very nice set of printed publications and host regular events. It's based in Dalston on the vibrant and refreshingly untrendy Ridley Road market. 51–63 Ridley Road, London E8 2NP, www.formcontent.org

GALLERIES AND CULTURE

TATE MODERN This isn't exactly an insider's secret, but it really is a must. On the South Bank in a spectacularly converted power station, it's one of the top modern art experiences. The Turbine Hall in the entrance has changing large-scale installations which have included crazy slides by Carsten Höller, a giant sun by Olafur Eliasson and a three-foot deep crack in the floor by Doris Salcedo. 53 Bankside, London SE1 9TG, www.tate.org.uk

THE PHOTOGRAPHERS' GALLERY Such a nice escape from the bustle of Oxford Street. This gallery is free and has some wonderful special edition photography books in their shop. 16-18 Ramillies Street, London W1F 7LW, www.photonet.org.uk

SERPENTINE GALLERY Another free gallery in the middle of Hyde Park. It has great exhibitions, a very good bookshop, and every summer it commissions a specially designed pavilion which hosts a series of interesting events. Kensington Gardens, London W2 3XA, www.serpentinegallery.org

VICTORIA & ALBERT MUSEUM The V&A Museum is largest museum of decorative arts and design in the world, and it has some amazing collections of ceramics, glass, textiles and jewellery. For designers it's also famous for its identity, created by the late Alan Fletcher. Every summer it holds a creative 'village fete' in the courtyard (see Events). Cromwell Road, London SW7 2RL, www.vam.ac.uk

HAMPSTEAD HEATH London has lots of green spaces – Hyde Park, Regents Park, Victoria Park etc... but nothing quite compares to Hampstead Heath. Known as the 'lung of London', it's massive (3.5km^2), and is partly cultivated and partly left to grow wild, incorporating meadows, woodlands and ponds – including separate sex swimming ponds. I can't speak for the men's pond, but the ladies' pond is a beautiful and serene refuge – especially mid-week. The top of Parliament Hill offers a great view of the city. If it's nice weather, put a couple hours aside to explore. You'll almost definitely get lost, but just enjoy the sensation – you'll find the city again soon enough.

THE BARBICAN The Barbican is a huge live-work-play housing estate built in the 60s and 70s, designed by architects Chamberlin, Powell and Bon. It's made up of concrete terraces and towers with the Barbican Centre in its middle – with theatres, cinemas and two art galleries. It's well worth a visit. www.barbican.org.uk

REGENT'S CANAL WALK The Regent's Canal was once an essential means of bringing goods into the London suburbs, but today it just offers a nice peaceful break from the city. It cuts from east to west, going underground briefly at Islington. If you're based in the east you can join the canal at Broadway Market, turn left and walk all the way to Limehouse, where it joins the Thames. There's a gastro-pub owned by Gordon Ramsay there, so you can refuel.

BRICK LANE WALK Brick Lane can get very busy at the weekend, so one of the things I like doing during the week is taking a stroll down this remarkable street. Brick Lane has been home to immigrant populations for the past 300 years – first the Huguenots, then the Jews and the Irish and now a big Bangladeshi population. Start your walk at the corner of Bethnal Green Road. This is the trendier end nearer to Shoreditch. You'll pass two bagel bakeries as you start. If you're hungry, pick up a salt-beef bagel for next to nothing. Delicious. If you go on a Friday, take a detour down Cheshire Street and check out the little design boutiques (they're closed the rest of the week). Then keep going down Brick Lane until you reach the mosque. This is the clearest indicator of the area's rich history – it used to be a synagogue and before that a church. Turn right, and nip down to Spitalfields to check out the stalls and the trendy shops surrounding them. Head back to Brick Lane and keep walking down towards Whitechapel Road. You'll see that after the mosque, it becomes a completely different street – almost completely Bangladeshi with not a trace of trendy Hoxton-ness. At the end of Brick Lane, turn right and check out the new Whitechapel Art Gallery. An important space for the East End that's recently been renovated and expanded.

V&A SUMMER FETE JULY The V&A Village Fete takes over the museum's courtyard for one weekend with a range of quirky and unusual stalls and games run by interesting designers. Lots of fun. www.vam.ac.uk

THE BIG DRAW A chance to draw with the genius Quentin Blake in Trafalgar Square www.thebigdraw.org.uk

NOTTING HILL CARNIVAL AUGUST This is the famous street festival in West London. Personally I hate it – lots of people and not much action – but many people seem to think it's very cool indeed.

OPEN HOUSE LONDON SEPTEMBER For one weekend 700 buildings across the capital open their doors to the public. Every type of architecture is on offer. And all for free. www.londonopenhouse.org

ST BRIDE LIBRARY This home of typography has a good range of talks and events, some of which are free. www.stbride.org

THE LONDON DESIGN FESTIVAL SEPTEMBER A big event and perhaps overrated – but do check the website to see if there are any worthwhile talks or events. www.londondesignfestival.com

EVENTS

THE RCA SHOW MAY-JUNE The Royal College of Art usually has an exciting graduation show. A good place to buy nice prints. www.rca.ac.uk

DESIGNS OF THE YEAR A competition in which the winner is chosen by the public and a jury. It's fun – even though the winner is usually not the one I'd choose. www.designmuseum.org

BIOGRAPHIES

CHRISTOF NARDIN
Vienna, Austria

Christof Nardin studied at the University of Applied Arts in Vienna, and upon graduation, he set up an office with colleagues and friends near the Naschmarkt. Taking an analytical and systematic approach, he works closely with a team of freelancers, attempting to find sensitive, individual and creative solutions for clients. Christof tries to keep his work fresh by taking on a broad variety of projects. He has a particular fondness for books and posters, but covers corporate design, identity and web design as well, and always tries to focus on substance before style. Although the resulting work is not always geared towards prizes, Christof has won plenty over the course of his career including a 'best of the best' Red Dot Award, a gold iF Communication Design Award, a European Design Award and awards from the Type Director's Club and Art Directors Club, New York.

In 2007, Christof worked on the book *Beyond Graphic Design* (Verlag Hermann Schmidt Mainz) with Fons Hickman. In 2008, he joined forces with Alois Gstöttner to establish the design network 'agcn', to develop, create and consult content, image, typography, space and code.

He takes an active interest in art, music and performance, and also in economics, science and politics.

www.christofnardin.com

TERESA SDRALEVICH
Brussels, Belgium

Teresa's Sdralevich's main passion is creating posters for plays, events, movie festivals, social and political campaigns... anything really. Sometimes she prints them herself in her silkscreen workshop, or she gets them printed in offset in big quantities and finds them spread across the city – legally or illegally. She also does illustrations for magazines, books and brochures for both child and adult audiences. She likes taking part in exhibitions – especially when they offer the opportunity to work on a large scale or address new subjects. She has a few book projects in the pipeline.

Teresa's country of origin is Italy, and although she is based in Brussels she maintains professional contacts in France and Italy and is involved in many cross-boundary projects. She has the good fortune to work from a beautiful space just behind her house. The workshop is shared with an artist, and the office of her partner – who writes and studies serious stuff.

www.teresasdralevich.net

BORIS BONEV
Sofia, Bulgaria

Boris Bonev is a young designer working in Sofia. He graduated from the Book and Graphic Design Department of the National Academy of Arts in Sofia, and has worked for two years at a creative studio on projects including a pack of graphic materials for the Picasso exhibition in Sofia, and the creation of typefaces for the city's communication system.

Boris's interests are primarily related to editorial design, specifically books, posters and catalogues. He loves typography and experimental type, and has been working a lot in this field lately. In addition to design, Boris is also an illustrator. His children's book, *A Dreamer's Manual*, which was part of his graduation project will be published soon.

Check out his work on the Behance Network, on typographicposters.com or on Flickr with the nickname borisbo.

bob1bonev@abv.bg

MARTINA SKENDER
Zagreb, Croatia

Martina is a 26-year-old graduate of the University of Zagreb School of Design. Throughout her studies she worked as a freelancer, and did her internship at the University of San Juan in Argentina, where she became interested in animation and web design. For her graduate thesis, she created a website for children illustrating the structure of an eco-system using a series of interactive animations.

Martina currently works as a graphic designer, web designer and illustrator at design studio Revolucija in the centre of Zagreb. Although her main focus is web design, she works on everything from interactive CDs, to learning software, game design, logo design, exhibitions and books.

Martina loves to observe, explore, learn and of course, create. She speaks English, Spanish and German, and enjoys travelling, reading and making things with her hands – especially ceramics.

www.mskender.com

EVRIPIDES ZANTIDES
Lefkosia, Cyprus

Evripides Zantides studied in Cyprus and the UK, and he is currently working as an associate professor at the University of Nicosia in Cyprus, a visiting tutor at the Cyprus University of Technology and as a freelance artist, graphic designer, and consultant for art projects around Europe. His work revolves around the study of semiology and its importance in visualising oral or written text.

Evripides regularly presents papers at international conferences and art and design biennials, and sits on jury panels of competitions including the 2006 Graphic and Illustration Awards (EVGE) for Greece and Cyprus. He also is the country delegate of Cyprus for ATypI, the International Typographic Association. Evripides' work as an artist has been shown in the UK, Italy, Greece, France, Canada, Lebanon, Russia and many other countries around the world. His papers and visual work have been included in numerous refereed conference proceedings and art and design exhibition catalogues internationally.

FILIP BLAŽEK
Prague, Czech Republic

Filip Blažek has been working as a graphic designer since 1993. In 2000, he graduated from the Faculty of Arts at the Charles University in Prague. In 2003 he established graphic design studio Designiq. It focuses on two main fields of work – creation of logotypes and corporate identity, and on the promotion of bodies focusing on cultural work.

Filip is also the co-author of the popular book *Typography in Practice*, and regularly contributes to professional periodicals in the field of graphic design. He is a founder and member of the editorial office of *TYPO Magazine*, which focuses on typography, graphic design and visual communication. He is an owner of the Typo.cz server, dedicated to Czech and international graphic design. He has delivered lectures on type and logo design since 1999. He is the Czech deputy of the international organisation ATypI.

Filip Blažek is frequent traveller, and over the past couple of years he has explored numerous countries in Asia, Africa and the Middle East. He loves to have leisurely breakfasts in cafes and long nights in pubs, bars or beer gardens.

www.typomag.com
www.designiq.eu

LA GRAPHIC DESIGN
Copenhagen, Denmark

LA is a design studio founded in 2007 by graphic designers Anne Strandfelt and Lizet Hee Olesen. They trained in London and Copenhagen respectively, and together they create bespoke graphic solutions for clients within arts and culture, fashion, publishing and advertising. Each project is dealt with individually, and in a personal and engaging manner. They pride themselves on their ability to listen to their clients, and on their thorough research processes, which allow them to anticipate the client's needs often before the client even knows what those needs are.

Anne and Lizet cite the influences of Charlotte Perriand, Eileen Gray, Niklas Luhmann, Maul McCarthy, Man Ray and the Fluxus movement, and there is a lot of humour and playfulness, as well as a quiet elegance to their work.

In the future they hope to work on large-scale publications for galleries and museums as well as continuing to work for exciting clients that inspire them.

www.lagraphicdesign.dk

VLADIMIR AND MAKSIM LOGINOV
Tallinn, Estonia

Vladimir and Maksim Loginov form the design company HMF (handmadefont.com), which was founded in 2008. Taking inspiration from the world around them, they create fonts that are totally unique and extremely visual – so much so that they can be used in the place of illustration. They have worked for a range of clients in all sorts of industries, and their work has featured in various magazines and journals.

HMF is always open to requests for developing tailor-made fonts across different budgets, but also has a wide variety of fonts readily available for purchase, and of a high enough standard that they can be used for anything from business cards to packaging to outdoor advertisements.

In their own words: 'We make ideas real through beautifully crafted design. We believe good ideas can be applied to anything'.

www.handmadefont.com

HILPPA HYRKÄS
Helsinki, Finland

Hilppa Hyrkäs works as a graphic designer for the Finnish Broadcasting Company, YLE, creating news graphics (maps, statistics etc.) as well as high-level illustrative work. She is used to working in a highly pressurised environment, working in shifts, thinking on her feet and making rapid-fire decisions. Whilst this can get stressful, at least it means she doesn't have to take work home with her!

Hilppa also runs her own design office (so that when the world of TV comes crashing down, she has a fallback option!) She mostly works on print graphics, and has a particular passion for poster design. She has received a number of prizes and honours in various international poster competitions, and has also sat on a few jury panels.

She loves simple design in one or two graphics and pencil drawings. Her other love and source of inspiration is poetry, particularly modern Finnish verse.

www.hilppahyrkas.fi

ELAMINE MAECHA
Paris, France

Elamine Maecha grew up in France, studied at the École Nationale Supérieure des Arts Décoratifs of Strasbourg and at SMFA School of the Museum, Boston. After graduating, he found a position as a trainee researcher at Atelier National de Recherches Typographiques, whilst simultaneously working as a freelance designer in Paris. In 2005, Elamine joined Studio Apeloig, working with them on a broad range of projects, including numerous book publications such as *Cave Art* and *Japan Style* for Phaidon. He also participated in a number of events and exhibitions, including 27 Graphic Designers for Europe and VU et 80+80 photo-graphisme at Galerie Anatome in Paris.

Since 2008, Elamine has been designing books for Xavier Barral Edition, and overseeing the design of *303 Art Revue*.

www.maecha.eu

CHRISTIANE WEISMÜLLER
Berlin, Germany

Christiane Weismüller was born in Germany in 1975. She studied graphic design at FH Munster where she co-founded the *Bianca 115* design magazine. After graduating in 2002 she moved to London to work for design studios Thomas Matthews, Why Not Associates and Coppenrath publishing house. During this time she also collaborated with different designers on various projects – including contributions to *Graphic Magazine*, and the exhibition *Stuck on Me*.

Christiane moved to Berlin in 2005 to work for Pentagram Design Ltd, joining the design team around Justus Oehler. The team's work embraces many disciplines, from signage systems and credit card design to print and packaging. Clients include Citibank, Villeroy & Boch, Stadthalle Wien, Serif Publishing, Philharmonie Luxembourg and the Museum for Communication in Berlin.

www.christianeweismueller.com

DIMITRIS KARAISKOS
Athens, Greece

Dimitris trained as a graphic and interactive designer in Athens and London, and after a couple of years working in London, returned to Athens to set up his own studio. He works in both print and screen media, and specialises in poster design. In 2007, he won first prize at the Greek Graphic Awards for a series of posters for jazz gigs, and in 2008, he represented Greece in the poster exhibition 27 Graphistes pour l'Europe. In 2009, he curated an international poster exhibition held in Athens.

Dimitris has also worked on book projects, including *Flotsam & Jetsam* – a collection of photographs of objects found on beaches, published in 2007. He has further ideas for self-published books, which he hopes to realise over the next couple years.

His only business partner is his dog Oro, who he consults on all serious matters. They like big walks, old books, surfing and the island of Tinos.

www.dimitriskaraiskos.com

DAVID BARATH
Budapest, Hungary

David Barath was born and raised in Novi Sad in the former Yugoslavia and has been living in Budapest since 1993. He completed his MA at the Hungarian Academy of Fine Arts, and worked for several years at various advertising agencies. Following his passion for photography, David then became the creative producer of publishing house Marquard Media, as well as outlining and producing fashion and celebrity stories for various glossy magazines. In recent years he founded a design agency called Visual Group Productions, of which he is creative director. This started as a boutique creative agency, and now represents and manages the best photographers, DOPs, movie directors and 3-D animators in Hungary, assembling tailor-made teams for any type of creative project. In tandem, David runs a design consultancy company, David Barath Design.

David's design philosophy can be summed up by Bruno Munari's quote: 'Simplification is a sign of intelligence – says an ancient Chinese proverb: what cannot be said in a few words, cannot be said in a lot of words either'.

www.davidbarath.com
www.visualgroup.hu

UNTHINK
Dublin, Ireland

Unthink is Noelle Cooper and Colin Farmer. Sometimes it's more, but most of the time it's just the two of them. They met in art college in 1998, and followed different paths. Noelle graduated with a degree and went on to work in the studios of XMi, Boyle Design Group and Dynamo. Colin on the other hand, being older and in need of money, did a diploma, freelanced (ie. watched daytime TV), and then got a job in Creativeinc. They both freelanced on the side for friends and family, and after a while they realised they had enough work to do it full time. In 2006 Colin robbed Noelle's idea and started Unthink and after a little while, Noelle came looking for a piece of the action.

The two of them share a passion for creative design, and Unthink strives to take on projects that offer the opportunity to produce original and exciting work. They are based in an old wool mill north of the river Liffey in the centre of Dublin. Their group of clients/ friends continues to grow, and generate more work through word of mouth, but perhaps in the future they might start hunting down people they'd like to work with.

www.unthink.ie

LUCIA PASQUALIN
Trieste, Italy

Lucia Pasqualin was born in Treviso in Italy in 1980. She graduated in industrial design from the Faculty of Arts and Design at the University of Venice in 2004 and took a second degree in visual communication and multimedia in 2007. For her final thesis, she looked at the work of Swiss graphic designer, Wolfgang Weingart, analysing the evolution of his work, and then with the use of processing, created a personal typographic experimentation inspired by his ideas and methods.

During her studies she worked with Cacao Design Communication Studio in Milan. She is currently collaborating with Studio Tassinari/Vetta in Trieste, where she now lives and works.

ARVIDS BARANOVS
Riga, Latvia

Arvids has always had multiple identities. He was born in Riga in 1983, and tasted the last moments of the Soviet Union, but mostly grew up in the new free country of Latvia. He studied languages and business at school, but in the evenings went to art classes. At the age of 15, Arvids bought his first SLR camera during a trip to Germany, and through its viewfinder began to find a visual language for himself.

At university, Arvids started out by studying IT, but shortly realised that it was all too geeky and literal for him, so he transferred to the University of the Arts Bremen, where he specialised in digital media. After graduating, Arvids returned to Riga to work as a freelance multimedia designer. He spent two years working on various commercial projects relating to web, print and broadcast design. However, ultimately the life of a freelance designer was not for him, and he decided to take the helm of his father's translation business, continuing to invest in his passion for design and new media art on the side.

www.arvidsbaranovs.com

ELENA DVORETSKAYA
Vilnius, Lithuania

Born in Vilnius, Elena Dvoretskaya studied graphic design in Denmark, and after a period of working in Moscow, she retuned to her native city to work as a freelance designer/illustrator. She works primarily on creative projects with advertising agencies, and is known for her playful, illustrative approach – rich in details and colours. Elena's work is often personal, and she aims to engage people by communicating emotions and associations, rather than literal depictions. She has won two Lithuanian Advertising Community awards and her work has been published in the German design magazine *Page*.

In the future, Elena aims to work more with surface design – specifically with textiles and fashion, to draw murals and to work on paintings in her summer house outside the city. Her inspirations come from nature; leaves, plants, earth and wildlife – and she loves handcrafted objects, hand-drawn illustrations and working with paint and clay. Elena is a great believer in the value of a happy carefree childhood, and would love to work on illustrated books for children one day.

www.mayagrafik.com

MARCO GODINHO
Luxembourg, Luxembourg

Marco Godinho was born in Portugal and moved to Luxembourg when he was nine. He studied in France, Germany and Switzerland, and currently lives and works between Luxembourg and Paris. His work revolves around creating maps that reflect the subjective experiences of space and time, global geographies, and individual and situation. Using drawings, sculptures, installations and videos, his post-conceptual art utilises a minimalist aesthetic and a playful, interactive element to illuminate questions of identity, multi-culturalism and immigration.

Over the past five years, Marco has won numerous awards and posts, including the Special Jury award at the 2006 Esch Biennial and a residency at FRAC, the Regional Fund for Contemporary Art for Champagne-Ardennes in Reims. He runs workshops in Luxembourg and Paris, and his work has been exhibited in galleries around Europe.

www.marcogodinho.com

PIERRE PORTELLI
Valletta, Malta

Pierre Portelli was born and raised in Malta. He studied graphic design at the Swindon School of Art and Design in the UK, and then returned to Valletta, where he lives and works today. Pierre's work focuses primarily on book design and installation art. It has been exhibited in Greece, Liechtenstein, Austria, Cyprus, Tunisia, San Marino, Italy, the USA and Malta.

Recent projects have included a collaboration with Lovedifference and Michelangelo Pistoletto at the 50th Venice Biennale, an exhibition at the 2008 Biennale Internationale du Design in St Etienne and a poster for the exhibition 27 Graphic Designers for Europe, curated by Phillipe Apeloig in Paris.

Pierre is a visiting lecturer at the University of Malta, a founding member of START, a Maltese contemporary art group and a founding member of No 68, an exhibition space in Valletta.

www.pierreportelli.com
www.68stlucystreet.com

STUDIO BOOT
Den Bosch, The Netherlands

'Dare to make something ugly, do not go for the results and the looks. Take risks to develop something special', reads the mission statement of Studio Boot, the design studio set up by Edwin Vollebergh and Petra Janssen. The two met at art school in the 80s and shared an interest in the post-modern approach to design – blending together street styles, advertising and stage-managed photography.

Founded in 1991, Studio Boot sets itself apart from more traditionally Dutch design philosophies. Taking inspiration from the warmth and gaiety of illustrator/designers such as Grapus, Alain Le Quernec, Perret and Mariscal, Volleberg and Janssen aim to incorporate humour, texture, colour and most of all empathy in all the work they do – from posters to books to branding and corporate design. Their distinctive combination of illustrative and graphic designs has grown in popularity, and they have a broad client base in Den Bosch. They also share their ideas and approaches with the students of the Design Academy, fostering creative independence in young designers

www.studioboot.nl

ANNAFRAGAUSDAL
Oslo, Norway

Anna was born in a small, snowy valley in Norway, and although she now lives in Oslo, she still holds nature dear, living a short walk away from the beautiful ski slopes with her soon-to-be husband Sigurd and beautiful son Nils.

She has a degree in Electronic Arts from Sydney College of Arts, and an MA in Visual Communication from Central Saint Martins, London. She works as an Art Director for the advertising agency McCann, where she has been since 2001, primarily focusing on new media.

Although a lot of her work is quite digital, Anna's interests as an illustrator/designer lie in the handmade. She comes from a family with a strong sense of craftsmanship, and takes inspiration from her roots and history, expressing herself through craft. In order to reconcile the differences between these interests and her day-job, Anna runs her own small agency, 'Annafragausdal' (meaning Anna from Gausdal – the valley in which she grew up). She takes on selected low or no-budget commissions that interest her, and this helps her stay focused in her commercial line of work.

The quirky or the unexpected is central to Anna's work, and she enjoys giving her audience a good surprise.

www.annafragausdal.no
www.pickles.no

JAN KALLWEJT
Warsaw, Poland

Jan Feliks Kallwejt is originally from Poland, but is currently based in Malaga, Spain. He worked for six years with agencies based in Warsaw and Hamburg, and is now a freelance graphic designer and illustrator working with clients from all over Europe and North America. His main focus is illustration, apparel design and personal art projects.

Jan's works revolve around simple yet sophisticated forms. He juxtaposes and multiplies them, creating complex and witty compositions with immense attention to detail. Usually operating within a limited colour palette of two or three tones, he employs multi-layered symbolism, occasionally dropping in an unexpected dose of perversion, just to keep things interesting.

www.kallwejt.com

R2
Porto, Portugal

Lizá Defossez Ramalho and Artur Rebelo formed their design studio, R2, in 1995 while studying at Porto Fine Arts University. They now have a wide client base including cultural organisations, curators, artists and architects. They also do self-initiated projects such as books, posters and installations.

Their work has won various design awards, such as the Red Dot Award for communication design in 2008, the 'Grand Prix' at the 22nd International Biennale of Graphic Design Brno, in 2006; 'Judges' Special Award' at the Taiwan International Poster Design Award 2005, and many more. R2 has also participated in the major design biennials, primarily with cultural posters and books. Their work has featured in magazines including *Eye, Print, Art and Design* and *Intramuros*, and books by publishers such as Gustavo Gili, Index Book, Rotovision, Die Gestalten Verlag and Victionary.

Their work also includes teaching, judging, writing and researching. Lizá Ramalho and Artur Rebelo have been AGI members since 2007.

ww.r2design.pt

LUCIAN MARIN
Bucharest, Romania

Lucian Marin worked for two years in advertising and branding agencies, and went freelance in 2006. He works in all design medias, specialising in brand identity and new media projects, collaborating with an expanding network of designers to deliver complete creative solutions, including website development and support. He has won two Internetics awards for his work on www.psst. ro. He has also participated in a number of exhibitions and one-off publications.

Lucian is an avid photographer – you can view photographs of Bucharest and Romania on www.flickr.com/photos/lucianmarin. He also loves antiques, travel, nature and beautifully designed stamps (which he collects).

www.lucianmarin.ro

MARCEL BENČÍK
Bratislava, Slovakia

Marcel Bencik was born in Žilina, northern Slovakia. He studied at Commercia Academy, and after working in the industry for a couple years, returned to university to do his Masters and then his Doctorate at the Academy of Fine Arts and Design (AFAD) Bratislava.
He currently works as an assistant at the Department of Visual Communication at AFAD, and freelances in graphic design and visual communications. He also organises the annual graphic design conference KUPÉ as well as other design events and workshops.

Marcel's interests are broad, but he particularly enjoys working on interdisciplinary projects relating to architecture and social impact in Slovakia and abroad. He has been living and working in Bratislava since 1998.

www.kupe.sk
www.afad.sk

RADOVAN JENKO
Ljubljana, Slovenia

Radovan Jenko graduated from the Academy of Fine Arts in Warsaw in 1981. Since then he has been working in graphic design and illustration, specialising in poster design. Over the course of his career, Radovan has won numerous awards for his work, including a silver medal from the Art Directors Club in New York in 1999 and a special jury award at the Taiwan international Poster Design competition, 2008. His posters are part of the permanent collections of the Israel Museum, Jerusalem; the Museum Die Neue Sammlung, Munich; and the Dansk Plakatmuseum, Aårhus. Radovan has also had his work published in magazines around the world and numerous books. He is the author of two design books; *Visual Thinking* (1999) and *Posters - Affiches* (LaLook, 2005).

Today, he is the principal designer in his own studio, which caters to a broad variety of clients from theatres and museums to banks. He is also a founding member of the Brumen Foundation, which sets out to promote visual culture in Slovenia, and is a professor at the Academy of Fine arts and Design in Ljubljana, where he shares his broad experience with the younger generations.

www.posterfestival-ljubljana.si
www.brumen.org

ASTRID STAVRO
Barcelona, Spain

Studio Astrid Stavro is an independent, multi-disciplinary design and communication consultancy based in Barcelona. Their work is based on distinctive, intelligent design that makes a difference and solves problems effectively. Their clients include the international music competition Maria Canals, Arcadia, DHUB (Design Hub Barcelona – the city's new design musem), Reina Sofia Museum, MACBA (Museum of Contemporary Art Barcelona), and the publishing houses Planeta and FAD Annual Books. The studio has won over 40 design awards in less than four years.

In addition to running the studio, Astrid also co-runs El Palace Editions, El Palace Exhibitions and El Palace Products, an independent product design and publishing company that explores ideas and their visual manifestations. These may take the shape of exhibitions, publications, or products.

Astrid regularly writes design articles and reviews for magazines such as *Étapes*, *Visual*, and *Grafik*. She teaches editorial design at IDEP, lectures on graphic design, and has been on the jury of several national design awards. She is also the proud mother of a baby called Marco.

www.astridstavro.com

NILLE SVENSSON
Stockholm, Sweden

Nille Svensson was born in 1970 and was educated at the Konstfack University College of Arts, Crafts and Design in Stockholm. Since graduating in 1997 he has worked as a graphic designer, illustrator and animator. His clients have included H&M, MTV, Sony, eBay and Volkswagen, as well as many local Swedish companies.

Nille's work has featured in numerous design magazines and books, and has also been exhibited all over the world. He is the co-founder of design agency Sweden Graphics, publishing house Pocky, art magazine *Konstnären* and the publishing technology startup publit.se. He also frequently teaches design, and his lectures have taken him to weird and wonderful places including Tijuana, Sydney and Kuala Lumpur, delighting workshopaholics far and wide.

Nille was pretty sure he was the best graphic designer in the world until his daughter grew old enough to start drawing.

www.swedengraphics.com

MERET AEBERSOLD
Zurich, Switzerland

Meret is an industrial designer born in Switzerland and currently living in London. She graduated from textile design in Basel and industrial design in Zurich, and lived in Zurich for seven years. Combining her skills in textile and industrial design, she specialised in accessory design, including bags and shoes.

Over the course of her career, Meret has worked within the textile and product industry for companies including Creation Baumann, Qwstion and K-Swiss. She currently works as a shoe designer for Puma in London. Shoes have been her great passion since she discovered her mother's high heels as a little girl.

BIANCA WENDT
Istanbul, Turkey

Bianca Wendt was born in Australia and has lived and worked in Sydney, Istanbul, Brussels and Antwerp. She currently runs her own studio in London, working across different media including books, magazines, identities, exhibition design and websites. She has a network of photographers, illustrators, editors and web-programmers who she works alongside on relevant briefs.

Her past projects include campaigns and printed material for Topshop, Topman and Comme des Garçons. Clients include Phaidon, The British Fashion Council, *Rubbish Magazine*, London Fashion Week and Nike. In Istanbul she worked for photography/fashion magazine *2 debir*, as well as lecturing at Sabanci University and freelancing on projects for *Biz* magazine and fashion label Eternal Child. She also undertook a personal project at this time called 8760 Hours in Istanbul, in which she took a photo out of her window every waking hour for a year.

Bianca's work has been published in *Creative Review*, *Grafik*, *The London Fashion Week Daily*, *Co-op magazine* and *One Hundred at 360 degrees: Graphic Designs New Global Generation* (Laurence King), amongst others.

www.biancawendt.com

JOANA NIEMEYER
London, United Kingdom

Joana is an illustrator and designer born
in Germany. She graduated from Central
Saint Martins in 2005 with an MA in
communication design and has been living
and working in London since then. She spent
four years working at Thomas Manss & Co,
where she was responsible for all Foster +
Partners publications and Bowers & Wilkins.

Her personal work combines illustration and
typography in the developmental stages and
is expressed through traditional skills such
as screenprinting or bookbinding. Joana
has also curated exhibitions such as the
badge show *Stuck on Me*, which was hosted
at the Notting Hill Arts Club, London and
the Galerie Walden, Berlin. The exhibition
included designers such as Jonathan Ellery,
Experimental Jetset and Spin.

In 2009, Joana and Lisa Sjukur set up the
design studio April in London where they look
after clients such as Alain de Botton, John
McAslan + Partners and the V&A. They have
also had commissioned work shown at Paris'
Aiports and the Athens Metro.

Joana shares a flat with Meret Aebersold
(see Zurich) and a smelly but inspirational
cat called Jones.

www.joananiemeyer.com
www.studio-april.com

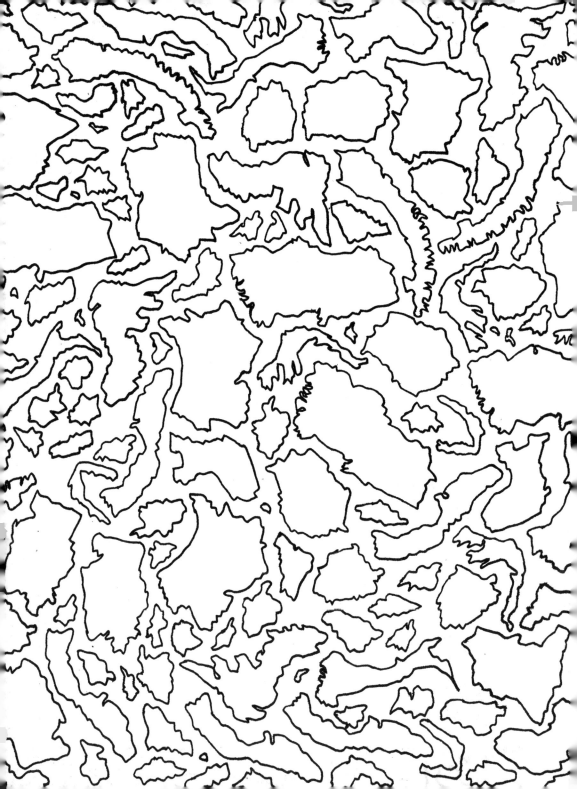